Read why others endorsing this boc

M000012686

"Bart Baggett's book, *The Success Secrets of the Rich and Happy* is **destined to become a classic**. With deep insights and great simplicity, Bart has created a manual for success that should be read by everyone. **If you read only one book this year, let it be this one.**"

—John Harricharan, award-winning author of the bestseller, When You Can Walk on Water, Take the Boat and creator of The Power Pause--3 Minutes, 3 Steps to Personal Success and Real Happiness.

"Great Book. **Intense, rich, profound, entertaining**... A book I would have liked to have read when I was 18."

—Cristiano Sileim Florence, Itali Ducati.com

"Very helpful in everyday life!" -Carol Sanders

"It was **excellent!**" -Michelle Hurr

"**This book changed my lif**e. There is sooo much information. I can't put it down. Thank you for writing it."

— Uma Devi, Austin, Texas, USA

"I have found Success of the Rich and Happy to be very thought provoking - you are **certainly 'in tune' with human nature** and how we tick! I have only read half way and loving it."

- Susan, United Kingdom

Bart, there are so many incredible secrets, lessons, tools in your book that once learned and practiced become priceless. The $20.00 I used to purchase *Success Secrets* has already and **will continue to pay for itself 100 times over** and more.

—Daryl S. Rembisz, Dallas, Texas, USA

I

"**You have done a world of good to my life.** I have studied throughout my life works by several authors including Robert Kiyoski, Shiv Kera, Wayne Dyer, Hans Jacobi, and even Edward De Bono. You are my number one favourite. **Your presentation style is unmatched by even these masters.**

I want all your products, but I need not worry about generating money now, for buying your other products, since I will use the techniques given in your new book. I will easily create abundance for myself and to share with others. I will update you with the results as I start following your techniques one by one. Thanks."

— Kumaravel Jagadeesan, India

"I have read many self-help books. **Bart's book is one of the easiest to read.** He has a very fluid style that complements his ideas and conveys it in an easy-to-understand way.

The handwriting analysis section was of particular interest as I am able to know a person on the first meeting better than many of their close friends. It also helps to see where people are coming from while not being so rash in my initial judgments (which are often misinformed.) I would just like to thank Bart from the bottom of my heart for sharing some of his many gifts. Thank you for all you've done to help me and others, so far. I know it's a river of abundance that will continue to flow... **This is a book you'll want to read over and over again. Guaranteed.** "

— Randy W. Hall, Detroit, Michigan, USA

"I just finished reading your new book, Success Secrets of the Rich & Happy for the second time. **I had trouble putting it down this time too.** I have read many books on "creating your own reality", but I have never read one **so in tune to me as an individual.** Instead of making me feel that by creating this reality I had made a serious mistake, it gave me a positive feeling of being able to change the negative aspects of my life. **I have never read a self-help book that gives you so many tools.** The timeline therapy was new to me and I found it really helped me to focus. Thanks for sharing your knowledge."

— Terry Shinabarger, Network Engineer, Plano, Texas, USA

"Looking back at past events in my life, I now know why I had the outcome that I did. I've read some chapters twice already and continue to refer to it as I gain new insight. I highly recommend this book to anyone who wants to make dramatic changes in their life."

—- Patty Yates, Tullahoma, Tennessee, USA

"I haven't taken the time till now to acknowledge my appreciation for your weekly newsletters and your books. I look forward to each one, as I've mentally absorbed your archives.

Thank you for the choices you've made in your life ... your results are unfolding more choices for me. Bravo! Encore! "

— Bonnie Luckey
Carthage, Missouri, USA

"P.S. The Success Secrets of the Rich and Happy is amazing! I can't put it down. "

"Dear Bart,

Your book is full of insights, and I could go through it again (I will!) and find many more, but the one which stands out to me is (I may have paraphrased it slightly) "We can't control the events, but we can choose the meanings we assign to them."

What impressed me about this was the concise way you stated it - I've heard people go on for hours trying to say the same thing, but **you have it all in just a few words**.

An example of how it worked for me is this: Just last week I knocked over my computer and damaged the main hard disk beyond repair - and lost everything! To replace the data I had will take a long time and a lot of work, but I can't believe how calmly I have taken what some people might consider a disaster. However, it has hardly moved me at all, and I feel sure that it is because I have taken your words to heart, and assigned a very limited sense of disappointment to this event.

There are very many outstanding ideas in your book, but this was one which showed its value most remarkably in the first few days after having read it."
Many thanks and kindest regards,

— Eric Silverstone, Caesarea, Israel

"Dear Mr.. Bart Baggett,

You were kind enough to offer your program and books through a scholarship at a discounted price. Your course had created a link of popularity for me including a lot of good luck. Is it luck? I happen to bump into quite a lot of handwriting cours-es and kits. Yours has been by far the best and most accurate. Also, thank you for the knowledge you have shared with through your work. It has changed the way I look at life. God bless you."

Your friend and forever a student.

— Loy Macedo

Dubai, United Arab Emirites

"I really enjoyed the variety of information you wholeheartedly were able to produce in one book. It is very obvious your greatest desire for writing this book was **to have an impact for the positive on many lives. I know it has for me and my family.** Having someone lay things down in a clear and precise way was just the push I needed to get me refocused on my goals.

Thank you for all the honesty, humor, life stories and experiences you put into one book. I know many people desiring a push or a positive plan of action will greatly benefit from reading this deeply personal book. Thank you for so much informative and useful information. "

— Karen Pennachi, Pelham, New Hampshire, USA

"P.S. I hope you find a strong sense of fulfillment from the response you receive from other readers. When you talked in your book about giving being true happiness I have to agree... I hope the happiness you gain from trying to touch others lives inspires you to consistently pursue a life of giving. "

"Bart,

I have **listed eight points** from your book that I feel, if a reader would focus on, **would change their life**. These are well written topics that have the power if one will master them **to turn failure to success.**

[1] The Six Human Needs

[2] Living in a No Drama Zone

[3] Overcoming Anger or Resentment

[4] Overcoming Fear of Success

[5] Self-Esteem vs. Confidence

[6] Personality Success Secrets

[7] The 10% rule

[8] The Secret of Rapport

This isn't to say these are the best parts of the book, but they are very **important for a quick fix out of failure or struggle.** These eight concepts reflect my life, but I never saw them written down until now. Wow. Insightful.
You have a very fine book Bart, and you should be very proud of it. "

Bob Massey,
Valley View, Texas, USA

"I've got an amazing testimony of my own to share. I have to once again thank you for sharing the success secrets in your book. One of the most important secrets for me was learning **that my brain is a "manifesting machine"**, and that money is nothing but energy traveling in waves all around us at all times. So I am able to

Introduction

contued from previous page....

attract the energy of money, directing it to me to fill my hands, my pockets, my wallet, my bank accounts by using the power of my brain through meditation and faith. And, boy, the money I spend certainly does come back to me ten fold.

I am now making in one week what I used to make in one month. Plus, my work week consists of three days a week between 5-6 hours each time. I just continue to ask the empowering question: "How specifically can I make more money and have more free time for myself?" **Now I am making money and enjoying what I do at the same time.**

Bart, thank you again for sharing your knowledge and wisdom in your book "Success Secrets of the Rich & Happy".

One more success testimony... **I SUCCESSFULLY completed my G.E.D. at age thirty.** Reading your book, Bart, gave me the tools for attaining the power and confidence to do so."

—Daryl S. Rembisz
Dallas, Texas, USA

"Really, your book *The Success Secrets of the Rich and Happy* is a blast. It is very inspiring and helpful ... **Giving me exactly the steps to take or the things to change**. I now feel more confident to produce my own happiness and success in life. The **clear and comprehensive information has saved hours of wasted time** and encouraged me to explore and exploit the knowledge I have accumulated over the last two months."

—Tatiana Velitchkov, owner/co-publisher
The Netherlands www.TakeYourFortune.com

"Bart,

After I got home from meeting you, I started to read your newest marvel, Success Secrets of the Rich and Happy. I must say that after utilizing the exercises in the first few chapters, **that I feel 20 times better already.** After meeting you, I now know that this book is written from your own success! **This book is a marvel, a blueprint for complete and total wealth, success, and most importantly, HAP-PINESS.** I eagerly await the completion of reading your book, just so I can read it again. I have already shown this book to people I know, and to my amazement, they are already asking to read it themselves. Thank you, Bart!"

— Kelly Wilkins CGA, MGA, Handwriting Expert/Analyst, Houston, TX

P.S. Just when I thought that you had it all in your Deluxe Handwriting Course, you come up with this book! Wow! **Tony Robbins...watch out! Your successor is here!**

Other Books and Course by Bart Baggett

(See appendix or website for complete descriptions.)

The Secrets to Making Love Happen! Mastering Your Relationships Using NLP & Handwriting Analyis! 304 page book

How to Analyze Handwriting in 10 Minutes or Less - Home Study Course

Handwriting University's Standard Handwriting Analysis Certification Home Study Course by Bart and Curtis Baggett

How to Earn a $100 an Hour or More Analyzing Handwriting! By Bart Baggett and Phyllis Mattingly

The Grapho-Deck Handwriting Flash Cards

Change Your Handwriting, Change Your Life Workbook for Kids. How to raise self-esteem, increase confidence, and improve grades through grapho-therapy.

Change Your Handwriting, Change Your Life Workbook for Adults Change your life in 30 days Grapho-Therapy Workbook.

Double Your Income Time Line Hypnosis Programming CD by Bart Baggett and Brett Thomas

Bart Baggett's ePublishing On-Line Marketing Machine for Authors, Publishers, and Speakers.

Sex Secrets Revealed! On-line adult sexual education home study course. by Bart Baggett and Stephanie Glenn

The "Success Secrets of the Rich & Happy" Abundance Course and Live Seminar Tapes ! by Bart Baggett

The Secrets to Creating Chemistry - NLP Romance & Seduction Home Study Course

You can purchase every product, book, or tape ever authored by Bart Baggett in one combined package at this special webpage:

http://bartbaggett.com/collection

or Visit: http://bartbaggett.com

1-800-398-2278

SUCCESS SECRETS OF THE RICH AND HAPPY

Happiness is a Choice
Wealth is a decision

**How to design your life with financial
and emotional abundance.**

Written by Bart A. Baggett

Edited by Brian Moreland

Empresse´ Publishing

www.bartbaggett.com

Success Secrets Of The Rich & Happy.
Happiness is a Choice, Wealth is a decision
How to design your life with financial and emotional abundance.

Written by Bart A. Baggett
Edited by Brian Moreland

Published By:
Empresse Publishing
PO Box 720355
Dallas, TX 75372
1-800-398-2278
http://www.bartbaggett.com
Copyright ©2001 by Bart A. Baggett

Second Printing August 2001

9 8 7 6 5 4 3 2 1

Library of Congress Cataloging in Publication Data

Baggett, Bart A.

Success Secrets Of The Rich & Happy

Happiness is a Choice, Wealth is a decision; How to design your life with financial and emotional abundance / by Bart A. Baggett— 1st Edition

Bibliography: p.

1. Millionaires — Psychology 2. Self-Improvement 3. Success — Financial 4. Spirituality 5. Graphology 6. Wealth — Psychological aspects I. Title

ISBN # 1-882929-01-2

Library of Congress Catalog Number: 2001086495

Printed in the United States of America

Table of Contents:

Acknowledgements

There are a number of special people that made significant contributions to this book, directly and indirectly. Over the past three decades, many mentors, heroes, and role models have crossed my path. Without the teachings and wisdom of each one of these men and women, my understanding of the life principles I am sharing inside these pages would be tremendously hindered. Thank you for sharing via your books, seminars, videos, and one-on-one chats.

In order to create the space and find the time to undertake such a task as writing a book of this depth, it was necessary to have support in many areas of my life. As usual, my father Curtis Baggett was always willing to lend a helping hand. Kay Keeton kept my training school HandwritingUniversity.com running smoothly while I was away writing. Honlee Beattie spent valuable time editing my early lecture transcripts into understandable literature. Mary Goldthorp kept me emotionally balanced and was instrumental in helping me make more leaps of personal growth during the peak of my writing sebatacle. And finally, the person who has contributed most to the completion and polishing of this work of art is Brian Moreland. Brian has not only been an outstanding editor and contributor to this book, but has been a coach, director, and close friend. Without Brian, this book would not have turned out on time or with the level of literary quality it is. Brian's contributions were nothing short of spectacular.

Thanks to all of you. Your contributions will touch many lives. I sincerely apprecieate all of you and the many others that were left unnamed. Thank you.

INTRODUCTION

Universal Truth #1

The past does not equal the future.

CHAPTER ONE

YOUR INVITATION TO GREATNESS

What do you really want? Seriously, take a moment and think about what specifically would make your life absolutely wonderful! What would make you leap out of bed early everyday with jubilance and anticipation equal to a six-year-old on Christmas morning? What are your passions? Is there anything you love to do frequently just because it's fun? What if ... you have the power within your own mind to create the things you want most in life? What would you create for yourself?

Well, I'm here to tell you that you do have the power. I'm talking mega brain power. You have the luxury of having an amazing mind that is essentially a "creative machine." Besides keeping your heart beating and lungs moving, your brain is a programmable machine. In fact, for those of us who learn how to tap into its unlimited potential, our brain can be a powerful "manifesting machine." Everyday your brain continues to manifest into your reality whatever it gets programmed to manifest. Sometimes what you want and sometimes what you don't want. Wouldn't you like to be able to create only what you want in life: Your highest choices? Well my friend, this is your lucky day! This book reveals a wealth of "Success Secrets" I have learned from numerous rich and happy people. You will naturally learn how you can de-program ineffective mental programs and "design" new mental programs that get the outcomes you really want. This book puts *you* in complete control of your own sub-conscious mind. How about that?

Most people do not really know what they want. They are not sure of their destiny and not clear on what will satisfy them at the deepest levels.

Most people can write down a list of the things they don't want in life. Do you have such a list? (Struggle, arguments, an angry boss, disease, screaming kids, mean people, etc.) This list can be useful, but it doesn't program your brain to attract what you want. In fact, the more you focus on what you don't want, the more you are programming your brain to bring more of it into your world. This is an example of an ineffective internal program. In this book, you will learn how to stop running negative programs and start running positive ones that attract what you really want. First, you have to write the new program. I'll show you how. Here is the first step.

I ask you again, what do you want? Here is a game. Please play along.

Imagine a MAGICAL WIZARD is standing in front of you right now. He is wearing a long silver robe, a pointy hat and holding his magic wand. He says, "I am your own personal wizard. When I wave this magic wand, instantly your deepest desire will create into reality. I have no limitations - just speak it and it will be manifested."

So tell me, what do you want? Would it be a bag full of cash, a paid college education for your kids, a life of champagne and caviar, lose four dress sizes, or would it be a better golf swing, a million dollars, or a new car … you name it.

Now, take a moment and pretend you did have a wizard, and you could create a life with no limitations. What would that life look like? It has been my experience, once I learned how to really run my mind, that I could work it as if I truly had a wizard inside me … waiting for the instructions in a way he could understand them. So I invite you to imagine that you have a wizard inside you, too, and expand your mind to the possibility that you can create anything you desire using the full potential of your mind. Now, on a sheet of paper, write down three things you want most in your life.

1. _____

2. _____

3. _____

MODELING GREATNESS

What does it take to become a millionaire, a billionaire, a world leader, a great dad, a peacemaker, happy, successful? Is it luck, education, family or money? With over sixteen years of experience as a handwriting expert, author and speaker, I've found that successful people have many personality and character traits in common.

Before we get into the nitty gritty of this book, let's find out if you can guess who these "great" people are. Let's take a brief look at three biographical profiles of well-known, influential and successful people. What did it take to accomplish what they've accomplished? What kind of character does it take to be this successful?

Throughout this book, we will take a look at the character traits of successful people, such as the three popular heroes below. I will also reveal to you the belief systems and thought processes typical of such influential individuals.

#1 WHO IS THIS GREAT MAN?

He was imprisoned in South Africa for 27 years, locked up in his cell during daylight hours, enduring the prime years of his life as a political prisoner. An opponent of the reigning government that endorsed apartheid, he wanted black people to have equal rights in their own country. He was peacefully working for a free and fair democracy in South Africa. When the South African government finally released him from prison, he led his country out of slavery as the new president of South Africa. He was later awarded the Nobel Peace Prize as a tribute to all who dedicate their life for peace. He single handedly stood against apartheid and racism. Two of the key personality traits he possesses are persistence and determination.

The real heroes are men and women who are friends of the poorest of the poor.

#2 Who is this great man?

He was the first man to ever see the earth from space. This former American astronaut was a renown hero all over the world in 1962. After that event, he went on to have a successful career as a politician -- a Democratic Senator from Ohio. Then on October 29, 1998, he flew back into space again, aboard the space shuttle Discovery. That trip earned him the title of the oldest man ever to

An innate, searching curiosity about all around us --
-- what do we not know?
-- how can we do it differently?
-- how can we do it better?

take a space journey. What kind of character does it take to be that successful and to have that much integrity? His personality could be described as brave, determined, and full of passion.

#3 WHO IS THIS GREAT WOMAN?

She was born poor and raised in a household where she was sexually molested. She could have chosen hundreds of excuses ranging from poverty, racism, prejudice, glass ceiling, etc. But she succeeded anyway. She is arguably the most influencial woman in America in an industry dominated by powerful men (television.) And, she is one of the wealthiest and highest paid women in America influencing millions of people daily via her TV talk show.

There are key personality traits that these three heroes have in common. The one central theme that great people possess is something all of us can have: a compelling mission. Each of these men made a decision to take on a mission that was greater than themselves. When you have a compelling and powerful mission that strikes an emotional chord in your soul, you can overcome many obstacles who otherwise would seem insurmountable.

These successful people are examples of the many great men and women that walk this planet that you can use to "model" your life. You sure don't have to free an entire country, topple a govern-ment or rocket into space to make a difference. You do have to find a compelling purpose that will drive you and allow you to satisfy all of your basic human needs. One of those needs is the need to make a difference and/or contribute to others. I will discuss the other five basic human needs in chapter 10. Once you find a career or purpose that satisfies all of these basic needs, you will find deep satisfaction effortless to achieve.

As you study the thought processes of great men and women, you will realize they have a predictable set of beliefs and values that run their lives. Likewise, miserable angry criminals who create pain and torment in the world have a very different set of values, beliefs and purpose. In the coming section, you will have an opportunity to elicit the beliefs and values that you currently hold. Then, you will be given the opportunity to decide if these are beliefs that will take you where you really want to go.

For most people, our beliefs and even our values were given to us in childhood without our permission. We simply adopted them without knowing we have a choice. People who are "in the flow" of lots of cash have very specific beliefs about the nature of money and how it works. Likewise, people who have wonderful marriages and close loving friends have specific beliefs about people, love and relationships.

Many people naively believe that the reason people have such positive ideas about money or love is because they have an abun-dance of it in their life. It actually works the opposite way. They have an abundance of love, money and happiness, because the beliefs, values, and ideas they hold about these things "attracted" them into their life. Their beliefs and values lead them to their desired outcomes.

Change yourself first. Your reality will follow soon after.

Answers to "Who is this great person?":

#1 Nelson Mandela

#2 John Glenn

#3 Oprah Winfrey

THE TOOLS FOR PROGRAMMING YOUR LIFE

Have you ever decided to fix things around your house? You might have had to change a light bulb, paint a wall, tighten a screw on a wobbly chair. When you do decide to fix things, isn't it easier to have all the tools you need within arms reach?

Do you have a tool belt or toolbox? Even though my house doesn't need lots of attention, I do have a red toolbox I go to as soon as I find an area that needs improving. If the tool I need is in the toolbox, the repair is quick and easy. If the tool I need isn't there, the repair problem becomes more frustrating, takes longer, and often doesn't get fixed at all.

For me, when I approach the human psyche, I picture the different avenues of psychology like a big tool belt. When I learned handwriting analysis, it became one of my tools in my tool belt. For instance, I could meet someone, and in about two or three minutes I would know what he's scared of, how emotional he is, how good his self-image is, even his sex drive and his integrity. All these different personality traits I can tell thanks to the science of handwriting analysis.

But if I wanted to help this person stop smoking or overcome depression, I probably wouldn't use just the tool of handwriting analysis. That would be like using a screwdriver to hammer in a ten-inch nail. There are better tools for that job.

I would turn to hypnosis to assist him to stop smoking. For depression, I might use some NLP (Neuro-Linguistic Programming) or Time-Line Therapy techniques as well as take a serious look at the nutritional/chemical side of that condition. There are many different tools to change ourselves and affect the quality of our lives. If your life is not everything you want it to be - right now - you will want to grab an effective tool and go to work on yourself.

If you're having a lot of energy problems, I'm not going to say, "Change your handwriting. This is going to solve your problems." I'm going to say, "Let's talk about getting you to exercise more or change your diet." Or I might refer you to a medical doctor who specializes in energy related disease. There are all kinds of tools you can use to change your life. You have to use the right tool for the situation.

Because I've been attending self-improvement seminars and reading these types of books since I was 13 years old, I have seen many theories on personal change. I have found that handwriting analysis always ranks in the top five of the most useful tools. It's like a crescent wrench in your toolbox. You can use it for so many different situations. But, handwriting analysis is just one of an assortment of amazing mental tools I will teach and reference in this book.

I encourage you to approach these new tools like you would approach me handing you a piece of equipment in a workshop. If we were building a wooden desk together what tools would we need? If I ask you to pick up the "automatic sander," what would you do? Just because you have never seen this tool before, you wouldn't assume it doesn't work. You would simply ask what it is for and how to use it. Most likely, you would want to watch a demonstration to prove the tool works as I claim. Once you have used it once or twice, your comfort level and *belief* in this tool will increase. Then, you would probably choose to add it to your own tool belt.

This book is a collection of tools that I have chosen to build your life of wealth and happiness the quickest. You don't have to use the "automatic sander," but trying to sand a desk by hand might take three times as long and won't look as good. The tools in this book are very effective and usually fast, as well.

Many of the successful men and women I reference in this book might never have heard of these tools. That doesn't surprise me. These tools are designed to adjust your thinking to be more like the person you aspire to be. If you already have a powerful "wealth consciousness," you wouldn't need to adjust it. If you grew up in a family that truly convinced you that you were worthy and loved, you might not need to boost your self-esteem. I have used each one of these tools to positively affect my life. I know from experience that they work.

Here is a brief description of some tools that I have found transform the mind very quickly:

• **Goal Setting** – Defining your highest goals

• **Changing Belief Systems** – Creating new beliefs that empower you to be the person you choose to be

• **Eliciting Values** – Discovering what emotion is most important to you, what you value most in life

• **Handwriting Analysis** – The science of determining personality and character from someone's handwriting

• **Modeling Successful People** – Doing what successful people do to be successful yourself

• **Grapho-Therapy** – Changing your handwriting to change your behaviors

• **Six Human Needs** – A model of your life and your interaction with people – also understanding the reasons you do what you do and how you feel fulfilled

• **Vibrant Health & Nutrition** – Tips on how to eat, drink and exercise to boost your physical energy, uplift depression and live a longer, healthier life

• **State Management** – A technique to help you be in control of your mental and emotional state in any situation

• **Building Rapport** – Learn to get along with anyone instantly

• **Toxic Vocabulary** – How to remove words that create ineffective emotional states in yourself and others

• **Abundance Mentality** – New ways of thinking and being that will put you "in the flow" of prosperity

• **Space Clearing** – A technique from the Chinese science of Feng Shui for letting go of baggage and creating space for positive change

• **Financial Strategies** – Effective strategies the super wealthy use to build wealth

• **Timelining Your Outcomes** – A powerful meditation to install desired future outcomes using your own interpretation of how you store time along your time-line. This technique is most effective while in a state of meditation or hypnosis.

If you are unfamiliar with any of the above techniques or theories, please keep a totally open mind about all of them. We are not reading tealeaves or leaving our destiny to the stars. Each mental technology I will discuss has proven its validity to my complete satisfaction. Each of the above techniques will provide another "tool" for you to use in your "success tool belt." However, I will not spend valuable time explaining the background, the research, and the statistics to why this stuff works. If you have this type of analytical mind, please reference the bibliography. I encourage you to research these incredible techniques on your own from the books of their creators and authors in the field. They have changed my life. I am sharing them, because I know they hold the power to transform your life, as well. I have extracted the "cream of the crop" information that applies to this theme of wealth and happiness. There is so much more.

Because I've been researching this half my life, I have some special insights as to what makes an individual successful and what makes him fail. I'm also a regular guy who is using all the information you'll be reading about. I am living the concepts that I'm writing about. Because of this, I am making more money today than ever before. I have more freedom, love and happiness too. My mission is to give you these insights, and hopefully you will embrace them as your own.

The big changes in my life only occurred when I began to change myself. It wasn't anything that I did. It was who I was *being* when I made those big changes. If I were sitting across from you now as your success coach, I would be more interested in **Who You Become** as a result of your journey, rather than the goals you have set. And more often than not, when you change yourself in a positive way - the goals come to you effortlessly.

I believe that people can change. I've seen dramatic changes in people in just a weekend seminar, an one-hour session, or in six months of training. Likewise, I've seen people get stuck in a ten year relationship having the same fights day after day after day - never learning a new way of being - never moving toward progress.

In this book, I'm going to share with you some of the tools to change quickly. Now grab your tool belt. Find a pen and paper and get ready to discover your innermost goals and outcomes.

PART ONE:

THE SECRET TO SEEING

WHAT'S REALLY POSSIBLE

Universal Truth #3

You may not always get your goal... but you always get an outcome. Choose your outcome wisely.

CHAPTER 2

YOUR GOALS & OUTCOMES

What is Success to You?

Any book on success or personal fulfillment should at least discuss the concept of goal setting. But, quite honestly, the task of setting goals sounds like a boring task and one I've heard before. Many of you have set goals and did not achieve them. Why is that? Most business workshops I've attended forced me to write down my goals. Well, sometimes I got what I wanted and often I did not create what I scribed. Statistics prove that writing down your goals dramatically increases the odds of being successful.

5% IS WORTH MORE THAN THE OTHER 95%

Harvard University conducted a study on the power of written goals. (It may have been Yale circa 1955.)

They asked the graduating class how many of them had written goals for their lifetime? Only five percent of the graduating class had written goals. Twenty years later, that five percent, (60 students) was worth 95 percent as much money as the rest of them. So out of the tens of millions of dollars that graduating class touched in their lifetime, this 5% controlled 95 percent of that cash. Why is that?

You can easily position yourself in the top 5% of the world. The simple act of getting clear on what you want gives your brain clear and concise instructions to follow. You are telling your unconscious mind where you want to go. I want you to get more clarity about some of the things that you want. Is it more spirituality, more time in your life, more love, improved health, more wealth, or something else? This chapter will assist you in "programming" your brain to be automatically compelled to move towards these goals. As effective as simply writing down goals can be, we are going to apply 21st century mental tools to eliciting your inner desires. You will learn how to do more than set goals. You will learn how to install them and build your personality around happily and effortlessly achieving them.

So, if goal setting only works for some... how can we improve on the process?

If I were lazy, I could just assume you are reading this book to experience more abundance of money and happiness in your life. We could skip right over this chapter and talk about ways to create exactly those two items. But, in truth, money and happiness are merely by-products of other areas of your life working effectively on autopilot.

Instead of setting goals, I am requesting you create a list of "outcomes." The reason we have changed the word is that your brain already knows it will always get an outcome. You brain is probably unsure as to whether or not it will reach a goal. So, by setting a list of "outcomes" you have easier targets to move toward. Your brain already feels more confident.

The other reason I want you to focus on your "outcome" is that you can most likely achieve an "outcome" through a variety of means. This gives the "universe" more options when looking for ways to create for you. For example, if your outcome is to have a loving monogamous relationship, then, your brain has the option of finding you a lover, a friend, or a spouse. However, if you tell your brain you have a goal of being married by next year, then your brain is likely to find you a spouse, but it may not include the real outcome (feeling the benefits of a loving monogamous relationship.)

So, instead of just writing down a goal, ask yourself what the outcome of having that goal really would be. In some cases, the goal and outcome will be the same word. In others, the outcome will reveal a deeper meaning. Be specific in describing your ideal outcome, and you'll be surprised at how focused your intention will become.

One thing is for sure ... you always get an outcome. In many cases, it might not be the outcome you were expecting. But, you will achieve an outcome. That's why I emphasize writing down specific outcomes. The more specific, the more likely you will achieve what you truly want.

How I Created My Goals and Forgot to Get My Outcomes

When I had just graduated from Pepperdine University, I had an interesting first hand experience with setting goals. I had lots of debt from the education and no cash savings. I said to myself, "Okay, I want to be rich." I didn't have an obvious opportunity to make tons of cash. I didn't come from a rich family, but luckily I had a good education. Because I truly believed I could become wealthy, I focused my mind on finding out *how*. Although I had already begun earning $100 per hour as a handwriting expert, the work had not been consistent and I wanted to do something different.

I moved to Las Vegas and took a job at a major casino in a management training program. During the first three months, I think I was earning just $6 an hour. Later, I was earning more, but nothing to brag about.

I knew I wanted to be a famous author and a well known speaker. But, I hadn't really accomplished anything to speak or write about yet. (Details, details). So, after working a few months I found myself thinking, "Bart, this is really going slow. I'm struggling financially. I'm not getting rich from working for someone else. What am I going to do?"

So, I signed up for a goal setting seminar. At 22-years-old, I set three goals for myself. They're not goals I would aspire to now, but at 22 I said to myself, "By the time I turn 23 I want a new jeep, I want to be on national TV, and I want a book with my name on it in the bookstores. I want to walk into the bookstore and see a book on the bookshelf that I wrote." To me, that would be success -- that would make me feel successful. That would be accomplishing something that would make me very proud. I thought those lofty goals would bring me happiness.

Let me tell you how it turned out. Sometimes when you write down your goals, you don't even have to work for them. They just kind of show up magically. This is the power of your unconscious mind. Your mind really is a "manifesting machine." Program it, relax, and know your outcome is already in motion.

In my case, all three goals were accomplished very close to the given date. One of the goals I worked my butt off for. Two of them just came to be as a result of forces outside of myself. (But, I'm sure I set those forces in motion.)

In 1991, I had not written a book yet. I had published the Grapho-Deck Handwriting Trait Cards and had appeared on a dozen or so small radio talk shows. I wasn't even a minor celebrity. How I was going to land a national TV show, I had no idea.

About two weeks before my birthday, a friend of mine named Ross calls me, "Bart, I'm going to New York to be on the Jane Pratt Show. One of their guests canceled and I talked the producer into letting you take his place. Do you want to go to New York, to be on national TV?" It happened that fast. We left three days later. I appeared as a guest expert talking about using handwriting analysis for dating.

As it turned out any TV show that airs in New York is a big deal. It actually wasn't aired to the entire nation. It just aired on the East Coast. However, that experience allowed me to eventually appear on the Montel Williams national TV show about a year later.

I later found myself thinking, "I got a free trip to New York. I just got one of three goals accomplished, and it was basically handed to me. They just called me." I felt lucky. But I knew my achievement was based on more than luck. Luck is when opportunity meets someone who's prepared. I was prepared and I had "spoken" the desire to my friend Ross. I set the dominos in motion - the universe delivered.

By the way, that appearance didn't make me any money. In fact, the next national TV show Montel Williams didn't send people rushing to book stores either. I had set a goal, not an outcome. I should have set an outcome to sell 10,000 books. But, instead I made the assumption if I land on national TV, I will automatically sell enough books to make me rich. That wasn't the outcome I got. But, I did get one of the goals I asked for – to be on national TV.

My second goal was getting a jeep. Now, I don't necessarily want to drive a jeep now, but when I was 22-years-old, a jeep was a really cool ride. At the time, I was driving a 1982 Buick Sedan De Ville. It was basically a tank built for a family of eight. It was so old I had to staple the headliner to the ceiling before each date so it wouldn't fall on her head when we hit a bump. I was really embarrassed to own this car. Many times I thought to myself, "Here I am writing a book on relationships, and I'm trying to convince a girl to like me, when I'm driving such a pathetic car."

I was still reading all the books on success and trying to think positive. But it was hard to maintain a positive mental attitude, when I thought the car was so ugly. So I asked myself, "How am I going to get a new car?" I wasn't making enough money to buy a new car, so, I simply wrote down the goals and forgot about it.

One day I was listening to a spiritual teacher discuss wealth and money. He said, "Everything in your life is a reflection of who you are. Whatever car you're driving is where your mind is regarding wealth. So if you're driving a cheap, ugly car, it's a reflection of who you are. It's a reflection of your self-esteem and your beliefs about money."

I thought, "Ooooh, I don't want to hear that. That's not me. I'm only 22. This is just temporary. Besides, the car was given to me. I'm really a total success." The spiritual teacher actually got me angry. I don't know if I was angry with him or myself. But the cruel reality of my world was that I was driving an '82 Buick with a broken window and the ceiling falling down. I thought maybe, just maybe, he's right. Perhaps my current world really does reflect the quality of my thoughts. No more excuses. Just look around and take inventory.

This is really what happened less than 30 minutes after hearing that lecture.

On my way home, I was sitting at a red light, in the middle lane. I had this unexplainable desire to turn right. So I crossed two lanes of traffic and turned right on a red light. Out of the corner of my eye I noticed a very large tow-truck heading toward my rear bumper. The tow truck missed my bumper and slamed into the left side of my Buick crumpling the side of the car from the rear to the front. The crash was loud and startling. But, since the car weighed as much as an army tank, I survived with out injury.

I thought, "That was about the stupidest thing I've ever done in my life" -- all for a right turn. I had no idea. It was like something possessed me to do this. I didn't put the two-and-two together until later. I got an envelope from the insurance company for $3,500 for the car repairs. So, I sold the old car for $500 and bought a $4000 used jeep.

This is a roundabout way to get a goal, but your unconscious mind has a way of giving you what you want.

I went, "New jeep. Whoa!" All of a sudden I had created this disaster, and ended up getting myself a new jeep. I know I didn't crash my car on purpose.

Those were two easy goals accomplished. Essentially, the universe just handed me my first two goals without a lot of effort.

Getting that first book written and published was not as effortless. I had at least 30 rejection letters in my file from publishers. It took nine hard months to write and edit. Eventually, I chose the option of self-publishing the first book The Secrets To Making Love Happen (Mastering Relationships using Handwriting Analysis).

Now, guess what? I wasn't rich. I wasn't famous. But I had achieved all three of my goals, so that was good. Yet for some reason I still wasn't happy. I learned from that experience, that you have to evaluate your goals very carefully, know exactly what you want, and be specific.

All of a sudden I had my books in bookstores and no one was buying them yet. I thought, "Oopps, I forgot to state a specific outcome." For instance, I should have set the "outcome" to sell 100,000 books or earn $1 million dollars from book sales. Because my ego wanted to see myself on TV and see my book on the shelf, I set goals that did not get my true outcome. My "outcome" for this book is to make a difference in over a million people's lives as a result of reading it. So, it really doesn't matter if I appear on national TV shows or if it ever sits on a bookstore shelf. Now, in order to achieve my outcome, it is likely I will reach those milestones, but not necessary.

Besides, the universe is much more likely to hand you gifts that help others than the ones that simply serve yourself.

WRITE YOUR GOALS, DISCOVER YOUR OUTCOME

Now it's time to discover what your personal outcomes are. Please take a few minutes to fill out the following information. Take your time, think about each question, be sincere, and answer each question as clearly and concisely as possible. You may want to use a separate piece of paper or your journal.

1. What goal or goals do you want to achieve?

(Be specific and concrete. State it in terms of what you will see, hear, and feel once you've achieved this goal. What would it look like on a movie theater screen?)

2. What is important about achieving or completing these goals?

3. Because?

4. So, ultimately, what would these achievements mean to you?

5. As a result of completing these goals, my outcome is...

6. I agree to do what it takes to accomplish this desired outcome!

Your signature / Today's Date

Universal Truth #4

Argue your limitations, and sure enough,
they're yours.

-Richard Bach, Illusions

CHAPTER 3

THE SECRET POWER OF BELIEFS

I was recently visiting with my 10-year-old half sister Jessica. She was proudly showing me her latest report card. She had pulled four A's and two B+ grades. As we sat and discussed the various challenges of Math vs. Language vs. Science, I asked her why she made A's in some topics and only scored B's in other topics. Her answer was typical for a 10-year-old, "I don't know." As I probed deeper, it didn't surprise me to discover she actually enjoyed Science, Physical Education, and Social Studies classes. Furthermore, she found Math and Language quite tedious.

I then asked Jessica, "Do you notice that you make better grades in the subjects that you like?"

She responded, "Well, I think Science is fun … and, I want to be a marine biologist. So, science is easier because I like it."

"Really? That sounds interesting," I said. "So you don't think you will need to know Math as a marine biologist?" I asked. "I think you will have to use lots of math as any kind of scientist. But you might change your mind. I think you already know that if you are having fun, the math won't seem that hard. How much money does a marine biologist make?"

"I don't know. They will pay me whatever they want to," was her reply.

"Well, if you are going to choose a career, you might as well pick one that makes you both happy and wealthy."

"You can't control how much money you make," Jessica responded with fervor.

I queried the slightly confused 10-year-old, "Who is in control of how much money you make?"

"Your boss decides."

"Really? Well, I work for myself, so who decides how much money I make?"

Jessica saw a debate coming and did the ingenious maneuver of answering a question with a question, "Well, who gives you money?"

"Customers who read my books and attend my seminars," I replied.

Jessica rallied. "So *they* decide how much money you make. You don't have any control over whether or not they will buy anything."

"That's not true. I've spent ten years learning the art of running a business. The smarter I run my business, the more money I make. It sounds to me that you don't really believe you can be rich. Don't you want to be a millionaire?"

She told me emphatically, "I don't want to be a millionaire."

"Really? You don't want to be rich? Why is that?"

"Because millionaires are snobs," Jessica said with conviction.

I responded with the question that is usually effective in destroying someone's generalization. "All millionaires are snobs?"

She looked angrily back at me, deciding not to answer for fear of being wrong. Her stubborn streak was showing.

I said, "Answer me this ... how many millionaires do you know personally?"

She thought for a minute and blurted out, "None."

So I asked her, "Are you a snob?"

"Of course not," she said defensively.

"No? So, why is it you think that if you become a millionaire you will become a snob?"

Just then her mother, Tracy, walked into the kitchen. I told Tracy the bad news. "Tracy, Jessica just informed me she is going to be poor the rest of her life, and she will not take care of you in your old age because she wants to be poor and work for a boss all of her adult life."

Jessica became hostile and blurted out, "I did not say that!"

"You said you refused to be a millionaire because millionaires are snobs. In this day and age a million dollars isn't that much money. In fact, if you plan to own a house, raise a family, and take care of your mom, making a decision NOT to be rich is the same as making the decision to be poor." I turned to Tracy, "Don't worry Tracy, perhaps your other daughter Stephanie will take care of you in your old age."

Jessica was fuming at the turn of events in this debate. She was determined to hold on to her *belief* that all millionaires are snobs. Ten-year-olds can be quite stubborn, so she stood up and asked knowingly, "I'm not going to win this one, am I?"

"Jessica, if you win this conversation and keep your beliefs you will lose in life. If you lose this conversation you will win in life. May I suggest you stop choosing to be right and start choosing to be happy?"

She took a moment to process my esoteric comment that I knew would most likely not be processed correctly by a stubborn, yet intelligent, ten-year-old. She then turned and announced, "I'm leaving. I can't win."

I enjoy discussing ideas and beliefs with children because they are generally more honest than adults. They also have not developed the exquisite levels of self-deceit and verbal sparring that can cover up true core personality issues. I had hoped that my one conversation with Jessica would jiggle or dislodge the limited belief that being a millionaire has bad ramifications. The problem with Jessica is quite simple. She had already associated a negative emotion, represented by the word "snob" with the concept of being a millionaire. Our emotions drive us in one direction or another.

Let's face it ... if a ten-year-old is already consciously choosing NOT to be a millionaire, what is the only destiny that is left for her? She will be firmly middle class (or worse) and overlook every opportunity that comes her way to earn big money. I was teasing her when I said she was choosing to be poor the rest of her life. Clearly that was not her intent. But by not choosing a path to wealth, you are taking the other road which leads to non-wealth.

Financial prosperity is not an accident. It is a decision followed by choices followed by specific actions.

You see, this conversation would not have been as much fun with an adult, because adults have better stories and better arguments. Jessica is just a ten-year-old with a few untested opinions in her mind. One afternoon spent with a kind, non-snob millionaire and Jessica's mind will be changed. However, you are already grown. You have a history and an ego to protect. Even if you had a chance to meet 100 millionaires that were kind and not snobs, you might have 200 more references in your past that that much money is either bad or simply not possible for you to attain. You might simply decide that the 100 non-snob millionaires you met were exceptions. It all depends on how deep your beliefs are set. Because you are reading this book, I will assume you are willing to dislodge and change the beliefs that aren't working for you. This will be a logical choice once you realize what a profound impact your beliefs and values make on the rest of your life.

I have started this chapter by discussing money - but the ingrained beliefs about being happy, spiritual, loving, and living life on your own terms follow the same pattern.

You choose a belief -->

You make decisions based on that belief -->

You take action or non-action based on those decisions -->

Your reality becomes a mirror to your adopted belief.

Furthermore, if I have this conversation with an adult about his present financial situation, it is common to hear the excuses - not the possibilities. Adults will convince themselves they are just victims of chance, luck, family, or bad timing. I'm wondering: *Are you one of those people who may deny you might have limiting beliefs in this area?*

Here is a test. If you are lacking in any area of your life: love, family, money, spirituality, health, etc ... you have some limiting beliefs or destructive thinking patterns in that area. Period. End of story. And you're not alone, because we all have limiting beliefs to some degree. Now, the proof of what is inside your mind is so clear all you have to do is look around you and take inventory. Take inventory RIGHT NOW. Be honest. Your thoughts have already created your reality. Do you like it? Can it be improved? Now, what reality are you going to create next?

The reason I start this chapter on belief systems relaying a conversation with a child is because most of our core personality traits, beliefs, values, and thinking habits were adopted during our childhood. There are exceptions to this statement, but I find it is true in most cases. I find it uncanny how a child will think, act, speak, and even physically emulate her parents' body, mannerisms, and language (unconsciously, of course). Even if a kid rebels from his parents, he often deals with the same limiting beliefs while sporting blue spiked hair and a nose ring.

I started with children as an example to illustrate a very important point: Time plus beliefs equal predictable outcomes.

Time + Beliefs = Predictable Outcomes

YOUR BELIEFS SET YOUR COURSE

Have you ever taken a plane flight? Did you know that the plane is off course 98% of the flight? The pilot is in constant communication with the towers on the ground to get new coordinates and current directions. If you are walking from your living room to your kitchen, a 5-degree angle might not mean much to you. So you arrive at the left side of the refrigerator door instead of the middle of the refrigerator door. No big deal. But imagine if you are piloting a 747 from New York City to Los Angeles.

If you are flying five degrees off course as you left New York airspace, you would find yourself way off course at the halfway point of your trip. You might find yourself over Kansas City instead of Chicago. Then, just about the time you are planning to land in Los Angeles, you discover that that 5% error has placed you squarely over Cozumel, Mexico with no place to land but a strip of beach.

CORE BELIEF GAME

Below is a simple matching game that illustrates the effect that a core belief has over time. Evaluate the five core beliefs that a child might have adopted. Then, choose the resulting identity that

that belief could have led to over time. Beliefs are like very strong blinders on a horse. They automatically filter thoughts, opportunities, and ideas that are not in alignment with that belief. Since your mind can only take in about seven bits of information at one time, your beliefs help you delete all the other information. Therefore, core beliefs tend to focus our mind on specific outcomes while avoiding alternative outcomes. This is extremely obvious if you run the core beliefs for twenty years starting at childhood. So, grab a pen and see if you can match the core childhood belief with the person the child grew to become twenty years later. Simply draw a line between the two columns.

Core Belief at Childhood	**The Resulting Identity as an Adult**
Life is unfair.	Vegetarian
Honest people can't have nice things.	Serial Killer
We are all equal regardless of color.	Thief
All animals have souls.	
Violence equals control and power.	Construction worker
I am a musical prodigy.	Civil Rights Activist
An honest day's work equals an honest day's wage.	Grammy Award winner

Diagram 3b- belief game
See Answers at the end of this chapter.

The lesson here is simple. Your beliefs, values and decisions are a predictable guide to your future. If we teach our kids useful core beliefs, when they arrive as an adult they will be *on course*. However, most of us must consciously go through a process of evaluating our core values and beliefs in order to locate and erase limiting ones. This may seem difficult because the more stubborn you are, the more you might want to cling to those old beliefs. The older you are, the more years of *proof* you have about how the world works. You might be fooled to think your own experience is truth. It's quite ridiculous, when you think about it. After all, there are over four billion people on this planet. And your unconscious mind has the audacity to think your limited experience is any proof of reality. As a child, there is less experience, so kids adopt new beliefs faster. So, be a kid. Imagine the world as new again.

As you read this book, I want to challenge you to consider this: Everything you already know might be wrong. I would also ask you to consider this: Everything in this book might be wrong. It also might be right. The only way to truly know is to be open-minded, try it out, and see how it works for you.

My mission for writing this book is to show you a simple, easy-to-follow map to living a life of wealth and happiness. The belief you must accept is "your thoughts create your reality." Once you accept that premise, we can start choosing our thoughts, beliefs, values, and events in our life from a position of choice and power. Most people just accept their parents' model of the world as truth. (Those of you who rebel simply accept the opposite point of view as truth. In either case, you might be wrong.) If you were not born to parents with abundant money, success, joy, love and happiness ... then I bet you have some mental clutter you will want to clean out. The first step to cleaning out the clutter is recognizing the clutter exists. By the way, I don't claim to know what the "true nature of reality" really is. However, I am going to share with you the beliefs that have assisted many people in creating a reality for themselves filled with joy, laughter, and abundance. You choose the beliefs that work best for you.

YOU WON'T EVEN SEE OPPORTUNITY

It's really kind of sad how toxic belief systems blind people from ever getting out of the rat race. Recently, a 27-year-old woman was cleaning my house. While she was taking a break, I turned the TV off of the talk show (*Jerry Springer*) and turned to a show on personal finances. There was a famous author talking about wealth, buying a house, and how to pay less in taxes. I thought this is useful for the cleaning girl with two kids to watch. I knew she didn't make very much money, so this advice could make a big difference. She ignored the TV and picked up a hair magazine.

I asked her, "Doesn't this interest you?"

She replied, "Oh, that's for people who have money, who are rich. This doesn't apply to me. I'll never have a house of my own."

I thought, Wow, how sad. And, because she believes that, she will be right.

Her beliefs are so corrupted she actually "turns away from" opportunities that could lead her to wealth. I had already looked at her handwriting before I hired her. So, I knew she had a low self-esteem and average intelligence. But no great personality trait could compensate for such a misinformed belief system. Because she so firmly believes she will never have money or own a house (unless she marries a rich man), she fails to set any goals.

Good beliefs can attract and magnetize any worthy goal to you effortlessly. Likewise, a limiting belief can actually blind you from seeing opportunity that is standing in your path.

I wonder how many opportunities you have missed as a result of a faulty belief system?

There are more obvious examples. I can think of many times when I was in the casual dating phase of my life and I saw an attractive woman but didn't introduce myself. I made the decision for her that she would not be interested in me. Sometimes I didn't introduce myself because of a fear of rejection or even a lack of "state management." Talking to strangers may require the ability to create an instant "state of confidence" if you are going to develop rapport quickly. I was younger then. Now, I have very congruent and useful belief systems about relationships, love, and money.

In business, I have missed opportunities too. When I was just nineteen, I taught a weekend seminar called "Change Your Handwriting, Change Your Life." I remember a guy who attended who was into TV marketing. He offered to talk to me about producing a 30-minute long TV commercial to sell me in the form of a video home study course. At the time, the term "infomercial" was new and cable air-time was cheap. Many millionaires were born as a result of those early infomercials. Well, I never called the guy to discuss it. I remember looking at his number and choosing not to call. I want to kick myself when I think about that today.

The only reason I can justify my decision to "miss that opportunity" was a limiting belief system. I just didn't have the confidence to go for it at age nineteen. I waited almost ten years to attract another person into my life who had the ability to promote me in the form of an infomercial. And, as it turned out, I had missed the "window of opportunity" to get in while the TV advertising rates were low. So, no TV advertising has been created.

I'm sure I could tell you many pitiful stories of how I lost millions or lived without love before I decided to change my limiting beliefs. Luckily for me, I decided to do what it took to change myself. I don't miss opportunities like that anymore. In fact, I continue to create more and more opportunities than I have time to pursue so I have lots of choices in getting my outcomes. Abundance mentality creates an abundance of options.

WHAT ARE YOUR CURRENT BELIEFS?

Before I give you any more examples, grab a pen and play a little fill-in-the-blank. The game is easy. I will give you a sentence and you fill in the blank to make the sentence true for you. Don't write down what you THINK I would want to see. Be honest. You are welcome to make a sentence with poor grammar if you must. The only point of this game is the belief system - grammar or punctuation doesn't matter.

Just fill in the blank with the first word that pops into your head. There are not right or wrong answers.

BELIEFS ABOUT THE WORLD:

Life is _____.

Work is _____.

There is _____ enough time.

People are _____.

Men are_____

Women are _____.

Bad things happen because _____

My reality is created by _____

My life is how it is because _____.

I am a _____.

My body is _____.

God is _____.

Sex is _____.

Love is _____.

When I make a mistake I feel _____.

Taking a risk is _____

BELIEFS ABOUT MONEY:

There is _____ of money in the world.

I find money is _____ to come by.

Whenever I see really rich people, I think

_____.

I was taught that money should be

_____.

My religious background taught me money is

_____.

My dad spent money like it was

_____.

My mom spend money like it was

_____.

Whenever I find extra money lying around, I immediately

_____.

Write down a specific amount of money that you consider "a lot of money." _____

In summary, if you could sum up your past relationship with money, what would that one sentence be? Money is

_____

Now, I'm not going to judge you or grade the above quiz. I do want you to judge your own answers. Ask yourself if those are the belief systems that will make you wealthy? Later in this chapter, I will reveal to you some commonly held beliefs from rich and happy people.

How Belief Systems Are Formed

Beliefs are formed quickly and can be changed quickly. The day you were born, you had no beliefs. You might have had a personality, fear, and emotions, but you had no beliefs. As you grew up, you formed an emotional attachment to certain people, emotions, and things. Things that made you happy were good. Things that made you unhappy were bad. If a puppy licked you on the face, then all puppies were good. If a puppy growled and bit you, then all puppies were bad. Thus your learning process really grew out of what was pleasurable and what was not so pleasurable. Your brain made connections and chose beliefs that you are not even aware of.

A firm belief can be formed two ways. It can be formed quickly by one very intense emotional experience of pain or pleasure. Example: A ten-year-old girl nearly drowns in the lake and watches her younger sister actually drown. Result: A set of beliefs relating to water: I can't swim. Water kills. I hate the water. Water scares me. And perhaps some other non-water related beliefs regarding death; "Life isn't fair. There is no God. Or perhaps she'll have a more positive slant like "I was saved by God because I am special." In any case, a strong emotional event can quickly establish a lifelong belief or an unconscious emotional response (fear, phobia, anger, joy, sadness, etc.) But it often takes more than one event to form a firm belief. It may take four or five pieces of evidence to form a belief.

Take a simple example of a child named Samantha on her first day of school. The teacher asks, "Who knows the name of the president of the United States?" Samantha proudly answers the question correctly. The teacher says, "Very good Samantha. You are so smart." Boom. One strong emotional experience has created one "association" with the word smart. Then a few weeks later she makes an "A" on a test. Another emotional "association" is created. Then her father tells her how "smart" she is. Etc. Etc. In this case, this little girl hears that she is smart over 24 times during the next six months. A core belief is established.

Then, something interesting happens. She is watching baseball with some boys. All the boys scream with delight at the action on the field. She turns to the boy next to her and says, "What happened? Did they score a touchdown?" The boy looks at her and says "Wow. You're stupid. Touchdowns are only in football, not baseball." One negative. 20 positives. What is her belief about herself? She might have her feelings hurt, but it is likely her brain says to herself, "No, I'm not stupid. I'm smart. And you're just a mean kid." Life goes on. The more emotionally laden evidence you can provide, the stronger that belief is against criticism.

Now, imagine a little boy named Billy has just the opposite type of event occur in his life. Billy missed the question the first day of class. A student calls him lazy. One teacher even suggests he join the remedial class for slow students. His parents call him stupid. Etc. etc. Then, one day at a different baseball game Billy meets Samantha. Billy explains all the rules about the game of baseball. Samantha is so impressed at Billy's intelligence she says to him, "Billy, you are the smartest boy I know!" And kisses him on the cheek.

Wow. Billy gets one extremely emotional positive affirmation that he is smart. The result is Billy will probably fall in love with Samantha. However, it is unlikely her one comment will de-stabilize the "stupid" belief that Billy now holds as truth.

Think of beliefs like this. Beliefs are like the top of a stool. The more "legs" you have, the more stable the stool will be to sit on.

Weak Belief   **Firm Belief**   **Stubborn Belief**

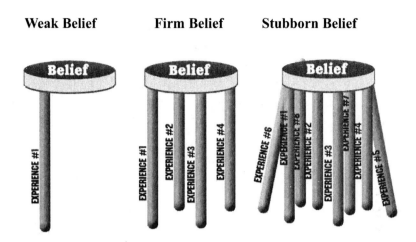

Diagram 3A: Belief Stools

The more "references" you have, the more pressure the belief can handle and not buckle under the pressure.

One way to change a belief is to provide many references to de-stabilize the current belief. However, if you are starting with a "Stubborn Belief" you might have an uphill battle breaking each metaphoric leg of each past experience or reference. In my experience helping people change their beliefs, I often took them into the past using time-line therapy. Instead of fighting the merits of each experience, I found that if I could take the client back to the very first experience and alter the decision they made during that experience, the other experiences just collapsed. They fell like dominoes. The Stubborn Belief became unstable like a barstool with only one leg. It just toppled. When it toppled, I picked a new, more useful belief and "looked for" new references and experiences so those would soon be accepted as truth.

TWO KINDS OF BELIEFS

There are basically two kinds of beliefs. The first belief is what I call a "CORE BELIEF". (Some books call this a global belief.) This is a belief that makes a broad statement about the nature of something. Usually core beliefs are expressed in our language after

the words IS, AM, ARE. For example: Life is _____. People are
_____. I am _____. Naturally, these can be associated with
any context: Love, family, money, career, church, sports, society,
gender, geography, etc.

Core beliefs are a bit more difficult to change, because they
seem to be true - despite your awareness that all beliefs are merely a
result of your limited and myopic experiences as one person in just
one body.

Here are some examples of some very limiting core beliefs: I'm
too young. I don't have the education. I don't have enough money.
I'm not smart enough. Men are pigs. Marriage is a bad investment.
All teenagers are trouble. Muslims are terrorists. Christians are dangerous. Americans are obnoxious. I'm fat. I'm broke. Life is hard.
Money is hard to come by. People are selfish. Life is a bitch and
then you marry one. All politicians are liars. Rock-n-roll is evil.

Accepting any of the above statements as a belief instantly
shuts down your ability to interact or learn anything from the subject of the belief. If you think money is evil, then imagine how
immediately "crippled" your ability to deal effectively with money.
If a man thought all women were evil, how "glorious" would his
marriage to a woman really be? Doomed from the start.

RULES

The second kind of belief is what I call a situational belief or a
rule. Don't we all love rules? Your life is full of rules, even if you
think you are a rebel. Rule beliefs are any statement or thought that
could be described as having an IF > THEN in the sentence. IF you
loved me, THEN you would marry me. IF I am smart, THEN I will
always get straight A's in school. IF I am educated, THEN I can be
rich.

Later in chapter 9, "Create Your Own Rules," I will discuss how changing the rules you have can dramatically increase the quality of your life. But, just to tease you, answer this:

What does it take for you to be happy?

What must happen for you to be successful?

What must happen for you to feel rich?

The answer to the above questions will give you insight into both your current beliefs and your rules for being happy, successful, and rich. So, are you happy with the rules of the game? If you are making the rules, make them so you can win. Heck, if you can choose your beliefs (and you did) and a rule is just a type of belief (and they are) ... what is stopping you from changing the rules so you can feel happy all the time?

Here is a secret. Shhh. Come closer. You don't want everybody to hear this.

You can change your own rules.

So, what are the belief systems of the rich and happy? On this page I have listed some of the most common beliefs of people who change the world, make a difference, contribute to humanity, have great family, love their spouse, earn millions, and even wake up every day and go to bed every day in a state of happiness.

Destiny is not a matter of chance, it is a matter of choice:
It is not a thing to be waited for;
it is a thing to be achieved.

-William Jennings Bryant

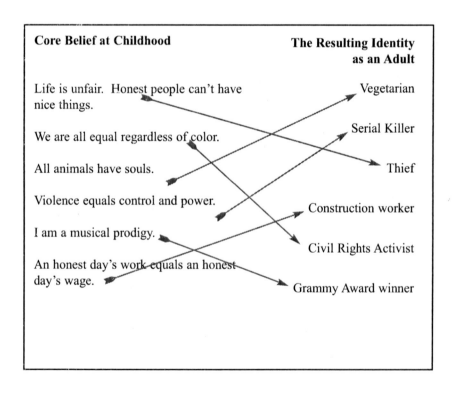

Core Belief at Childhood	The Resulting Identity as an Adult
Life is unfair. Honest people can't have nice things.	Vegetarian
We are all equal regardless of color.	Serial Killer
All animals have souls.	Thief
Violence equals control and power.	Construction worker
I am a musical prodigy.	Civil Rights Activist
An honest day's work equals an honest day's wage.	Grammy Award winner

As you read these, notice which ones resonate with your soul and which ones offend you. The ones that offend you, make you angry, or you have a need to argue ... those are the beliefs you need to work on the most. I'm not making any claim that these statements are right, accurate or true. All I know for sure is that these beliefs are VERY USEFUL in living a life of abundance and happiness. What beliefs do you aspire to hold as true?

In my humble lifetime, I aspire to hold all these statements as my own core beliefs.

Everything happens for a reason, and it is an opportunity to learn.
There is no such thing as failure, only results.
I will take full responsibility for whatever happens in my world.
I am at cause.
My thoughts create my reality.
Other people are my most valuable resource. I must attract and maintain strong relationships throughout my life.
I feel passion for my career - work is play.
I must first believe it before I can see it.
Making money is easy.
The more value I create in the world, the more money flows to me.
Money works for me, I don't work for money.
Money is abundant.
There is enough money in the world for everyone to win.
I am worthy of abundance.
When I give money away, I get back ten-fold in return.
God wants me to be rich.
I am grateful for what I have.
People are generous. I am generous.
I will always have enough money to get by.
My basic needs will always be met, no matter what.
Money is my friend.
Making money is fun!
I deserve and expect to be rich.
People are basically fair and just.
What goes around comes around.
Honesty has its own rewards.
I am lovable.
People like and respect me.
I am attractive.
I am a good person who lives my word.

Universal Truth #5

The emotions you value most
are the compass which reveals
the direction your life is headed.

CHAPTER 4

THE SECRET TO TRUE FULFILLMENT AND EFFORTLESS MOTIVATION

Have you ever wondered how some people accomplish so many amazing things in their lifetime? I think most people would love to make a difference or be a hero. I don't think they go through life not doing it because they are morally corrupt. No. I think it is much simpler than that.

Answer this question. If the New York Times ran an article about your life, after you have died, which life summary would you prefer to have in print to summarize your life?

1. You are an individual who freed the nation from the bounds of slavery. Without you, thousands of children would have needlessly died of hunger. People will be free for generations to come thanks to your leadership and fight for justice.

2. You spent your days in a dead-end job working just hard enough not to get fired. You spent most of your free time sitting on the couch eating moonpies watching television re-runs and sports events.

Hmmm. Which history would you choose?

Now I admit that I have chosen two extreme opposites along the spectrum of contributing to society, but I have a point to make here. I imagine most people reading this book would want to claim #1 as his or her biography, even though many of you could relate more to #2. Then why don't we all become heroes? There is a very

He who has a why to live can bear almost any how
- Nietzsche

simple reason. We don't know how. We all know how to sit on the couch, watch TV, and eat junk food. But how do you feed hungry children or free a country? If you could ask Gandhi or Martin Luther King if they knew *how* they were going to accomplish the great missions they did, I would guess they would admit to having a rather foggy plan, if they had a plan at all. But, they were very clear on one aspect of their mission. They knew why.

GET A BIG WHY

The secret to learning ***HOW*** to do anything is to create a big enough why.

Before I tell you how to set up your brain and your nervous system to automatically "wire " in a compelling *WHY*, please imagine taking this test.

THE $100 TEST

This is one of my favorite demonstrations in a live seminar. I ask who would like to win $100 cash? Imagine you raised your hand and came up to the front of the room.

Here are the rules of the game:

You must hold your arm and hand in front of your body, palm facing down, for 90 seconds without moving it. That is how you win the $100. Are you willing to play? Good. Ready?

Hold out your arm and start the timer. 89 seconds. As the seconds tick away, imagine I then pull from my pocket a large cigarette lighter. I light the lighter and a 4-inch flame rises from the top of the tiny butane tank. I then start moving slowly toward your hand. With each inch I get closer, I ask, "Are you sure you want the $100?" 55 seconds to go. Remember you can move your hand at anytime. When you move your hand away, you forfeit the cash. The flame moves closer. The lighter now sits 12 inches under your open palm. 30 seconds to go. You can feel the heat rising from the flame. The lighter now moves up toward your palm. The heat is now a focused beam of flame searing your tender flesh. 25 seconds. You can handle the pain. It hurts, it hurts. 20 seconds. Sometime between 20 seconds and 19 seconds your brain decides the pain of the flame is greater than the pleasure of the $100 cash. You move your hand.

So, the secret to motivation is having a large enough *why*. What if you were going to win $1 million dollars? I would burn my hand for $1 million bucks, no hesitation. When your *why* gets compelling enough, you are willing to go through larger amounts of pain to accomplish your goals.

PAIN VS. PLEASURE

Your life is motivated by a constant assessment of *pain vs. pleasure*. You might not be aware of it at the conscious level, but almost every decision you make is designed to move you either away from *pain* or closer to *pleasure*. When you understand this basic truth of the mammalian brain, your life is easy to direct. Think about a dog. How many times does a dog have to get shocked by an electric fence before he learns new boundaries? These boundaries are taught by the simple principles of pain or pleasure. He rolls over for a doggy bone repeatedly. (Pleasure)

Almost all the personality traits or "roadblocks" to success you will learn about in chapter 7 were formed as a result of a painful experience early in life. Being embarrassed at age 6 could result in the *fear of ridicule*. Being told you were stupid at age 10 could result in a *low self-esteem*. Being alienated for being the smartest kid in the class could have resulted in the *fear of success* rather than in a strong sense of self-worth. Our emotions are very serious and important to whom we become. Our early experiences create links between certain actions and specific emotions. Most of these early decisions are made completely outside or our awareness. The class clown learned early on that being loud and funny brought him pleasure. While, the shy girl sitting next to him learned that speaking her mind brought her embarrassment (pain). Etc. Etc. So, when you learn to analyze yourself and your friends' personality traits in chapter 6 and 7, please have empathy. Even the really dysfunctional personality traits like dishonesty or temper are based on a child's innate need to avoid pain and move toward pleasure.

Our brain actually makes new neuro-associations with each new experience. Biologically, a new neuro-pathway is actually created in your brain. In non-medical terms, this means that a new cellular "road" is formed to assist in having that specific thought or feeling. The more often you feel a specific emotion, the bigger and stronger that cellular road becomes. Eventually, that road becomes a habit. So, your hundreds of cellular roads are what make up your personality. Your brain opts to take those big paved highways, because it is much easier than creating a new road across untamed land.

However, in order to form new personality traits and create new habits, you must force your brain to build new cellular roads. Most of the exercises, including all the grapho-therapy based handwriting suggestions in chapter 7, are designed to "build new cellular highways" in your brain. When you do these, change can happen faster.

Your own perceptions of what equals pain and what equals pleasure are the driving forces behind your life. By the way, very few people have the exact same definition as someone else. For some people, giving public speeches represents positive emotions like acknowledgment, respect, and contribution. However, for most of the world, giving a speech sparks emotions such as humiliation, embarrassment, failure, etc. So, which one is real? They are both real to each person.

One of the most important steps to discovering how to live in a

There is more to life than increasing it's speed.
—Mahatma Gandhi

state of wealth and happiness is to establish how much you value specific emotional states. By understanding how much you value each emotion, you can then determine what has been stopping you. You can also create an extremely compelling mission that works with your values.

Take this simple test:

Which of these emotions do you value most? (Security, adventure, success, peace, fun, love, trust)

No, you do not value them all the same. One pops out as being the most rewarding. And, one probably stands out as being the least important. Take a moment and rank them in order of your preference. #1 being the most desired emotion and #7 being the least important emotion to feel.

The above seven words are actually just labels to describe an emotional experience. Whether that label is #1 or #7 is really the amount of value you have assigned to this emotional experience. Your brain has already assigned a VALUE to almost every possible experience. The problem is, you don't know what value it has assigned. In many cases it assigned a value to some experience when you were seven years old. Today, your brain still perceives that emotion as a #1 value, when in fact you want it to be #7.

For instance, when I was a kid, my parents got divorced. At the time, I associated marriage with emotional pain. Although my mom's second marriage has been 20 years of love and bliss, whenever I got into serious relationships, my brain still remembered the pain of the divorce. So even though I wanted love, I spent my twenties valuing freedom over marriage.

Most people have conflicting values that make them feel stuck or pull them in two different directions: security vs. adventure, love vs. freedom.

The seven-word test above was a simple learning tool. There are probably hundreds of words you can think of that describe your emotional states. Let's explore which of your values move you *toward* pleasure. I encourage you to take a few minutes and really answer the following questions as completely as possible. First, answer them in your own words. If you get stuck, I have provided a list of common values a few pages away. Use your own words. They contain more emotional juice than words you choose from a list. You can choose values that pertain to your whole life. Or you can be more specific and elicit your values about being in a relationship. If you are really serious about making all areas of your life work, I suggest answering the question five times- once for each category; Life, Career, Relationship, Health and Family.

HOW TO ELICIT YOUR "MOVING TOWARD" VALUES

What has been most important to you in life?

Or, another way to phrase this question:

What's most important to me in _____? (Life, Career, Relationship, Health, Family, etc)

What else is most important to me in _____. (Same category as above)

Now, this question will guide you to rank the value of each emotion from highest to lowest.

What has been most important to you , _____ or _____?

In order to get the proper values, you must be careful to choose the actual "ends value" and not the "means value." I'll explain.

Have you ever heard the Machiavellian phrase that says, "The ends justifies the means."? Essentially, words like money, family, relationship are means to experience specific emotions. The emotions are the ends values. For example, having *money* gets me the emotion of freedom, security, and peace of mind. Having family gets me the emotions of love, passion, and contribution.

SOME COMMON "MOVING TOWARD" VALUES

(Feel free to add your own in the blank spaces provided)

Achieving	Adventure	Career
Comfort	Contribution	Creativity
Freedom	Friendship	Fun
Happiness	Investment	Making money
Health	Helping others	Honesty
Intimacy	Knowledge	Love
Learning	Growing	Making a difference
Passion	Power	Respect
Security	Spirituality	Strength/vitality
Success	Wealth	

_____   _____   _____

_____   _____   _____

_____   _____   _____

_____   _____   _____

Do not read on until you have elicited your major values for the above questions.

The above two questions elicited values that you are drawn *toward*. These tend to be positive emotions that you want more of in your life. Remember the test I did with the $100 bill and lighter? Which one was a more quick and compelling motivator... the flame or the cash? (Pain or pleasure?) That's right. Pain tends to get our attention quicker. And most people will work harder to avoid pain than to gain pleasure. How urgent do you get to earn $200? Is the motivation more when you want to buy a new dress or when you have an eviction notice stapled to your door? Many people live in a state of *drama* and *urgency* because pain is the only motivational strategy that gets them to take action.

Therefore, it is equally important to know what emotional states your brain is currently programmed to avoid at all costs. What we want most and also what we fear most shape our lives.

Example: if you really want success, but you are programmed to avoid the pain of rejection, you will have trouble succeeding in a sales job. People struggle with value conflicts all the time and don't know why they feel torn or stuck.

HOW TO ELICIT YOUR "MOVING AWAY FROM" VALUES

So take a moment to answer this question. The resulting list will be your primary "moving away from" values.

What have been the feelings or emotions you would do almost anything to avoid having to feel?

Once you have your list, rank them in order.

Would you do more to avoid feeling _____ or _____?

(Which would you do more to avoid having to feel?)

Keep asking the above question until you have ranked them in order of highest rank to lowest rank.

Here are some common moving away from values: Frustration, anger, depression, humiliation, embarrassment and physical pain.

WHAT DID YOU LEARN?

Now, look at both of your lists in ranking order. Do you see any conflicts? Ideally, your "moving away from" values will push you toward your goals, and your "moving toward " values will pull you toward your goals.

If you know a person's value, you can predict a person's direction in life. Your values are like the walls of a pinball machine. They "bounce" you from one direction to another. Some "push" you in a direction and others "suck" you into another direction. If all your values are "pushing" you back and forth, you might begin to feel like a pinball. Moving very fast, but not getting very far.

Just as your goals can change, so can your values. If values are merely the ranking you give to the value of the emotional experience, your values will change with your level of experience. Don't despair if you find a value conflict. Just be grateful it has come to your attention, and you can begin to change yourself so that success will come easier than before.

EXAMPLE #1:

If you are a 21-year old virgin, the value of "sexual stimulation" might be ranked #1. But, after that same person has been married for 20 years, the value of "sexual stimulation" might rank lower on the value scale than love, connection, commitment, etc. We tend to change our value of something given the rarity or the abundance of that experience.

*Some people die at twenty-five and aren't buried
until they are seventy-five.*
—Benjamin Franklin

EXAMPLE #2 BOB AND NANCY:

I once knew a guy named Bob. Bob had a self-confessed fear of commitment. His girlfriend, Nancy, was getting impatient with his resistance to getting married. Upon eliciting Bob's values, it was clear why Bob had such a difficult time making the long-term pledge of his love.

Bob's #1 Toward value was **freedom**.

Bob's #2 Toward value was **love**.

Bob's #1 Moving away from value was **loneliness.**

Bob's #2 Moving away from value was **being controlled**.

You can imagine the inner struggles Bob was having. Bob desperately wanted to avoid feeling the emotion of loneliness but was ranking freedom as the #1 positive value he thought he needed to feel in order to be happy. Once this ranking came to his awareness, he was able to work through why he felt being married was a sacrifice to his freedom. When he realized that in order to keep his version of freedom he must sacrifice his love and feel lonely, he felt pulled in two different directions. From his past both freedom and love had been very deep and important, and he associated pleasure with it. So, with his new awareness of his values, Bob began to reassess his rules about having freedom. When he began looking, he found the evidence.

Bob had unconsciously adopted a rule that marriage = no freedom. Hmm. Bad rule for Nancy. She had a belief that marriage = freedom (freedom to express, to be authentic, to be vulnerable, etc.) Bob began to look for married people who experience freedom and

asked them how they did that. He began to look for evidence to dislodge his limiting beliefs regarding marriage and freedom.

So, both people wanted love and freedom. But, they had different rules about how to achieve these states. Bob eventually decided
that love was a more compelling and rewarding emotion than this
old version of freedom. Then, he and Nancy discussed all the ways
he could feel free within a committed relationship. Once Nancy
agreed to those rules, Bob felt comfortable moving forward with the
engagement.

EXAMPLE #3: 40-YEAR-OLD MAN

Here is an example of the values chart of a 40-year-old man
who wants to be more financially successful. The first chart is how
his values appeared to him after taking the above quiz. The second
chart is how we "designed" them from out of his own power of
choice. I have included only the top six values. Your chart may
include 10 - 15 values.

OLD VALUE RANKING:

Toward Pleasure Values	Away From Pain Values
Love	Failing
Fun	Loneliness
Freedom	Being Controlled
Security	Physical Pain
Adventure	Risk
Success	Being Bored

What changes would you suggest?

NEW VALUE RANKING

For example, here are the newly designed values from this 40-year-old:

Toward Pleasure Values	Away From Pain Values
Love	Being Bored
Success	Physical Pain
Fun	Loneliness
Adventure	Being controlled
Freedom	Risk
Security	Failing

For this demonstration only, I re-arranged all six values. In your life, you don't have to keep any values you don't want to. In the above example, I would most likely suggest he put fear of failing at the very bottom of his list of twelve *moving away from* values and put new values such as "being mediocre" or "feeling broke" near the top of his *moving away from* values.

Do you think he will find achieving success much easier now than before?

Notice how his life will change. First, I didn't suggest he re-arrange his #1 life value of "love". His wife might not appreciate that. So, he kept Love as #1, but we moved "loneliness" from #2 down to #3 moving away. This slight change will make it okay to spend more time working and less time with his wife in order to be successful. (If that is okay with her.)

Second, we moved "fun and freedom" down on the list so "success" could rank higher. He obviously had a habit of choosing the short term "fun" instead of working toward a long-term success. Fun is still in the top three, but now he has balance.

Third, we moved "freedom" down to #5 so he has the choice to work for a company that pays him big money, if he so chooses. For many people that have "freedom" so high on the scale, they avoid any type of career or opportunity that compromises their freedom. He might choose to work a high paying corporate job for three years and earn four times the salary. He now has that option.

Fourth, we moved "security" down to the bottom of the *moving towards* list. This would be a difficult transition if it was #1, but since it was #3...it could be accomplished. Now, the concept of "security" is less attractive and he is free to take more risk.

Fifth, we adjusted the moving away from values so he isn't so fearful of risk or failure.

This isn't the ideal value structure. It is just an example. I was tempted to include the value structures of self-made millionaires and other successful and/or happy people. But, out of respect for your individual mission, I will not do so. You might be tempted to "program" their values with the assumption that will make you happy. Nope. You have to choose your own value chain based on your own desired outcomes. I will give you hints throughout the book to which #1 or #2 values tend to make people the most happy.

I will relay this piece of advice that I learned from Dr. Tad James many years ago when I was struggling financially. Tad assisted us in eliciting the values of the participants in the workshop. He specifically asked us what was important in a career? Therefore, we were eliciting the emotions that made us most satisfied in a working environment. He then ask people to raise their hand if they ranked the value of "making money " or a similar phrase in the top three career values? As we looked around the room, only a few raised their hands. He said, "In my experience talking to thousands of people, the people that have "making money" in the top three values always do well financially." And, it makes sense. If you value "freedom, teamwork, or fun more than making money... you will consistently choose those values before you grab the cash. You don't have to make it #1, but if you work to earn money, then put that value at #1, #2, or #3. Why? Because you make decisions based on what you value most. When you put making money that high in your value chain, you begin to sort opportunities with "cash flow" as a priority and not as a hope. You will choose which business people to spend time with based on your financial best interest. If you are serious about making money in your career - consider moving around some values to make your work pay off.

HOW TO CHANGE YOUR VALUES

Changing your values can be as complicated or as easy as you make it. The awareness of where your values are today is the first step to effectively changing them. On a daily basis, being aware of the decisions you make is a good place to practice living within your chosen value structure. Now, I will share with you an easy and effective way to move values higher on your list.

For this demonstration, let's use "Money" as the value you would like to move higher on your list. Many people see money as merely a means-value. They feel money is merely the means (the path) to a more important value found in the end. That's okay. They don't particularly get much emotional satisfaction in earning money. They do it to get the other values.

Other people experience a strong positive emotional charge when they earn money. These people feel money is an ends-value. Because of this emotional charge attached to money, they often have an easier time earning money.

If you want yourself to experience a more positive emotional charge to money, all you have to do is associate the same positive emotions of your top three values with the act of making money. This mental conditioning will train your brain to feel the same good feeling when you earn money as you get from your other top values. Essentially, this process changes the way you value money.

When you place a high value on money,
you begin to naturally attract money.

All you have to do is begin seeing "money" using the same mental processes as you are currently seeing your #1 value. You do this by eliciting your submodalities. Submo-what-alities? Submodalities is one of those big scientific words that took me awhile to fully understand and to grasp the level of significance they can play in effecting the quality of my life. Now that I do understand the incredible power of submodalities, I have more direct control over all my emotions and internal thoughts. Submodalities are the fastest method to re-ranking values and changing anyone's emotions related to any past or future event.

Submodalities are the various ways your brain forms memories and emotions (loud or soft, in color or black & white, bright or dim, big or small, moving or still, fuzzy or clear, textured or smooth, panoramic or bordered, rectangular or square, you see yourself in the memory vs. seeing the event through your own eyes, etc.) Submodalities exist in every thought, memory, or emotion you already have. If you were to close your eyes right now and imagine yourself eating last night's dinner - that memory will have submodalities to it separate from other memories: you may see yourself at the table or see through your own eyes all the food on the table; you may hear voices of people you were talking to or music in the background; you may feel the chair you were sitting in or sensations in your stomach; you may even smell the food and taste it in your mouth as if you were eating it right now.

Research shows that by simply shifting these submodalities, you can have a dramatic effect on the emotional charge of that memory. I encourage you to elicit the submodalities you currently have relating to your lover, your ex-lovers, your job, your daily chores, and your dreams. Shifting the size, color, or location of that image or sound can have a profound effect on the emotion you feel. This simple concept has applications in every area of your life. Now you will learn how to elicit submodalities relating to values and change them.

COMMON SUBMODALITES

Visual
location in space
quantity of images
distance
crisp & clear/ fuzzy or blurry
bordered/ panoramic
color/ black & white
moving / still
speed
shape
size
horizontal & vertical perspective
see event through your own eyes (associated)
see event from outside yourself watching event (dis-associated)
3D or flat
brightness/ dullness
foreground background contrast

Kinesthetic
temperature
intensity
pressure
vibration
expanding/ contracting
spinning
still/ moving (where to where)
location inside body
moisture/ dryness
texture
rhythm
smell
taste

Auditory
quantity of sounds/ sources
distance/ location in space
style: music/ noise/ voice
rythm & cadence
mono/ stereo / surround sound
speed
clarity & intelligibility
pitch
volume (loud, soft)
echo /reverb
tinniness
bass/ treble

*See chapter 11 for more
information on submodalities.*

3 STEPS TO MOVING VALUES

The process of moving the value up the hierarchy of values has three steps. First you must discover the submodalities that are present with your # 1 value. Second, you must discover the submodalities that are present with your "making money" value. Third, you must adjust your "money" value to exactly match the submodalities of your own #1 value. When you do this, you will instantly feel that making money can be an easy and efficient way to feel your #1 value.

Here is an example of the actual questioning process that I would have taken a seminar participant through. You will want to ask and answer the same questions for yourself. I have chosen the name Susan as an example.

Bart: "Hi Susan. What you told me you wanted is to make more money. Is it okay with you to change the relationship of money in your hierarchy of values?"

Susan: "Sure. Anything to make more money. Let's do it!"

Bart: "Okay, I will guide you through a simple exercise so you can feel for yourself the changes. You can always put them back in the original order if you choose. You are in control."

Susan: "Great. What do I do?

Bart: "I am just going to ask you a few questions based on the hierarchy of values we just created. Ready?"

Susan: "Yes."

Bart: "You have on your list that being happy is your #1 value. When you think about being happy... is it a picture?"

Susan: "Yep."

Bart: "Is it black and white or in color?"

Susan: "Color"

Bart: "Is it bright or dim?"

Susan: "Bright."

Bart: "That's nice. Does it have a special location in your mind?"

Susan points to the front and says "I haven't really thought about it before, but yes. It's up and off center to the right. Over there."

Bart: "Nice job. Does that image have a border around it or not?

Susan: "Yes. A small border."

Bart: "What color is the border?"

Susan: "Black Border."

Bart: "Is the picture still or in motion?

Susan: "It's moving."

Bart: "Is it focused or blurry?"

Susan: "It's crisp and clear."

Bart: "Good job. I think I can now see why "being happy" is so compelling to you. You have painted a great picture of how you see it."

STEP #2: DISCOVER THE CURRENT SUBMODALITIES OF THE "MONEY" VALUE.

Bart: "Okay, Susan. Put that image aside for a few minutes while we talk about something different. Can you clear your internal screen? Are you ready to move on? "

Susan: "Sure."

Bart: "Okay, now I want you to again think about what is important to you in a career. Think about your value of making money. On your list here you have it listed at #8. What do you think about money?"

Susan: "Okay. I'm not getting a clear image of it."

Bart: "Really. What are you getting?"

Susan: "I am just getting a foggy dark feeling that it isn't fun."

Bart: "That makes sense. I realize your not exactly sure what image you see, but if could guess. What image would be there regarding making money?"

Susan: "It is me cashing a check."

Bart: "Good job. Is that a still picture or moving image?"

Susan."Still. I think."

Bart: "Okay, is this image bright or dull?"

Susan. "It's about medium. Not as bright as my being happy image."

Bart: "Where, inside your mind, is the making money image located?"

Susan: "It's a bit lower and to the left. The entire image is also smaller."

Bart: "Good job. Now what I am going to ask you to do is simply take the image of you cashing that check and view it using the same features as you told me the being happy image was in. So, when you think of money now... I want you to have the same process occur as you did before. I will guide you based on what you told me earlier."

Susan. "Okay."

Bart: "First, move the making money image up and to the right."

Susan: "Done."

Bart: "Make the image big and bright."

Susan: "Nice. It feels better."

Bart: "Put a nice black frame around the motion picture image of you cashing that check."

Susan: "Okay. Interesting."

Bart: "Now, make the image crisp and clear."

Susan: "Wow. It looks like money could really help make me happy."

Bart: "Exactly. Nice job. You might want to continue tweaking the features until you get totally excited about making money."

Susan: "This is fun. Can I do that with all my internal images, feelings, and voices about making money? Just think about them using features of a value that is naturally compelling."

Bart: "That is the idea."

This simple visualization exercise will literally force the "money" value to be moved to #2 directly under your #1 value. You will feel that now "making money" will be more compelling to assist you in feeling the other top 5 values. The concept of sub-modalities are the key to making this work properly. If you want to learn even more about submodalities, check out the NLP book called *Using Your Brain for a Change* by Richard Bandler or The Tad James book *Time-Line and the Basis of Personality*. I reviewed both books while writing this section.

The emotions you value most are the key to unconscious sustained motivation.

PART TWO:

PERSONALITY SUCCESS SECRETS &
OVERCOMING ROADBLOCKS

Universal Truth #6

You Change — Reality Changes

Your world is a reflection of who you are.
Reality is the mirror of your soul. As you change,
so does the world around you.

CHAPTER 5

THE SECRET TO DISCOVERING TRUE PERSONALITY — QUICKLY

One of the wonderful gifts my father gave me was the belief that I could be anything I wanted to be. I feel blessed that from an early age I felt very few limitations as far as my future was concerned. As empowering as that belief is, it still took me many years to figure out what I wanted to do and how to do it. The first step is having the empowering belief. The next step is asking the right questions. If you ask the right question enough times, you will find the answer. I was on a mission to find out how to be what I truly wanted to be.

So, in my early teenage years, I found myself voraciously reading autobiographies of famous men and women. I especially was intrigued with Benjamin Franklin, Thomas Edison, and Leonardo da Vinci. I found myself imagining what it must have been like to be these men. As I imagined what kind of men they were, I began to imagine their life through their eyes. I asked myself what habits or personality traits they must have had to accomplish great things. As I studied these men and dozens of other self-help books, certain traits came to light. Even as a fourteen-year-old, I realized that these were self-made men. They created their own legacy by *being a certain way*. Ben Franklin taught the value of honesty and hard work. Edison was the poster child for persistence. Leonardo was not afraid of failure. I also noticed their lifestyles and habits. Ben Franklin was a strict vegetarian. He lived to be 89 years old in an era when most men didn't live past 40. Hmm. That was clue to the value of health in successful people. (Ben Franklin also had a proclivity for young French women - oh, I digress. Never mind that trait.) Ben did reveal to me the strategy of saving a percentage of every coin earned. Etc. Etc. So, I too was convinced that if I could "model" successful men, I too could become a success. However, it wasn't easy to get a clear "map" of their thoughts and strategies. It was especially difficult because I lived in a different century than they did. The 1930's book called *Think and Grow Rich* gave a good road map to the mindset of success. The author, Napoleon Hill, interviewed dozens of rich men near the turn of the century. His work was revolutionary at the time. But, in a nutshell, he told me to "Think and Grow Rich." Okay. Got it. Now what? It is my intention, in this book, to give you actual mental "tools" which show you exactly "how to think" in order to be successful.

One thing was clear to me at an early age. My success wasn't simply a matter of what I accomplished. My primary focus was on *who* I needed to become. I intuitively knew that, when I became the kind of man I wanted to be, success would follow as a natural law. So I focused on changing myself and expected the world to change with me. It did.

THE CAR RIDE THAT CHANGED MY LIFE

One hot summer day, my father and I were driving toward East Texas. I was just fourteen years old. My dad was taking me to spend a week at Camp Red Oak Springs. I had been to this camp two years in a row, and I looked forward to it. During the car ride, Dad handed me a piece of paper and a pen. He said, "Write me a paragraph in your cursive handwriting. Sign your name. I'm going to analyze your handwriting." I said, "What?" He said, "Just do it." I complied. I thought perhaps that this was some kind of joke. It wasn't. He glanced at the chicken scratch I just handed him and started to describe part of my inner most soul that only I knew about, and many traits I was not proud of. He described my stubbornness, low self-esteem, over sensitivity to criticism, self-consciousness, and even my tendency to be obnoxious and rebellious. Hmmm. Was he just saying all this stuff because he knows me? Or, could handwriting analysis really reveal all that just from one paragraph? My dad had recently met a man named Dr. Ray Walker. Dad had started attending weekly classes to learn this 100-year-old science called handwriting analysis. And, it seemed to be the real deal. Knowing my prove-it-to-me attitude, my dad offered me a challenge. He said to me, "Take this textbook with you this week to summer camp. Get handwriting samples from at least ten different kids and adults. Go back to your bunk and just compare their writing to the handwriting samples in the trait dictionary at the back of the book. If you get a match, write down the trait. If it doesn't match, ignore it. Show your list to the author of the writing. They will tell you if it is true or not. Then, you be the judge if this stuff works or not."

To make a long story short, I ended up analyzing over thirty samples that week. I even stood up on stage and did a handwriting analysis of the Camp Director. I told everyone that he was sarcastic and unorganized. They laughed and gave me a standing ovation. Not only did I have fun at the camp, but also I made more friends than every before. I had the cutest girlfriend and even received a trophy for best camper! Wow. What a gift my father gave me.

I learned a few very important lessons that week. 1. Handwriting Analysis really works. 2. People behave the way they do because of their fears, desires, and personality traits. I learned empathy. 3. Handwriting Analysis can get me a lot of positive attention and popularity. 4. If a fourteen-year -old can do it, anyone can learn it.

When I returned home to Dallas the next week, I enrolled into Dr. Walker's Handwriting Analysis Certification Course. I have been hooked on this science ever since that day. Dr. Walker passed away in 1991, but we carry on the education through www.HandwritingUniversity.com.

As I have stated before, life is a bunch of beliefs. I don't know what 's true or real. Rene Descartes' even had me convinced I wasn't even reading his book. ("I think, therefore I am"... I am confused!) I think if you open your mind, you will find handwriting analysis an amazing and useful tool. I do whole-heartedly believe in this science. But, don't just take my word for it. Test your own eyes.

Below are two handwriting samples. You tell me whom you would feel most comfortable hiring to baby-sit your six-year-old daughter? Now take some time to really think about this – this is a hard one. Who would you let baby-sit your child?

Sample: 5A:

hello !

Dave Angie + Pat,

You and your silly monkey Should be happy to leave the little room.

Sample 5B

Even if you've never heard of handwriting analysis, you can probably tell that there's something wrong with the man in handwriting sample B. If you could pick this sample apart letter by letter, you'd find he has a number of what I call "Hell Traits." Hell traits are personality characteristics that indicate the person will be harmful to himself or others emotionally, mentally or physically. This letter is compliments of the Arizona State Prison. There's a reason he's in the Arizona State Prison. This person is a loony and potentially dangerous. He probably should never be let out of jail. But, I do like the happy face. Nice touch. That makes me really trust him ... just kidding, of course.

The point of showing you these handwriting samples is to show you how obvious it is that handwriting analysis reveals some clue to the character of the writer. Most people intuitively know that the person who wrote sample B is very different than the person who wrote sample A. If I took the time, I could break this handwriting sample apart into hundreds of individual strokes and explain every detail. But you don't have to be a handwriting expert to intuitively know that sample B is not the person you would let baby-sit your child.

Most handwriting samples are not this interesting. You don't have to be a genius to know there's got to be some truth to handwriting analysis when you see this extreme example. In our daily life we meet a lot of normal people, therefore we often see similar personality traits or handwriting characteristics. If you want to really prove this science to yourself beyond a shadow of a doubt, it helps to study crazy people. For this book, I studied successful people. They have different writing styles, too.

When I was a guest expert on The Leeza Gibbons Show, I analyzed Ted Bundy's handwriting and other serial killers. Serial killers have distinctive handwriting traits that reveal part of their psyche. Just as criminals tend to have predictable personality characteristics, so do entrepreneurs, engineers, pilots, accountants, salespeople, public speakers, radio hosts, and self-made millionaires. But before I reveal to you some of the personality traits of successful people, I want you to give yourself a quick self-test using just a few of the handwriting traits one could locate in your own handwriting. This book is not intended to teach you handwriting analysis. In fact, I'm only going to reveal to you the traits that directly relate to success, failure or happiness. If you want to learn more, you will have to reference some of the other books, cards, tapes, or home study courses I have authored. Log onto www.myhandwriting.com.

Okay, we're going to have a little fun here. Are you ready to have some fun with your own handwriting?

ANALYZE YOUR OWN HANDWRITING

Write down this sentence in your own handwriting. Use a ballpoint pen on unlined paper if you can. This sentence has all the key letters we will need for this simple demonstration.

The purple people eater said, "You and your silly monkey do not go home from the zoo on Tuesday. Instead they go to the racetrack on Friday!" - Signature.

Sign your name. If you print all the time, please write a little cursive. A professional can analyze printing. Cursive handwriting always reaveals more. Even if you think your cursive looks like a 5-year old, write cursive for comparison purposes over the next three chapters.

If you or someone you know cannot write cursive, they only print, then this gives us a general clue to their character. People who only print tend to put up emotional barriers so people don't see their insecurities. Men who only BLOCK print usually have problems in the area of intimate and inter-personal communication. There's nothing inherently bad about printing, but it takes longer to get this person to open up. I can analyze printing, but for a beginner, I always recommend asking for cursive. It's okay to do a bit of half print, half-cursive. For this exercise, please write cursive - even if you haven't written cursive in twenty years.

If you were sitting in the front row of a seminar, I would grab your paper out of your hand and bedazzle you with my insights. You might even be "blown away" at the sheer number of personality secrets I can extrapolate from your penmanship. In other words, if I had the privilege of analyzing your handwriting, in person, you would be a true believer in this science. Since this is a book and I am not able to look at your handwriting in person, you will have to do a little more reading before you become a convinced of the glories of handwriting analysis. I'm not assuming you might have been skeptical. Nope. I just realize the stronger your belief is that handwriting analysis has value for determining personality, the more likely you will be to use it as part of your own personal transformation. The study of handwriting is one of the most important "new tools" that I am going to share with you that can change your life. If you are not whole-heartedly convinced handwriting reveals character, then the next step, grapho-therapy, will be met with deaf ears.

Compare your writing to the samples on the following pages. Pay specific attention to the aspect of the writing I point out. There are literally hundreds of different strokes one could make in this one sentence. In order to accurately determine the trait, you must look at the individual stroke. If you just look at the overall "look or feel" of the writing, you will not be accurate. The following self-test is designed to give you a quick introduction to what your handwriting reveals.

Is your slant to the right or to the left... or in between?

The slant reveals how expressive you are. If you slant really far to the right, you respond and express more emotionally than people who have a leftward slant do. You are more touchy-feely and more in touch with your feelings, more expressive, more emotional. You are the kind of person who might cry at sad movies. People who write like Sample 5-C are more impulsive shoppers than 5-D.

Sample 5-C

I said you and your silly monkey do not go home to the zoo.

Jennifer

You and your silly monkey do not go to the zoo.

Sample 5-D

If your slant is straight up and down, this indicates you are more logical and rational. These people are cool under pressure and respond less irrationally in emotional situations.

And if you slant backwards to the left, which most people do not, you have some emotional issues that force you to be more withdrawn. You're the kind of person who would say, "Honey, I told you I loved you last week. Why do I have to tell you I love you again?" You're very logical, almost cold at times. Now, in my other books and courses, I explain that there are actually six possible slants and an exact measuring tool to establish the emotional outlay. In this scenario, just decide if you are emotionally withdrawn, detached, or emotionally expressive.

ARE YOU INTROVERTED OR SOCIALLY EXTROVERTED?

The size of your writing indicates how social you tend to be. Judging extroversion or introversion can be a bit tricky. You must balance the size with the indicators of the slant as explained previously. People who tend to write very small have outstanding "focus and concentration." Many pilots, mathematicians, and engineers have this tiny focused handwriting. Likewise, those professions are not known for their social skills. The really big, large, fluffy handwriting is much more fun at a party. Receptionists, exotic dancers, and high school girls typically have large "social" handwriting.

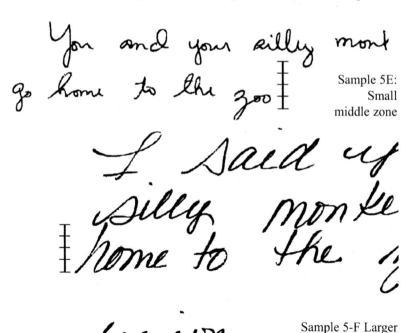

Sample 5E:
Small
middle zone

Sample 5-F Larger
writing = more social

Being fun at a party does not require a high level of intense focus and concentration. Which one are you? Or, are you in the middle?

LEARN ABOUT TRUST, ENERGY, AND SEX DRIVES.

Take a guess at which one of the people below has a more fulfilled sex life? Which one has the ability to open up and trust other

I said that you and your silly monkey do not go home to the zoo.

Tiny y-loops

Sample 5-G

people faster? Which one has more energy, which permeates all areas of her life, work, and relationships?

Sample 5-G : Small y-loops and controlled copybook writing

wife's handwriting
You and your silly monkey, do not go home to the z

Sample 5-H:

indicates conservative nature with low level of sexual expression.

Sample 5-H: Large lower zone loops with sloppy right handed

slant indicates impulsive and a highly sexual nature. Open minded and adventurious in the arena a sexuality.

"Y's"

Look at your "y's". Look at the word "monkey." Is your "y" really huge compared to the rest of your writing? Do your lower loops come back up and touch the baseline? Do you have a really, really big lower loop? The truth is the depth of your "y" and "g" down stroke is an indicator of your sex drive and your energy level. So the bigger the "y," the more energetic and the more physically natured you are. If you have a little tiny y-loop, it means that you're not very energetic, or sex isn't very important to you at the moment. In fact, I have noticed that when I have a cold or I am feeling very "under the weather", my lower loops literally shrivel up. Some aspects of my handwriting actually change with my moods or health. Wow. What an amazingly accurate personality test!

The next chart, Diagram 5-I, reveals various ways people can make the letter y-loop. Choose which examples best fit your writing. Don't be surprised to find more than one match. We are not robots. We often have contradictions and paradoxes in our own personality.

If your "y" goes straight down with no loop whatsoever, it means that you have a tendency to want to be alone. You can be a loner. It doesn't mean you don't like people, but it does mean you will want to make it on your own, you will like to work alone, and you'll probably like some private time. For a complete discussion of the lower loops and the "sex drives" revealed in handwriting, read Chapter 8 of my first book *The Secrets To Making Love Happen*.

THE SECRET JOY OF BEING DEFIANT

Do you follow your own rules or do you make your own? I have found one interesting personality trait in a vast majority of

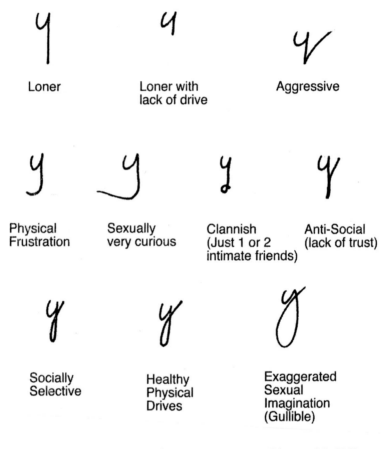

Diagram 5-I: Y-Chart

successful entrepreneurs: defiance. The tendency to break the rules, rebel, or defy the status quo seems to be a re-occurring theme in literature of heroes, superstars, and the super successful. Dr. Thomas Stanley's research in the book *The Millionaire Mind* indicates that most millionaires claim one important skill helped them achieve success. That skill was to "Think differently from the crowd."

Clearly, you don't have to break rules and get into trouble to think differently. But, research firmly indicates that people who make straight A's, have perfectly legible handwriting, and have perfect spelling are the least likely students to become self-made millionaires. Shattering statistics. Isn't it?

I'll show you two personality traits in handwriting analysis that proves this point. The first trait is called a "go to hell K". A capital "K" in a word that should contain a lower case "k" indicates defiance. Look around at the entrepreneurs and pioneers of the world. Many of them have this type of K. (So do the class clowns, criminals, and trouble-makers.)

Which of the below handwriting samples is more likely to become an entrepreneur?

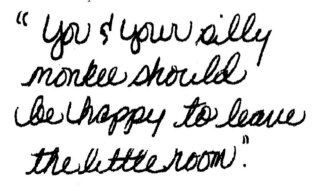

Sample 5-J: A person who follows all the rules and proper protocol. (Notice the legible handwriting, small lower loops, curvey m tops, beginning hooks, and normal sized "k.")

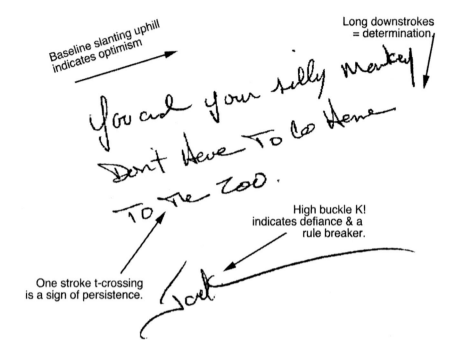

Baseline slanting uphill indicates optimism

Long downstrokes = determination.

High buckle K! indicates defiance & a rule breaker.

One stroke t-crossing is a sign of persistence.

Sample 5-J: The above handwriting is that of a very successful man in his mid 50's. A defiant rule-breaker in his youth, he still bucks the trends. His optimism is critical to his success. His pointy m's are a sign of quick thinking and intelligence. His high buckle "k" reveals his defiant rebellious streak. Even his sharp t-point indicates some sarcasm. This is the writing of legendary radio host Jack Diamond. Jack has hosted one of the longest running morning radio shows in the USA (in Washington D.C.) A career in morning radio is about as close to being a creative entrepreneur while still having a boss as you can get. In reality, Jack is both a successful on-air personality and off-the-air entrepreneur/ businessman. Morning Radio and other forms of performace comedy tend to attract people with defiance, sarcasm, and other fun but trouble making qualities. Don't we love them?

THE SECRET SCIENCE OF GRAPHO-THERAPY

After I started to study the science of handwriting analysis, I realized that all great men and women were within my ability to study. If I could just find a sample of their handwriting, I could get a clue into their characters. If I knew which habits or personality traits they possessed, I could "model" them. Upon embarking on my research, I discovered that Benjamin Franklin had this idea 200 years before I did. It is said that he would go as far as copy a great man's penmanship to get a feel for who he was. Maybe Ben was the first Grapho-therapist.

One of the most effective tools I have used or taught for people to change themselves is the science of Grapho-therapy. During the first meeting with Dr. Walker, this concept was introduced to me. When I was just fourteen years old, Dr Walker suggested that I begin to immediately raise my t-bar. As I sat in awe of this wise man, my brain thought, "You have got to be kidding?" Dr. Walker spoke with congruent confidence about the hundreds of clients and friends over the past 20 years who have seen profound results using this technique.

In my case, I had more than just the "t" to fix. I had to de-program my stubbornness, over-sensitivity to criticism, self-consciousness, and boost my self-esteem. Dr. Walker was probably praying that my "sarcasm" would find it's way to the exit, as well. Luckily, at the age of just fourteen, I listened. I thought about the simple risk vs. reward system for making a decision.

Step one: What happens if this succeeds?

Step two: What happens if this does not succeed?

My answer was simple. If Dr. Walker's advice succeeded in transforming me (this insecure, weak, scrawny, smart-ass, defiant, obnoxious teenager) into a world class self-made millionaire who attracts the ladies ... Wow! On the other hand, if this "changing the handwriting trick" did not succeed, I would be stuck with a funny looking letter "t" for the rest of my life. Not a tough decision. Hmmm. Wealth, Women, and Wisdom vs. a silly t-bar. The reward was clearly worth the risk. In fact, I couldn't think of a downside. My handwriting sucked anyway. It was illegible, so now it would be illegible with different letter formations. So what?

As it all turned out, my handwriting actually became more legible over the coming years. My t-bars are still crossed at the top of the stem. And the strokes of stubbornness, self-consciousness, and over-sensitivity to criticism have been gone for over a decade. The real test was what I found in the results. The first thing I noticed was my tendency to think more of myself. I wasn't a student who actually liked to study. However, I found myself walking into the school counselor's office one day requesting I be moved to a "more challenging" English class. I was bored. Then, I found myself asking the prettiest girl in school out on a date. She said, "No." But since I had begun to erase the fear of failure, I just asked out someone else. It didn't take long to develop some better rapport skills and the girls started saying, "Yes." I even noticed my grades were improving.

I clearly remember the day I knew "Grapho-therapy" had worked for me. I realized it when I made an "F" on my first English paper. What? That's right. It was a horrible paper. In fact, my teacher actually suggested I go back to the "non-advanced" class, because it was unlikely I was ever going to excel at writing. Hmmm. I would say my defiance was a useful trait during that conversation. I re-wrote that "F" paper and turned it into a "C-." It wasn't the teacher's false opinion. She was right about one thing: the paper sucked wind. I deserved a "C" or an "F." But she was wrong about my abilities.

Later that day, I sat and meditated upon my future. Because books had such an impact on me, I refused to believe I couldn't contribute something to the world in the form of the written word. I remember clearly sitting on my porch on a rainy winter day in Dallas, Texas. I must have been fifteen years old, trying to grasp what my life would be like over the next fifteen years. I had a vision. I made a decision that would shape the direction of my life. I decided in that moment that I was going to write a book and become a famous author. Thanks to my new and better t-bar, I actually believed this was possible. I made that decision despite having a respected teacher tell me I had no skill. I made that decision despite having no firsthand knowledge of publishing, writing, TV, or radio. I just knew I was going to do it.

Once you get clear on WHAT you are going to do ... the HOW finds you.

Less than 8 years from making that decision, I had my first book in my hand. At the age of 23, it was published. I'm sure I could have accomplished it much faster, but I had to take care of a few minor tasks such as puberty, high school, and college. Over the past decade, I appeared on over 1300 radio and TV talk shows promoting my book, tapes, and the science of handwriting analysis. I lived my dream.

WHY IT WORKS

I had a lot of faith in the technique of programming your brain via handwriting changes. In fact, I had even written a fill-in-the-blank workbook on the topic called *Change Your Life in 30 Days* that I used in my live seminars. However, I was unable to explain it. I even had my own doubts it could be nothing more than the "power of positive suggestion"... the placebo effect.

It wasn't until I began studying other forms of psychology, therapy, and personality tests, that I discovered some scientific evidence that explains what I had been witnessing in myself and others. The

*"Any sufficiently developed technology is
indistinguishable from magic"
- Arthur C. Clarke*

field of NLP (Neuro-Linguistic Programming) is revolutionizing the world of change therapy. NLP is teaching therapists how to cure life-long phobias in half an hour. It is teaching sales people how to have "instantaneous rapport" with clients. It is explaining the delicate balance between our body, our subconscious mind, and our behavior. It is so much more than a set of tools to improve your communication. I was sitting at an Anthony Robbins seminar in 1989, when he began to discuss how our brains learn information. He said that learning is really a function of our brains establishing new "neuro-pathways." Each time we have the same "experience" a spark of electricity moves along the neuro-pathways thus making the pathway twice as strong. If you have the emotion or experience 100 times, the brain creates 100 micro-strands along that neuro-pathway. This is how we establish habits.

Now, if you have studied any brain biology, you realize this is a simplified metaphor for the complex neural-cortex. However, it is an accurate big picture description. Anthony Robbins referenced a study at UC Davis using macaque monkeys to establish a connection between repeated physical movement and cellular development. Upon researching this study at UC Davis, I discovered that Dr. Amaral has been the man instrumental in this research. On the website, Dr. Amaral states that "our research program is divided into three major efforts that use neuroanatomical, behavioral, electrophysiological and clinical studies to investigate: (1) organization of memory systems in the mammalian brain, (2) the organization of brain regions that contribute to social behavior in the macaque monkey, and (3) human neuroscience."

The UC Davis M.I.N.D Institute (Medical Investigation of Neurodevelopment Disorders) explains the various advances in brain research like this, "Advances in imaging technology are enabling researchers to unravel the complexity of brain function. Functional magnetic resonance imaging (MRI) permits researchers to identify areas of the brain at work during specific activities and to compare the brain activities of normal patients with those with neuro-developmental disorders."

"New computational models of brain function are now available so that the activity of the brain can be measured and recorded, facilitating comparisons between healthy and diseased brains. On the horizon are other technologies that will allow researchers to analyze the interactions of particular brain cells during specific activities."

The website continues, "The use of animal models to study neuro-developmental disorders has also been expanding, particularly here at UC Davis, which has schools of medicine and veterinary medicine, as well as a primate research center. Monkeys and other nonhuman primates have brains organized comparable to humans, making them ideal research models for the study of neuro-developmental disorders."

What I found revolutionary about the research is this: Repeatedly moving a macaque monkey's fingers in a slightly different motion path creates a totally new and separate neuro-pathway. A separate neuro-pathway means you have a totally new and different thought or experience. (You are literally building a habit at the cellular level.) The MRI can reveal this exact pathway each and every time the movement occurs. Then, when the scientist forced the monkey to move the same finger in a slightly different motion (as little as a centimeter different), the MRI revealed an entirely new neuro-pathway was forming. According to Mr. Robbins, they did this experiment by taping up the other fingers on the monkey's hand and giving him an MRI. In plain English this means ... moving your fingers actually affects the brain at the cellular level.

Now, please don't misread the above research. Neither Dr. Amaral nor Anthony Robbins is claiming that changing your handwriting can affect your personality. However, if you put the three different fields of study together (neuro-science, NLP, and handwriting), there is a strong biological argument as to why we are getting the results we are getting. For me, I didn't need to read all the neuro-scientific research to know it made sense to me. Furthermore, the risk seemed quite low. Heck, I was just changing the way I crossed my "t" and looped my "d." So, I chose to go for it. I give you the above research so that you can tell a loved one there is some logic behind the madness.

In the next chapter, I will show you the results of my research. I'll reveal to you the personality traits that are consistent among very successful, well-adjusted people. Wouldn't that be interesting to know? Naturally, not all rich or happy people possess these traits. I think you will quickly see how incorporating these personality traits into your own character can immediately "PUSH" your life to a higher level.

Now, are you ready to find out what handwriting traits are found in rich and happy people? Are you ready to see how well you already stack up the world's great minds? Grab your pen and paper and turn to the next section!

References:

Dr. David G. Amaral, Ph.D (the Director of Research for both the Department of Psychiatry at the University of California at Davis and the M.I.N.D. Institute.

http://myhandwriting.com/change

http://psychiatry.ucdavis.edu/faculty/amaral_david.html

http://neuroscience.ucdavis.edu/

http://mindinstitute.ucdmc.ucdavis.edu/

Universal Truth #7

*Success is not a destination,
it is a journey.*

CHAPTER 6

PERSONALITY SUCCESS SECRETS

In the next two sections, you will discover which personality traits contribute to absolute success and which traits are stumbling blocks. Upon taking inventory of your own character, you will then want to choose which traits to adopt as your own and which traits to eliminate from your personality.

Personality is a non-specific science. The subset of psychology called Personality Theory is an attempt to categorize and label clusters of thoughts, habits, attitudes and behavior. It has been a successful scientific pursuit. Some scientists still argue as to the origin of personality. Some will claim your personality is purely genetic and you have little control over your introversion, extroversion, or stubborn attitude. Other, more enlightened scientists realize there are hundreds of factors in determining a person's character. Most of the factors are a direct result of the "nurturing" or the environment you grew up in. The reason this argument is important is to point out that if you believe you are the way you are because of genetics or destiny, you have a very low chance of changing.

However, if you believe that personality traits such as stubbornness, argumentativeness, self-consciousness are *learned* behaviors, then you will have an easy time *unlearning* them. I have read numerous long-term studies that reveal a baby's "temperament" seems to be partially encoded from birth. However, no evidence I've ever seen indicates the "success traits" I am about to reveal to you cannot be learned at any age. Furthermore, the "personality roadblocks " described in the next chapter are all changeable. Research in physiology tells us that it takes between 21 and 30 days to change a habit. Physical repetition and mental imagery accelerates the process. The following chapters reveal handwriting strokes in successful and non-successful people. If you make a conscious effort to adjust your handwriting to match the "success traits", you will feel a noticeable difference in your thinking process in less than 30 days. I have tested this theory and experienced successful results firsthand, and I have seen many of my students change dramatically by heeding this advice. Start changing your handwriting now, and you will transform your life. I guarantee it.

Now, the following personality traits are typical of rich and happy people. Clearly, there are many exceptions to this list. In fact, only a handful of people I've studied have ALL of them in their handwriting. (Nobody's perfect.) Just because it isn't "in their handwriting" doesn't mean they don't sometimes display the characteristic. Handwriting analysis shows us the personality traits that are "most prevalent." I've never met a miserable, impoverished, mean spirited person who displayed these success characteristics. Once you read the list, I think you will agree these "success traits" would provide a powerful foundation for anyone's journey toward success and happiness.

ESSENTIAL SUCCESS TRAITS OF THE RICH & HAPPY:

High Self-Esteem / Sense of Self-Worth

High Goals   Persistence

Strong Self-Confidence / Healthy Ego

Determination   Optimism

Enthusiasm   Strong Physical Drives

Integrity /Honesty

VISITORS PASS

BRUSH PARK
BOWLING CLUB LTD.
A.B.N. 94 742 534 267

Cnr Marsden Rd
& Rutledge St, Dundas 2117

Phone: 9858 1166
Fax: 9858 1535

Email: brushparkclub@bigpond.com

TEMPORARY MEMBER ☐

MEMBER'S GUEST ☐

- I declare that I have attained the age of 18 and if required shall show identification, details of which may be recorded.
- All Temporary Members and Member's guests must adhere to the directions of the management of the club and also the club's house policy on responsible service of alcohol and gaming.
- All visitors and guests must assume the consequences of entering into club premises where smoking is permitted.
- This slip must be carried whilst on Club premises and shown on request or when claiming poker machine payouts.
- This slip is valid only for day of issue

18907

SUPPORTIVE TRAITS

DEPENDING ON THE CAREER CHOICE:

Desire for Responsibility	Intelligence
Deep Enduring Emotions	Imagination
Diplomacy	Flexibility
Sense of Humor	Acquisitiveness
Self-Reliance /Leadership	Pride

THE ESSENTIAL ELEMENTS:

HIGH SELF-ESTEEM / SENSE OF SELF-WORTH

This is the most important personality trait in the entire book. Your belief system about what you can accomplish, who you are, and what you are worth is the single most important aspect of success and happiness. Because our thoughts create our reality, doubt and insecurity simply hold us back from taking action toward our goals. Your sense of self dictates the minimum acceptable level of "crapola" you will tolerate in your life.

A t-bar crossed on the upper 3/4 of the stem indicates high goals and a good self-image. The higher the better; but keep it touching the stem. If someone crosses the t-bar over the stem, they have lost touch with reality when setting goals. t-bars consistently above the stems indicate a dreamer.

Notice in my own signature I have a high t-bar. I changed my signature to incorporate enthusiasm, confidence and leadership abilities. (I write a long t-bar, high t-bar, and underline my name.)   I even make the first letters of my name a healthy bold size. Not too

101

*The power to shape the future is earned
through persistence. No other quality
is as essential to success. It is the sandpaper
that breaks down all
resistance and sweeps away all obstacles. It is
the ability to move mountains
one grain of sand at a time.*
— Anonymous

big, but not too small. Naturally, the tilt of the baseline is up toward the right (optimism).

I started changing my signature when I was fourteen years old. It seems to have worked for me.

Having a high t-bar is no guarantee of success in life. In fact, those who take more risk, tend to experience more rejection and loss. But, they don't notice it. They keep their eye on the prize and keep going. It's like the military slogan, "You can lose a battle and still win the war." High self-worth allows you to separate your actions from who you are. It is the difference from failing at something and taking on the identity of being a failure.

So look for the high t-bar in your own handwriting, and if you don't have a high t-bar, go ahead and change it now. Literally, changing the way you cross it can affect your future. At first, I suggest you draw the t-bar lightly across the top of the stem, even in the middle of a word. Only after you have practiced this for 30 days do you begin to draw the t-bar heavier. After 30 days, you will notice that your beliefs about who you are and how much you can

the strong self-esteem

accomplish will change for the better.

HIGH GOALS

The ability to plan ahead is essential. In handwriting analysis, the personality traits of high goals and self-esteem are revealed in the same stroke: The position of the cross bar on the letter "t." In traditional psychology, there are many distinctions between a good self-esteem and having ambitious goals. For some unexplained rea-

JOHN GLENN
OHIO

UNITED STATES SENATOR

An innate, searching curiosity about all around us —
— what do we not know?
— how can we do it differently?
— how can we do it better?
is at the heart of excellence.

Then, human progress and excellence comes when someone goes beyond "why" to "why not?"

John Glenn

Senator John Glenn's handwriting shows extremely high t-bars (ambition and high self-esteem) and a very straight baseline (perfectionist). The rest of his handwriting reveals integrity with the combination of retraced d-loops (dignity), clean o-loops, and balanced upper and lower loops (organization and emotional balance). He even connects his letters together with one pen stroke which indicates fluidity of thinking and intelligence. He is a real hero.

son, the height of the letter "t" gives us clues to both personality traits simultaneously. In my experience, the height of the letter "t" indicates a strong sense of "certainty" in accomplishing any goals, rather than merely the "bold nature of the goal." I have met many individuals who claim to have high goals (medical school, movie stardom, graduate school, etc.) and yet they have low t-bars. Upon closer examination of their life, they don't see those "goals" as particularly risky. In fact, they function with all the elements of a low self-esteem (emotionally adverse to risk, defensiveness, fear of change, etc.) So, if you analyze other people's handwriting, you must be sensitive to their definition of "high goals." A Zen Buddhist may have high t-bars and have aspirations for a happy marriage and a healthy garden this year. That is success, too. It is a safe conclusion that people with high t-bars have a stronger, healthier sense of "self confidence" than those with low t-bars.

U.S. Senator John Glenn is also an American national hero. He was the first man to orbit the earth way back in 1962. He wasn't a one hit wonder. He went on to hold a seat in the United States Senate and then go BACK into space near his 77th birthday. Do you think he has ambition, confidence and personal power? Check out his t-bars and think about his success. We could all learn a thing or two about success from Mr. John Glenn.

STRONG SELF-CONFIDENCE / HEALTHY EGO

Now this may sound obvious, but if you lack self-confidence - your lack of belief in yourself is your worst enemy. If you lack the belief system that you can achieve what you want, you sabotage any future effort. Confidence and self-esteem are closely related but actually different terms. In handwriting terms, I am guilty of lumping them together and referring to the trait interchangeably. Actually, we can all experience confidence as a specific "state." You are likely to have one or more arenas that you feel very "confident" while performing. (Tennis, golf, negotiating, computer programming, speaking, etc.) However, self-esteem is really a "cumulative rating" of the various levels of confidence you feel in your entire life. Self-esteem is also tightly tied into the actual "beliefs" you hold about your own value and your own expectations. A confident baseball player could lead the league in home runs and still suffer a low self-esteem. This athlete has mastered the mental art of being confident. He feels confident by successfully controlling his internal images, voices, and feelings related to hitting a baseball. At the same time, some of his internal past wiring guides him to tolerate an unhappy relationship, turn to drugs, and lash out at those close to him. Confidence is contextual. Self-esteem expands across all contexts of your life. When you raise your self-esteem, you will feel a higher level of confidence in all areas of your life.

For example, if you come up to the plate to hit a baseball and you lack the confidence to know that you can hit it, here's what happens. Instead of hearing that voice inside your mind saying, "Bring it on you crummy little ball. I'm going to hit you out of the park!" What often happens is the dominant thought is based in negativity or fear. So your internal voice might say, "I'm going to strike out. I just know it." Now that thought actually predicts the future because it sends signals to your muscles to miss the baseball when it's thrown.

You can only visualize an event. You can't visualize a non-event. If you lack confidence in any situation, then you put pictures in your mind of failing. And often, your body (physiology) becomes weakened because of the thoughts and beliefs that you have allowed to run your brain. In baseball, if you have doubts, here is what happens. You imagine yourself missing. You swing. You miss. Therefore, you meet your expectations. On the other hand, if you have true confidence that you are going to achieve, your mind works for you, not against you. When you get to the plate, your body follows the pictures that you had displayed in your mind. This means you hit the ball in the proper direction, at the proper force. You may even hit a home run.

In handwriting analysis, esteem is seen in a couple of places. The most important location is the height of the crossbar in the lower case letter "t." The size of the ego, sense of self, is seen in the signature and the personal pronoun "I." All are important factors when assessing someone's overall sense of self-worth.

Write the word "cat" to check your own t-bar. (See "cat" below.)

MICHAEL J. FOX

Take a look at actor Michael J. Fox's handwriting. Michael is a world famous actor. Most people don't know he is a Canadian who moved to Los Angeles when he was just eighteen years old with five dollars in his pocket and a dream. He lived over his aunt's garage and started going to auditions. He made it. He broke into Hollywood playing a conservative, Reagan loving Alex Keaton on the TV sitcom *Family Ties*. He went on to star in the blockbuster hit *Back to the Future* and many other hit movies. His most recent success was ABC's sitcom *Spin City*. In my view, the greatest success is his ability to maintain a loving marriage and family life among the challenges of a fickle Hollywood casting couch and a forgetful American viewing audience. He has succeeded, failed, and re-emerged a winner time and again.

In the December of 1998, he received a lot of media attention because he has been silently living with Parkinson's Disease for many years. I think his story is just another testimony to the power

Michael J. Fox

The only thing that separates any of one of us from excellence is fear, and the opposite of fear is faith. I am careful not to confuse excellence with perfection. Excellence I can reach for, Perfection is God's business.

of the mind over adversity. I began using his handwriting sample in 1997, as just another case of "young actor moves to LA and makes it big." Now his life story becomes a more significant example. In 1999 he retired from TV at the top of the ratings. I have no doubts Michael J. Fox will come out of all this smiling. Winners always do.

Look for the success traits I discussed in his writing. He has most of them. Take special note of the t-bar. Remember, he didn't learn that t-bar in third grade writing class. It is just natural. He also has optimism (baseline tilted uphill) , fluidity of thought (connected words), desire for responsibility (large beginning loop in M), and a nice overall rhythm and balance. (Rhythm and balance suggest a balanced life with good common sense.)

EGO - BOLD SELF-CONFIDENCE

Another way to look at your self-mage is the size of your signature. A very tiny, tiny, tiny signature could mean a lack of confidence in yourself and/or a lack of confidence in your place in the world. (Capital letters and in "I" specifically, must be tiny, too.)

Liberace

On the other hand, a signature that is incredibly too big indicates a drastic need to be noticed. A bit of arrogance, too.

I see a lot of rock musicians and movie stars with huge signatures. Some are illegible. I'm fairly confident the "illegibility" issue tends to be a result of signing their name in a hurry, frequently, and while walking in a crowd. Speed equals sloppiness. Often, when you see very big, bold strokes of handwriting or when a signature is much larger than the rest of the writing, that is a sense of pride and ego, saying, "Hey! I'm worth it. Give

Bill Mahr

me the spotlight." But I tend to think that one of the reasons a musician works so hard to become famous is the need for "recognition." A large ego has special needs. Some psychologists will claim a big ego is merely a result of an insecurity complex. I think that depends on the person. As with all generalizations, there are many factors that could contribute to the healthy or non-healthy expression of an ego. I personally recommend people choose a signature that is somewhere in between large and tiny. However, the capital letters in your signature should be strong, bold, and larger than the lower case letters.

Elizabeth Taylor

To be candid, I also have a healthy ego. I am someone who had the audacity to write a book on relationships when I was 22 years old. I've been under the spotlight on hundreds of radio, TV shows, and newspaper articles. If I didn't have a sense of self-importance,

Drew
Carey

Elisabeth Shue

Gilbert Gottfried

an ego saying, "What I have to say is important. So listen up," there's no way I could have succeeded in those arenas. A healthy ego is essential to success and leadership.

PERSISTENCE

Strokes that double back over the letter and end toward the right indicate persistence. This trait is usually located in the "t" and "f." This person has the quality of not giving up when confronted with temporary setbacks. He will persist until he completes the task.

When you see this in someone's handwriting, realize they are very powerful people who tend to hit the wall and then break through it with great triumph and success. The only downside is they often stay on the same path too long when they realize there could have been another path with less resistance.

Persistence is shown by a double-crossed t-bar, much like a star. If you think about drawing the star on the side of the Dallas Cowboy's helmet, you go down, up to the left, never pick up your pen, and back to the right. One metaphor for remembering this trait is someone hitting difficulty head on, going back into the past evaluating what works and what doesn't, and then coming back toward the issue head on. Of course, all the while never picking up the pen.

Ben Affleck's signature shows persistence in the letter "A", not in the t. He also has optimism and a perfectly straight baseline (perfectionist.) Notice he underlines his name, too.

General Colin L. Powell, USA (Retired)

You have Achieved excellence
As A leader when
People will follow you
Anywhere, if only out
of curiosity.

General, USA (Ret)

General Colin Powell's handwriting is full of successful person-
ality traits. The long downstrokes on the "y's" indicate both mas-
sive determination and the desire to make it on his own - an inde-
pendence streak. The tall "d's" indicate a high level of pride and
dignity. (He gets insulted with any form of disrespect.) Honor is
everything. You might also notice the very large capital letters in
his first and last name (healthy ego). If I were at war, I would want
a man with confidence, honor, determination, and power leading my
troops into battle.

See: www.HandwritingUniversity.com/newslettersamples/colinpowell.html

DETERMINATION -- OVERCOMING ADVERSITY

The next trait is very important, and you'll see different variations of this personality trait, sometimes with different labels. I think they all work together. The three traits that reveal various aspects of determination are: enthusiasm, persistence, and determination. We have already discussed persistence.

Enthusiasm is shown by a very long stroke, often in the crossing of the letter "t." If the t-bar is extra long, it means lots of enthusiasm. You ought to notice that the opposite of enthusiasm is a very short t-bar, perhaps on the left side of the stem, and that would be someone who procrastinates. Obviously if you procrastinate excessively you may never get around to achieving your goals.

The third trait is determination. Again these all sound similar, and they are distinctly different in the handwriting. If you combine them all together you get a massively powerful result.

Determination is more of a physical drive rather than simply setting your mind on something and achieving it, like persistence. Persistence tends to focus on local goals and long-term goals. Drive is an addition of strong energy. If you have a strong drive, you might get up at 5:30 in the morning and go home at midnight in your work. You could do that for weeks on end. You often see drive even in letters like "y" and "g" that have complete loops, but the down stroke is very heavy -- a lot heavier than the upstroke. What you look for is any down stroke that is substantially heavier or even longer than other handwriting samples or other strokes. I often see it in the letters "t" or "m" which is an unusual way to end a letter. Superstar athletes tend to have a strong determination. I've shown handwriting samples here of some famous people. Notice that the last letters "t" and "n" go down far below the baseline.

This is a reproduction of what I remember Curt's signature to be like. The last letters of his t and n extended far below the baseline (determination). I didn't have an original.

sending you one of my photographs
for publication in your Album
Yours Very Truly
Thomas A. Edison

Inventor Thomas Edison found over 1000 ways not to make the electric light bulb. Energy and enthusiasm was his trademark. Notice the perfectly straight baseline (meticulous).

Superstar Basketball player Michael Jordon's signature reveals long hard downstrokes, too. He also reveals diplomacy and a small loop in his letter "d". A sensitive guy who knows how to talk to people.

Troy Aikman. Dallas Cowboy 3-time superbowl winning quarterback. (American Football) Notice the long downstrokes and the persistent "cross" in his first name. That cross starts as part of the y-loop.

114

My friend Curt Hanson has the most dynamic sense of determination I've ever seen. Curt had a unique experience that formed his strong sense of determination. In fact in his case ... survival. When Curt was less than age three, he was diagnosed with a form of cancer that the doctors considered fatal. Up until that point in the early '60's, no one had ever survived this form of cancer. He survived through the chemotherapy, the drugs, the surgeries, and the months of recovery strapped to a bed unable to move his spine. He has felt more physical pain than most soldiers could endure. He has been in and out of hospitals until the age of 20. I believe the development of the trait determination was a direct result of his physical ailments and his mental decision to survive. I tell you this story with his permission, because he is so thankful that he is alive to tell it. He's one of the most happy, optimistic, and playful people I know. He says his attitude is such, because every day to him is a gift. His determination is unlike any I've seen. Therefore, in his life, in his business, everything works out fine. Nothing is a struggle for him, because he has overcome so much more. Is he a self-made millionaire? I'm not sure of his net worth, but he will be if he sets his goals in that direction. Is he successful? Absolutely. A great marriage, a great business, and he is happy.

I've also discovered that determination of this magnitude is often a result of physical challenges when someone was young. So when you see determination in other people's handwriting understand that they are determined to meet all their goals, and that it's also a level of energy in addition to persistence.

I believe the Dallas Cowboys' quarterback Troy Aikman displays many elements of determination. As you know he's a very successful athlete in the very competive world of the NFL. He also lost many games on the way up to the top. He had to consistently endure, and throughout his career he has been one of the best quarterbacks, considering he has won three NFL Super Bowls. One of his autobiographies references a medical problem that he had to overcome when he was a child. So, I do believe that strong determination is often dealt with and learned through physical challenges, which is often why athletes become successful in business. They learn to overcome setbacks and they take the same route in their business. NFL Champion quarterback Troy Aikman's handwriting is on the previous page. Notice the double cross capital letter "A" ... persistence and the long straight lower zone strokes - determination.

OPTIMISM

All the classic self-improvement books say a positive mental attitude is the key to success. As general and ambiguous as that statement is, the trait of Optimism comes closest to capturing the essence of this skill. If you have a sample of handwriting written on unlined paper, you can quickly determine how optimistic someone really is. The more the entire baseline is tilted up and to the right, the more positive this writer is. This "slanting uphill" is an easy trait to remember and accept, because both our body language and our spoken language hold parallels to this written subconscious expression. Ever heard the phrase, "things are looking up?" How about the song, "Always look on the bright side of life!" sung by Monty Python in the final scene of the satirical comedy *The Life Of Brian*. How about the description of someone feeling "down" - pessimistic? Even your body language goes limp, down and saggy when sad or depressed. When you are optimistic, you tend to stand up, look up, and tilt your head above the horizon. Just holding your head straight and staring at the ceiling fires optimistic thoughts to your brain.

As far as your handwriting goes, you can start writing uphill, since your physiology affects your mood. So start tilting your handwriting at a 45-degree angle right now. See how much better you feel. I find this lifts me up really well when I feel down.

Look at the handwriting sample of Ebby Halliday. Mrs. Halliday was a pioneer as a female entrepreneur. (Real Estate in the North Texas, USA area). Ebby was one of the first female self-made millionaires in Texas. A pioneer for working women in the 1950's and 1960's, she had a wonderful marriage and a fabulous career. She was one of the first women ever to keep her own last name during marriage. She is a legend in the real estate circles of Dallas, TX. Ebby has created a total successful, rich, and happy life.

Handwritten lecture notes of Ebby Halliday. (Circa 1998)

ENTHUSIASM

Enthusiasm is a result of lots of mental and physical energy. It is revealed in extra long horizontal strokes anywhere in the writing. The most common location to spot enthusiasm is in the cross bar of the letter "t". Martin Luther King has an abundance of enthusiasm and ambition. Making the cross in your t-bar long is always a positive personality improvement. In addition to the long t-bars, Dr. King has lots of pride and dignity.

A long t-bar indicates enthusiasm as shown in Martin Luther King's signature. Enthusiasm is one common trait of great leaders.

Also people whose handwriting have very short t-stems tend to start projects and not finish them. Which of course would be a lack of enthusiasm. Enthusiasm is the enduring emotion of excitement. (Some men with ... you know, a short endurance sexual problem ... have t-stems that are just a dash - no lasting energy.) Similar to enthusiasm would be traits like determination and persistence, although a little different in behavior. They are very useful traits, and when they're all tied in together, you have someone who's very powerful and usually achieves what they desire.

STRONG PHYSICAL DRIVES / BIG SEX DRIVES

Some people may disagree with this success trait. I have noticed a strong correlation between high achievers and big sex drives. This does not mean that in order to make money you have to have lots of sex. (Although there might be a correlation to how much money you have to how many sexual offers you get!) What it does mean is the same part of the brain that creates energy, drive, and ambition is the same part that leads to sexual adventure. So if you find yourself needing to travel, yearning exercise, getting restless and bored easily, you are feeling "the drive" calling.

I have read that the same region of the brain processes energy, fitness, and sex related thoughts. This might explain why super powerful men often get into trouble from their

Jennifer Tilly

overactive sexual appetite (Bill Clinton, Senator Gary Hart, Howard Stern, Senator Newt Gingrich, Robert F. Kennedy, Donald Trump, etc.) So ladies, you can blame his brain for his wandering eyes! But all seriousness aside, not all men with strong sex drives have affairs. Napoleon Hill, author of *Think and Grow Rich*, did a study where he interviewed several of the most highly successful men in America over a twenty-year period. What he discovered was that all the men over 50 in his study successfully redirected or "transmuted" their sex drive into their careers.

IMAGINATION

The ability to see things that do not exist

Jon Lovitz

is essential to achieving long-term goals. The term imagination can refer to an artist's mind, an architect's vision, or a broad open mind. The term imagination is usually referred to as a description of the amount of new ideas one allows in or generates. Sometimes, even

*I am different from Washington; I have a higher, grander
standard of principle. Washington could not lie.
I can lie, but I won't.
-Mark Twain*

the negative term gullible is used to describe someone who allows too much information in without effective discernment. In handwriting analysis, we see one clue to the amount of imagination one has by the width of the loops. If the d-loop is wide, we see the person has an unrealistic imagination relating to people's criticism. (Not healthy). In the h-loop, a big loop reveals a tendency to be open and investigative about philosophical and religious concepts. If the loop of the lower case cursive "e" is large, the person is called broad-minded. The most common location for a healthy imagination is the size and width of the lower loops in the "j," "g," and "y." This is often combined with an assessment about someone's sex drive or sexual imagination. But, imagination can clearly exist exclusive from any sexual connotation. Imagination is the width of the loop. Physical drive is the heaviness and the depth of the downstroke in these letters. Many handwriting samples contain both elements. Thus, it is easy to confuse a healthy imagination for an adventurous sex drive. In general, a healthy size y-loop is a positive thing. Refer to the y-chart in chapter 5 for more information on the letter y.

INTEGRITY /HONESTY

One indicator of honesty is found in the lower case letter "o." The way the lower case "o" is formed indicates traits such as blunt-ness, secrecy, self-deceit, and lying. Although true criminals and thieves may have other more devious handwriting traits not revealed in the letter "o," you will find the letter "o" a valuable asset in searching for someone's level of integrity and honesty. There are many ways to make a lower case "o": the less inner loops, hooks or squigglies inside the oval increase the person's propensity to be candid, blunt, and truthful. So, look for the letter "a" and "o" with no inner loops or only small inner loops on the right side. The cleaner the inside of the a and o is.. the more blunt and candid the person tends to be.

Interviews with millionaires have stated that "honesty" is the most important element to their success. Honesty builds trust and is essential in maintaining long-term relationships. Research indicates 98% of millionaires have a supportive spouse and have been married for over ten years. From a spiritual perspective, all the great philosophies have preached the value of honesty and integrity as having its own rewards in this lifetime and after this lifetime.

From a linguistic perspective, the question of the honesty of your "word" is very significant. Your unconscious mind is constantly receiving programming from your own internal voices. The consistency of your spoken word dramatically affects your ability to successfully program your unconscious to assist you in manifesting your goals and dreams. If you have a habit of not keeping your word to others, your unconscious mind knows this and then lowers its own commitment to follow your own orders and requests. In essence, your unconscious stops believing what you say. Therefore, it stops working for you as effectively. If you lie to others, you will lie to yourself. If you lie, you are sabotaging your future.

Integrity and honesty in handwriting are characteristics that are not easily spotted in any single letter. Entire books have been written on this one element of personality and how to spot it in handwriting. It takes an advanced eye to know all the subtle clues. The letter "o" will give you a good head start and assist you in noticing any red flags. Read the following chapter for more information about the letter "o" and how it relates to dishonesty.

Supportive "Success" Traits That Complement the Above Traits

In my research analyzing handwriting samples of successful people, I discovered a number of personality traits that I found repeatedly in certain careers. However, they did not show up all the time - so it isn't fair to say you will want them. They did show up consistently in certain careers and always seem to be a positive compliment to the previously mentioned traits. In other words, if you have them, they will help you, not hinder you. You can add these to your writing or just look for them in others for an additional clue toward success.

DESIRE FOR RESPONSIBILITY

People who have a need to be responsible tend to gravitate toward leadership roles and get their sense of significance from contributing to the good of a team. This personality trait is revealed in a signature or a capital letter in the form of large loops at the beginning or ending of strokes. The larger this hook the more the person desires to be responsible or in the spotlight. This trait sounds like it is a desire for attention, but it is less self-serving.

I also coined the term "desire for fame" which is the same stroke on a large signature. The reason I associate fame with this stroke is because of the shear number of famous people I have noticed that use this stroke compared to the rest of the population. It seems that a large signature and this hook stroke are common among famous musicians, actors, and celebrities. This same stroke is also found without the big ego in civic leaders, organizational presidents and volunteer leaders. This stroke indicates a deep need to win the love, affection, or respect of a group.

DEPTH OF FEELING OR EMOTIONAL INTENSITY IN HANDWRITING

123

Depth of pen pressure is a handwriting trait I have found in a majority of self-made millionaires. I wouldn't suggest you change your own level of pen pressure, but I felt obligated to mention it as a spur to achievement. Pen pressure is easy to notice if you just run your finger lightly across the backside of a sample of handwriting. I just flip the paper over and feel if the pen made an impression on the backside. The harder you press on the paper, the deeper your emotions run. The more intensity - the more depth of feeling. One descriptive metaphor is "You may forgive but never forget." One good aspect of someone who writes lightly is that they get over angry situations much faster. Light writers never brood as long as heavy writers.

Now, interestingly enough, deep enduring emotions are not always a positive element. In fact, most traits are not judged good or bad viewed separately. But, when you combine the many traits together they have a dynamic result. You would probably agree that persistence, enthusiasm, and determination are wonderful personality traits. Of course, like anything ... those traits could become a detriment if in the character of someone evil.

Emotional intensity, determination and persistence would not be good for society if it was part of a psychological profile od a homicidal maniac. That desire to "kill" would then be supported by a deep burning emotion, determination and the tendency to try again and again to satisfy his dark desires. If you ever get a chance to view an actual serial killer's handwriting, you might be surprised what you would see. (Always heavy handwriting.)

What I find in most successful self-made millionaires is that they get an urge to achieve something, and it drives them. It obsesses them. They think about it day and night. An accurate indicator of this trait is heavy pen pressure.

So, do you think emotional intensity is a benefit or detriment for the state of happiness? Since happiness is an emotion, the ability to feel deeply would be an asset. The secret is determining how to control which emotions you feel on a regular basis.

Test yourself: If your hand hurts from pressing too hard on the pen and paper, you are a heavy writer. If a copy machine has trouble seeing your pen marks because you write so light, you are a light writer. For example, if you have strong emotional depth, and someone angers you to the point of revenge or hatred, you will still hate that person many years later. Likewise, if you fall in love with someone you'll probably still feel deep feelings many years later. Even if the relationship has long ended. In some cases, as you know, the deep feelings are just as intense, but we label them differently after an ugly breakup. If you have lots of break ups in your love life, you will handle it much better if you are a light writer.

In your case you have to look at your own handwriting, evaluate your own personality, and decide which traits you have now that support your success in a positive, ethical way, and which traits do not. If you do not have heavy handwriting, it doesn't mean you have to put it in there to be successful. If you do want to add this intensity to your life, please make this addition only after you look at all other aspects of your personality. Remember, you are just intensifying what you've got. So make sure you have changed anything negative or bad or you're turning up the heat on the ugly part as well as the wonderful part.

DIPLOMACY

The ability to get along with people is essential to both financial and interpersonal success. The ability to gain rapport with people quickly will be discussed later in this book. One element of rapport is the ability to choose your words carefully in a way not to offend anyone. We call this way with words: diplomacy. Diplomacy is revealed by a noticeable decrease in the height of the second hump compared to the first hump of an "m" or "n." If the humps go

I said you and you Silly Monkey do not go there to the Zoo

Notice the difference between these two handwriting samples. The bouncy baseline and lack of structure translates into a more free spirited flexible personality with less "rules." The top handwriting sample is someone who can handle unexpected events with ease. He also tends to be more sloppy and have less discipline.. The person below writes similar to what people are taught as children. This "copy book" style has a perfectly straight baseline and even spacing. He expects people and events to follow a prescribed set of rules. In fact, when things don't go according to plan, this kind and simple person can go temperamental. (especially with a low self-esteem). Tight and perfect handwriting sometimes indicates some form of neurosis or at least an anal retentive "uptight" quality. This person is not very flexible when things go haywire. There is no better or worse style. Each type of baseline and structure has its strengths. Thomas Edison and John Glenn's writing have perfectionistic even baseline qualities. How many rules do you follow?

You and your silly Monkey should be happy to leave the little room.

Basketball player Michael Jordon is still a worldwide celebrity years after his own retirement from sports. Part of the reason is his kind and diplomatic demeaner.

downhill this indicates diplomacy.

You might want to realize the opposite stroke is not the opposite of diplomacy. If the second hump is higher, it indicates self-con-sciousness - which is a fear of being ridiculed. I have not found downward humps in a majority of rich and happy people's hand-writing. However, I believe it would add to your repertoire. As a side benefit of programming diplomacy, you will be de-program-ming the fear of ridicule. Nice side effect.

FLEXIBILITY

It has been said the person with the most flexibility wins. This is obviously true in the physical manifestations of conflict such as the martial arts. Tai Chi and Hop Ki Do teach the student to move with the attacker's energy and simply re-direct it. They teach the metaphor that wood breaks, water bends. Whether you are pursuing a goal or having a discussion with your spouse, the ability to change on the fly is essential. Flexibility is the tendency to have many options to succeed.

In handwriting analysis, the lack of rigidity in the baseline reveals flexibility. On the other hand, excessive control is revealed when someone writes a sentence that appears to have been typed by a typewriter (each line is exact and perfect, the baseline could have been drawn on a ruler). The term "anal-retentive" comes to mind when I see pretty, precisely spaced, copy-book style, totally bal-anced writing. This tells me the person follows all the rules way

Common sense is not so common.
-Voltaire

too closely. If they follow rules, they demand other's to follow their own rules, too. When you set up rigid rules, you experience frequent frustration when those rules are not followed.

Naturally, there will be anal-retentive neurotic people who can achieve wealth and happiness. If I were flying a spaceship that required zero mistakes (John Glenn) I would want an anal retentive controlled personality. However, these people don't have the happy-go-lucky, change-paths-on-a-dime attitude that makes being around them fun and easy. Because I have a bouncy baseline, I don't want other people's rules imposed on me. I have a tendency to want these people with too straight of a baseline to just loosen up. I've never seen anyone try to change their own baseline. (I have seen other people's baseline and overall slant or spacing change dramatically as a result of taking prescription medication such as Prozac or Paxil. Isn't it interesting that the handwriting reflects the personality shifts when a drug intervention is effective? Those drugs are often prescribed for either obsessive compulsive disorder or depression. I tend to suggest taking a middle of the road approach. Not too perfect, not too sloppy!

INTELLIGENCE

Many people have very limited belief systems about their own level of intelligence. In the past thirty years, there have been many intelligence tests that have come and gone as far as validity. Even handwriting analysis has many subjective areas relating to judging intelligence. There is not just one, easy-to-identify handwriting stroke to spot intelligence. Therefore, instead of showing you geniuses handwriting and having you wonder if you stack up, I'm going to allow you to believe you are a genius. And, even if you never choose that belief, you will know it doesn't really matter. Wealth and happiness just take enough intelligence to choose them over poverty and misery.

MILLIONAIRE'S SUCCESS FACTORS

PERCENTAGE OF MILLIONAIRES
Indicating % Factor Who Ranked Very Important (Important)

Being honest with people all the time	57 (33)
Being well disciplined	57 (38)
Getting along with people	56 (38)
Having a supportive spouse	49 (32)
Working harder than most people	47 (41)
Loving my career / business	46 (40)
Having Strong Leadership Abilities	41 (43)
Having a very competitive spirit / personality	38 (43)
Being very well organized	36 (49)
Having the ability to sell my ideas / products	35 (47)
Making wise investments	35 (41)
Being my own boss	29 (36)
Willing to take financial risk given the right return	29 (45)
Having good mentors	27 (46)
Having an urge to be well respected	27 (42)
Investing in my own business	26 (28)
Finding a profitable niche	23 (46)
Having extraordinary energy	23 (48)
Being physically fit	21 (44)
Having a high IQ / superior intellect	20 (47)
Specializing	17 (36)
Attending a top-rated college	15 (33)
Ignoring the criticism of detractors	14 (37)
Living below my means	14 (29)
Having strong religious faith	13 (20)
Being lucky	12 (35)
Investing in the equities of public corporations	12 (30)
Having excellent investment advisers	11 (28)
Graduating near / at the top of my class	11 (22)

*This survey from *The Millionaire Mind* by Dr. Thomas Stanley

There is no statistical correlation between good grades and success in life. For most of us, our performance in school was a major measurement device for establishing our own beliefs about our level of smarts. Book-smart people sometimes lack the common sense others seem to have so naturally. There seems to be a correlation with the level of "emotional intelligence" and happiness in life. The book *Emotional Intelligence* has forced many people to reevaluate their own definition of intelligence. Dr. Thomas J. Stanley's book *The Millionaire Mind* states that in a self-assessment of over 733 American millionaires, the success factor of "High Intelligence / Superior Intellect" was ranked just 21 out of 30 key important factors of success. In fact, only 21% said it was very important and 47% said it was important. But, it fell considerably behind other more attainable qualities such as honesty, hard work, and discipline.

Dr. Thomas J. Stanley's book *The Millionaire Mind* revealed some interesting statiscal facts about millionaire's and their thinking processes. One of the questionairres asked participants which personality traits were most imortant in being successful. The #1 response was honesty and discipline. You can read for yourself how someof America's millionaires judged their own success factors.

Intelligence is not found in just one stroke of the pen. It is a combination of many various strokes in various letters. Because of the advanced nature of this trait, intelligence in handwriting will not be discussed in detail. Furthermore, we don't have any evidence that any single handwriting change can make you smarter.

Here are a couple hints to assist you in spotting thinking styles.

New York Real Estate Tycoon Donald Trump

People who make fast decisions and tend to be impatient often have angular middle zone letters. Needle point "m's" and "n's" are typi-

sending you one of my photographs
for publication in your Album

Yours Very Truly

Thomas A. Edison

Thomas Edison has round, almost square top "m" and "n" humps.
This cumulative fact-upon-fact thinking style assisted him in his
own creative process. Note the enthusiasm revealed in the extra
long t-bar!

Dr. Laura Schlesinger

Larry King

Steven Bochco

Fluidity of thinking is commonly found in radio or TV talk show
hosts, professional speakers or writers. Steven Bochco is one of
America's most successful television writers. Larry King and Dr.
Laura Schlesinger are Talk Radio /TV hosts. All highly intelligent.

cal. For example, Donald Trump's handwriting reveals his lighting fast mind. Many CEO's have this trait, because they have to make quick decisions all day long.

On the other hand, there are very successful men and women with more round, curvey handwriting. These people have a more cumulative procedural type of thinking, but intelligent nonetheless. For example, Thomas Edison was took his time when experimenting with his inventions. Yet no one would argue he wasn't a genius.

INTUITION

Truthfully, intuition is also a sign of intelligence and a lot of people are not familiar with the concept of intuition as a part of intelligence. But remember, intelligence is processing information and coming up with a good decision. Intuition is a 6th sense. It's taking information from your gut feeling. Research indicates that people who do follow their gut feeling, in addition to well-researched advice, often make better decision makers.

In fact, after interviews with some top executives, many of their best hiring decisions are made "going by their gut." Intuition is shown in handwriting by frequent lifts of the pen, rather than solid connected handwriting. Interesting.

SELF-RELIANCE / LEADERSHIP

An underline in a signature is usually a positive sign. Underlining one's name is adding a bit of "boldness" to your public image. You are saying, "I am here. Take notice. I mean business." I have seen great leaders with and without an underlined name. Therefore, there is no statistical pattern to prove it will help you. I think it is a positive trait that helps people succeed in leadership roles. If you look at my signature, I underline my name and make

Make a start and sustain the effort! Inspiration will follow with excellence becoming the eventual result.

Take the Time to Listen to the Trees. That is where the Music is!

John Williams

Composer John Williams has many success traits. The long and high t-bars reveal his self-confidence. The extra tall t-stems show us he is full of pride and dignity. People with this level of pride tend to be sharp dressers and are concerned with their reputation.

Small beginning hooks in the middle zone indicate a desire to acquire. This seems to motivate these people to acquire security, money, and even shoes. If they appear in the upper zone, it indicates a desire to acquire knowledge (not shown here.)

my t-bars as high as I can. At the same time, I don't want to have a signature too large. I don't need my ego to get any bigger.

PRIDE & DIGNITY

Pride & dignity are revealed by tall narrow "t" or "d" stems. As a grapho-therapist, I don't recommend people intentionally make their t-stems taller. If a stem is 4 times the size of the middle zone writing, the writer is often arrogant. This excessive pride and unnecessary concern about the opinions of "society" (What will they think?) is usually excess baggage on the trip to the top. So, I feel programming pride via handwriting changes carries the risk of accidentally programming vanity. Therefore, limit yourself to removing the loop in a "d" or "t" stem, but keep them in between 2-3 times the height of the surrounding lower case letters. By the way, as you start to raise your t-bar, you might find the t-stem growing taller. Stop it. Avoid letting your t-stems grow too tall.

ACQUISITIVENESS

The desire to acquire is a trait that will accelerate someone's tendency to accumulate physical stuff. This may include money, cars, and shoes. Depending on your philosophy in life, this might be a positive trait or a negative one. Feng Shui experts say keeping too much stuff around the house compromises the flow of the chi. Therefore, acquiring too much stuff can stiffen your ability to earn more. I can't say this trait will increase the odds of you becoming rich and happy. I do know this fact. Acquisitiveness is a handwriting trait that I often see in people who have acquired lots of wealth. It is only a supportive trait. It indicates a burning need. When people have a burning need, they usually find a way to fill this need. Acquisitiveness is revealed by beginning hooks in the middle zone.

When I see this in a woman's handwriting, I always tell them they have more shoes than they could ever wear. Most of them are amazed that I knew they were shoe collectors. Naturally, buying shoes is just an outlet for the desire to acquire. And when speaking to an American woman, this is a high percentage metaphor to use. However, the underlying motive is a need to collect things. I also find a significant correlation between a high value on security (chapter 4) and the occurrence of repeated acquisitiveness hooks.

SENSE OF HUMOR

Who doesn't feel happy when they laugh? I have the unique characteristic of making myself laugh whether I am alone or with friends. Both of my parents had a very highly developed sense of humor and have no fear of expressing it. I have studied hundreds of people with a highly developed sense of humor. I have not discovered one handwriting stroke that promises to improve your sense of humor.

Humor is fun. Learn to laugh more. You'll figure it out. Because there are so many different types of comedy, it is difficult to paint a personality profile of the funny person. (Sardonic, witty, outrageous, obnoxious, dark, satirical, childish, etc.) Handwriting analysis isn't the most effective tool to spot funniness or learn humor. Here are two tips. If you see a long wavy t-bar, this indicates a silly sense of humor. The sharp pointy t-bar indicates sarcasm. Often sarcasm can be very witty. It can also be very caustic.

CONCLUSION

Becoming a successful leader, entrepreneur, or just plain old multi-millionaire is so much more complex than we could possibly get into in this chapter. I want to remind you that your personality and your character are essential in becoming successful, both financially and in other areas of your life. It is more than just crossing your t-bar high... but that is a good start. Enjoy the following pages of actual handwriting samples of people that have made an impact on society through their outstanding personalities.

strong RNC Victory 2000 program.

Your support for Victory 2000 right no is Essential to advertise our compassionate Conservative message, identify voters who support our candidates, and turn them out.

These crucial programs are expensive

With your help, we can achieve our dreams, end Clinton Democrat partisanship, and together, renew American purpose through an across-the-board GOP victory.

Please, renew your commitment to our cause and send a donation today. It would mean a lot to me, as leader of our ticket. Thank you again for all your support.

Sincerely,

George Bush

P.S. Having been officially confirmed as the Republican Party nominee, I look forward to leading our team to victory. Please help as generously as you can. Thanks again.

President George W. Bush has handwriting of a leader. High t-bars, sharp pointed "m" humps, and a steady disciplined baseline. His closed dotted "i's" indicate a good memory and loyalty. He really has no "bad" personality traits. I am especially proud of the height of his t-bars. Naturally, he connects many of his letters into the next word indicating a fluid mind (including some lower case t-bars which do not mean low self-esteem.) For a complete analysis of America's President George W. Bush, see this webpage:

HandwritingUniversity.com/newslettersamples/candidates/gbush/

JAMES A. BAKER, III

Excellence doesn't happen without dedication and hard work or without always taking the time and effort to cross the "T's" and dot the "i's".

I always try and remember my father's advice: Prior Preparation Prevents Poor Performance!

Jim Baker

James Baker III was the Secretary of State under United States President George Bush from 1988-1992. He is a man of unquestionable integrity and accomplishments. Notice his high t-bars, persistence, and determination.

The Jane Goodall Institute

Every individual matters, non-human as well as human. Every individual has a role to play. Every individual makes a difference.

We cannot live through a single day without making an impact on the world around us. And we all have free choice - what sort of difference do we want to make? Do we want to make the world around us a better place? Or not?

Jane Goodall

©Mark Maglio 1990

"Fifi fishing for termites"
derived from Hugo Van Lawick, 1964 photo

Jane Goodall is a pioneer researcher of primate communication and a true hero for ecological & animal preservation. Dr. Goodall's research was the basis of my first ever term paper in high school. Recently, I met Jane in person and asked her this question,"Do you feel primates understand the concept of God?" She responded by telling a story of a chimp who sat by a waterful with the obvious sensation of "awe" while noticing the rainbows appear in the mist. She concluded primates have the sensation of a higher power, but lack the language skills or vocabulary to make the concept tangible. Jane Goodall is one true hero for the planet. She has written many profound books. She is an amazing woman who also has high t-bars.

#1 THE PURPLE PEOPLE EATER TOLD ME AND MY MONKEY DON'T GO HOME TO THE ZOO.

THE Purple people eater told me and my monkey don't go home to the zoo

The purple people eater told me and my monkey don't go home to the zoo.

Actual writing of Howard Stern submitted for Bart Baggett's live interview on his radio show in December of 1997.

Radio Host Howard Stern is both offensive and very successful in his career. He pioneered syndicated morning radio shows in the United States and starred in a hit movie <u>Private Parts</u>. *His high t-bars, fluid S, sharp pointed "m" humps, and tall "d" and "t" stems are the most telling of his traits.*

For a more in depth analysis of Howard Stern's writing, see this webpage:

www.myhandwriting.com/audiofiles

140

Tom Landry
Dallas, Texas

Thoughts on Excellence
" The quality of a man's life is
in direct proportion To his
Commitment of excellence. "
Tom Landry

*Football coach Tom Landry was known for his cool demeanor
and kind nature. He was the first head coach for the Dallas
Cowboys and held the position for over 20 years. His t-bars clearly
reflect the winning style of the 70's Dallas Cowboy teams. He
passed away in 2000 to an outpouring of emotion from family and
friends. Notice the fluid thinking in the T and L of his name and the
high t-bars throughout the writing.*

Maya Angelou

My grandmother told me that every good thing I do helps some human being in the world. I believed her fifty years ago and I still do.

Joy Maya Angelou

Maya Angelo is one of the prolific poets of our time. She was invited to write and read the inaguration poem for president Bill Clinton. She is a friend and mentor to Oprah Winfrey and a champion to the spirit of humanity. Notice her enthusiasm, determination, intelligence, and of course... high t-bars.

RUBY BRIDGES
A CHILD OF COURAGE,
A WOMAN OF DETERMINATION

Don't follow the path. Go where there is no path & begin the trail. When you start a new trail equipped with courage, strength, and conviction, the only thing that can stop you is you!

Ruby Bridges
Civil Rights Pioneer

Ruby Bridges was just a child when she had the courage to become one of the first black students to attend an all white-school. Years later, she has grown into an even more determined and proud woman. Notice her optimism, honesty, and fluid thinking. Most of her t-bars are high. When t-bars connect to the next letter, that indicates fluidity of thinking and it is not a reflection of the self-esteem.

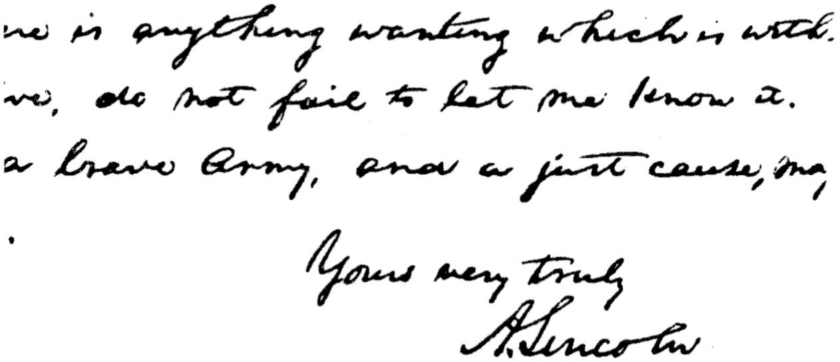

* no is anything wanting which is with.*
vo, do not fail to let me know it.
a brave Army, and a just cause, ma,

Yours very truly
A. Lincoln

Abraham Lincoln

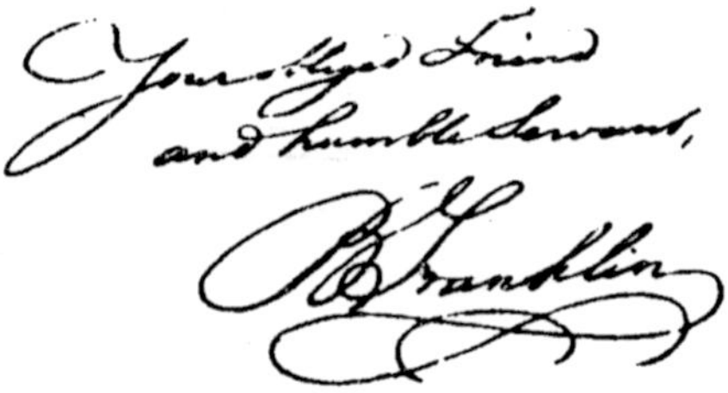

Your Affec'd Friend
and humble Servant,
B. Franklin

Benjamin Franklin

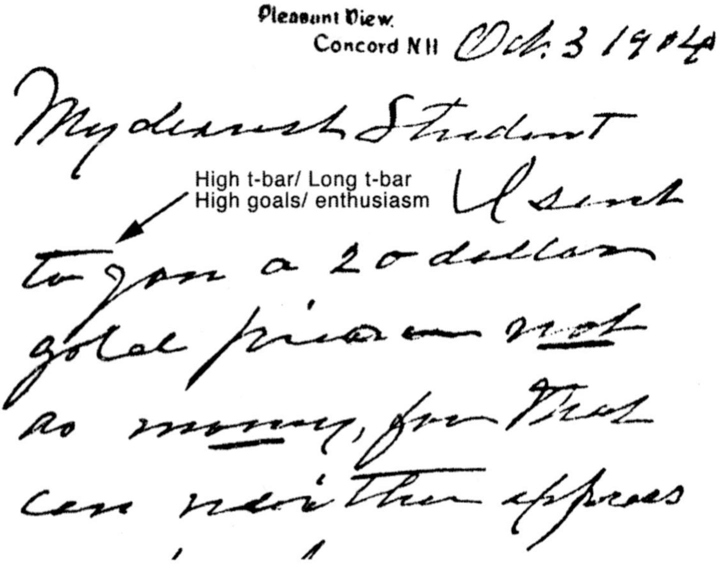

Pleasant View.
Concord NH *Oct. 3 1904*

My dearest Student

High t-bar/ Long t-bar
High goals/ enthusiasm

U sent to you a 20 dollar gold piece and not as money, for that can neither express

Mary Baker Eddy

ROBERT SCHULLER

Excellence! The attitude generates enthusiasm, attracts top people & becomes the basis for real optimism.

It will generate powerful self esteem without falling into the trap of perfectionism.

For me its spiritual, God gives me the dream & I owe him a finished achievement worthy of a gift to him. ~Schuller~

Robert Schuller is one of the world's most inspiring and motivational speakers. He is a preacher with a gift of wisdom and the ability to connect with millions of people through his words. No matter your spiritual leanings, one must respect his success and admire his personality traits such as enthusiasm, deep emotions, optimism, fluid thinking, intelligence, and of course... high t-bars.

President   Republic of South Africa

The real heroes are men and women
who are friends of the poorest of the poor.
Mandela

Nelson Mandela is a hero's hero. He single handedly freed South Africa from Apartheid in the 1990's and then became its first black president. He sat patienty and purposely in a South African Prison for over 30 years for political crimes of speaking the truth. His handwriting reveals very sharp M humps (high intelligence, quick thinking) and a logical emotionally reserved slant (vertical). His t-bars are always at the top of the stem. He also has very short d-stems which reveals an independent thinking style or strong internal frame of reference for what is right and wrong. Very short no-looped d-stems indicate the writer doesn't really care if you approve of him or not... he knows right from wrong and will live that way through any type of criticism.

THE DALAI LAMA

THEKCHEN CHOELING
DHARMSALA CANTT
KANGRA DISTRICT
HIMACHAL PRADESH

༄༅། །རྗེ་སྐྱིད་ནམ་མཁའ་གནས་པ་དང་།
།འགྲོ་བ་རྗེ་སྐྱིད་གནས་གྱུར་པ།
།དེ་སྐྱིད་བདག་ནི་གནས་གྱུར་ནས།
།འགྲོ་བའི་སྡུག་བསྔལ་སེལ་བར་ཤོག །

The 14th Dalai Lama fled his country under the cover of night when he was just a child as the Chinese Government invaded Tibet. He has lived in exile working tirelessly to reclaim Tibet from the Chinese rule. His unique version of Tibeten buddhism teaches that the purpose of life is to be happy. He has joined hands with spiritual leaders of all faiths in an effort to create a more peaceful, joyous, and loving planet. His efforts have raised awareness worldwide of the horrific atrocities still going on in occupied Tibet. He has written some wonderful books including The Art of Happiness *which I recommend. Truthfully, I can't make heads-or-tails of his handwriting... but it's my book and I get to choose who's writing I put in here. He is spiritually wealthy and happy despite all he has suffered through. He is a real hero.*

If you want to help his cause...send a donation to :

http://www.SaveTibet.org/

Handwriting Analysis Resources

If you are curious and would like to learn more handwriting analysis, Grapho-therapy, or even hire a professional handwriting analyst to tell you exactly what your handwriting reveals...

Please visit these websites and shop the on-line catalog.

http://www.myhandwriting.com

√ Free Special Reports

√ Free Weekly Newsletter by Bart Baggett

√ Shop on-line catalog

√ On-line self-test

http://www.HandwritingUniversity.com

√ Get Trained and Certified as a Handwriting Analyst

√ Hire a professional Handwriting Analyst

√ Take an on-line course or tele-class

√ Enroll into the Certification Home Study Course

√ Earn $100 per hour or more in your spare time.

And much, much more.

Handwriting questions, comments, or true stories...

email to: mail@myhandwriting.com

Learn Handwriting Analysis:

How To Analyze Handwriting In 10 Minutes or Less Beginner Home Study Program

Includes 60 minute Amazing Personality Secrets, Grapho-Deck Handwriting Flash Cards, 4 Audio Soundtracks, and the Special report. All by Bart A. Baggett (Best Seller!)

This course is all you need to get started today deducing people's character just from a sample of handwriting. You'll be surprised at how fast you learn using this system. It includes the best information available today about the science of handwriting analysis, presented for you in both a visual and audio format so you learn interactively! If you just listen to the tapes and watch the video, you can't help but appear to be an expert the next time you look at someone's handwriting.

Visit our on-line catalog for current prices and availability:

http://www.myhandwriting.com/learn/

Universal Truth #8

You already have all the resources within yourself
that are necessary for you to change.
All you must do now is
make the decision to change.

CHAPTER 7

ROADBLOCKS TO SUCCESS

What is stopping you? I doubt this is the first time you've been asked what you want in life. So, in the past, what has stopped you? Fear, anger, people, laziness, health? Naturally, there might be many reasons you haven't already accomplished your goals. Actually, I don't want you to focus on your past or even your past excuses. I have found most people that consistently achieve simply take full responsibility for the outcome they get. If the outcome doesn't meet their expectations, they re-evaluate, create a new plan, and do it again. No worries.

In the last chapter, I introduced to you many personality traits that increase the odds of experiencing success effortlessly. I even encouraged you to change your handwriting to adopt some of those handwriting strokes. Simply adding those traits to your handwriting is like adding nitro glycerin to your car. It will supercharge your engine and send you rocketing down whatever path you are already on.

However, putting a turbo charged engine in a 1964 Ford Dart might not be a great strategy. I doubt the steering, tires and brakes are designed for that kind of speed.

HOW DO YOU GET A LAND SPEED RECORD?

Have you ever seen the long rocket cars that compete for the world record in land speed? These daredevils build these super fast cars that basically look like a space rocket on four wheels. One man straps himself in and cheats death at a speed of 600+ miles per hour. Every few years someone else attempts to beat this record for a place in *The Guinness Book of World Records*. No matter how fast the car becomes, the driver must choose a track with miles and miles of flat, obstacle-free land. There is no 20 mile paved highway that is straight, flat, and empty of all other cars. So, the team races their cars across huge dried lakebeds in Nevada and Utah called the Great Salt Flats. The ground is smooth as silk. No obstacles are in the path that might slow the car down. Imagine the distress of clicking on your turbo charger just before you come upon a broken down Chevy in your lane. You must find an obstacle-free road.

Your path toward your goals is similar to these racers looking for a new record. In order to be successful, they must have a clear path free of roadblocks. In your life, you must take a look at the unconscious programming and remove the "personality roadblocks" that might be holding you back. Luckily, in the field of handwriting analysis, many of the most important personality roadblocks can be easily identified and changed through grapho-therapy.

Grab a sample of your own handwriting and begin looking for areas of your internal programming that match the traits explained in this chapter.

PLAY ALONG WITH THIS GAME.

Before we jump into explaining and eliminating roadblocks, please play along with this simple game. Imagine that you and I are standing in the middle of a basketball court in an empty gymnasium. As we are chatting about your life's purpose, you notice about twenty feet above your head is a shiny blue gift box with a bright yellow ribbon. You ask me what that box is for. I tell you, "Inside that box is proof positive that one of your goals has already been achieved."

You look at me sideways. "That's impossible. I haven't even started working on it yet." I tell you that that gift box is a metaphor for all the things in life that you want but don't have yet.

So, I'll ask you, "What is in that box for you? "

You say, "A new car."

Diagram 7a-Prize

"Don't be silly. A new car can't fit inside a two-foot box. But, a set of keys to that new car can fit. And, wouldn't a set of keys and a title with your name on it be positive proof that you had already manifested that car?"

You might then comment, "Hmm. Well actually there is something I want more than a new car."

I say, "Then stop and write it down. But, you must decide on something that will either fit inside that box or whatever in your mind will prove to you that you really have it must fit inside this box. For example:

If you want to attract and marry your soul mate, then visualize a wedding picture of the both of you with real wedding rice sprinkled in the package.

If you want to live in a large new home, then visualize the front door key, a photo, and a signed contract stating you own it.

If you want to be a successful entrepreneur, then visualize your checking account statement, your corporate charter, letters from happy customers, and your daily schedule where you get to sleep until 9 a.m.

For this exercise, please just pick a goal and make it fit inside this blue gift box.

Grab a pen and write down that goal and the proof positive elements inside the box here:

_____

_____

Okay, you have decided what you want. You have decided exactly what has to occur in order for you to be convinced you have it. Now, you have to create a plan to get the darn blue box.

Again, we are about twenty feet away from just grabbing the box. But it is just too high to reach. How would you suggest we get the box the fastest?

BRAINSTORM SOME STRATEGIES. MAKE A PLAN.

1. Stand on my shoulders.

2. Find ten people and build a human pyramid.

3. Throw basketballs at it until the rope snaps and it falls down.

4. Jump really really high.

5. Pray it will just fall into your lap.

6. Find a gun and shoot the rope.

7. Find a pole-vaulter to vault up and grab it.

8. Give up because it seems impossible.

9. Don't even make a plan because you don't deserve to get what you want.

Any other suggestions? Congratulate yourself if you are even playing along. Most people in life would see that prize and think something along these lines:

Some lucky person is going to have a nice prize.

The person who owns that must be rich.

Wouldn't it be nice to have that. Oh well, that's not my destiny.

I don't want what's in that box anyway. I'm perfectly happy without it.

If I got that box, someone would just steal it from me anyway.

But, you are different. You are determined to find a way to get what's inside that box? So, what's your solution? Did I hear someone say, "Get a ladder!" A ladder. Now that's a great idea. Good suggestion.

Diagram 7b-ladder

What the ladder really represents psychologically is that we need a plan. Any time you have a goal, if you get a plan, you're on your way. Half the people out there do not even have a goal and most of the other half don't have a plan to get there.

We are in luck. There happens to be a maintenance crew outside the gymnasium. We walk outside to borrow a ladder. We bring the ladder into the middle of the basketball court. We position it right under the hanging blue gift. And I say to you, "Okay, you have your plan in place, now go get the prize."

Isn't' it that easy? Well, most people might not even start because they might have a fear of falling, a fear of the ladder slipping, or they might be physically unfit to climb. You are different. You jump up onto the first step of the ladder with enthusiasm, but your foot doesn't take hold. You look down and notice someone has placed a huge bag of cement on the first step. You have hit your first roadblock.

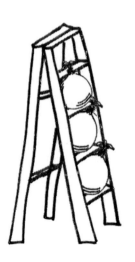

In life, deciding what you want and making a plan isn't enough. You must have the flexibility to see the roadblocks, clear them, and start again.

From a psychological angle, roadblocks are those habits, fears, or personality traits that hold you back from accomplishing your goals. I will use the analogy of a big, black bag of rocks for each fear that holds you back. Whether you try to navigate around the bags or you pick it up and carry it with you, those bags of rocks will slow you down.

There are nine key roadblocks that we will discuss in this section. If you will, imagine that for each of these personality traits, a bag of cement has been placed on the ladder. This personality baggage is a major stumbling block to simply climbing up the ladder and grabbing your prize. Your job now is to re-program your mind to avoid seeing these roadblocks in the future.

By the way, if you are wondering who put the cement bags on your ladder ... you did.

ROADBLOCKS TO SUCCESS

Fear of Failure / Low Goals

Low self-esteem / Weak Ego

Fear of Success / Sabotage Goals

Fear of Ridicule/ Rejection (Self-consciousness)

Fear of Criticism

Self-Castigation

Guilt and or Living in Past

Lack of Integrity / Honesty

Resentment or Anger

Naturally, we could add dozens of emotions or psychological traits onto this list of roadblocks. However, this list is special in that we can both spot and affect this personality issue through the power of the pen. Thus, if you have one or two of these strokes in your own handwriting, don't despair. Nobody is perfect. If you find all nine in your writing, you are so lucky to be holding this book in your hands. Because, to be frank, you are a mess. And now there is hope for you.

ROADBLOCK #1: FEAR OF FAILURE

The fear of failure is revealed by the location of the cross bar on the lower case letter "t". This one handwriting stroke might be

the most significant single stroke in the alphabet. This same stroke also reveals insight into someone's self-esteem, self-image, and confidence. A low t-bar is defined as a t-bar that is crossed inside the middle zone, not above that zone. The middle zone is defined by the typical height of all the single height letters such as "a, o, e, i, n, m" or the humps on such letters as "h". It would be easier to say the t-bar is below the halfway mark, but this wouldn't be accurate if someone made his stem 8 times as tall as normal.

In the last chapter, you noticed most of the super successful men and women crossed their letter "t" near the top of the stem. Those who cross their "t" above the top of the middle zone are more practical, but still able to handle change well.

In the ladder metaphor, someone with a fear of failure might imagine falling off the ladder or simply getting to the top and being unable to get the box. Because this fear is so real, people choose to stay in their current situation instead of taking any risks.

Remember the pain vs. pleasure exercise in an earlier chapter? You take action easily because the pain of taking action is so much less than the pain of not taking action. It amazes me how much discomfort people will tolerate in an effort to avoid failing. Think about the number of friends you have known who stay in a very bad relationship long after it became very painful? They don't get out because they imagine the pain of leaving (loneliness, financial hardship, physical threats, etc.) as being worse than suffering in the relationship.

cat at esteem

If you find that half of your "t-bars" are crossed at the bottom and the other half at the top, this means that your self-image fluctuates with what you're doing. For instance, you might have a lot of confidence in certain areas, your job, but then personally you've got insecurities to deal with. Does it make sense? So you don't have to be 100% consistent. We are humans not computers.

Handwriting is really brain writing. It's basically a projection of your neurology on paper. So if a trait is present only 20% of the time, it only occurs 20% of the time in your life. Handwriting can be very statistical.

Ryan Waton's parents purchased my workbook for kids when Ryan was just 10 years old. This book *Change Your Life in 30 Days for Kids* was designed to effectively guide a child into erasing some of these personality roadblocks while programming the success traits. Ryan worked diligently for 30 days straight. I know he worked hard because he wrote me a letter telling me how much fun it was to complete the workbook. Like a good student, every t-bar was crossed at the top of the stem. Ryan told me that within weeks of starting the grapho-therapy, he began doing his homework without his mother forcing him to. His grades began to rise as a result of his improved habits and higher expectations. A year or so after that nice letter, Ryan's father called me to thank me. Apparently, as a result of the changes in Ryan's esteem and test score grades, Ryan was admitted to a prestigious private school. Both Ryan and his parents believe he wouldn't have achieved that honor without the simple yet powerful tool of grapho-therapy.

I could tell you hundreds of other true stories. But, you already know the reward for changing your t-bar is tremendous and the risk is minimal. Change it and be my next written testimonial.

Elizabeth
Taylor

SELF-ESTEEM VS. CONFIDENCE

The next roadblock to success is low self-esteem / weak ego. This is very much the same discussion as the previous trait fear of change. So similar, handwriting analysis uses the same stroke to reveal it: A low t-bar. Because self-esteem is such a complex problem, I feel I am oversimplifying it just spotting it in the t-bar. In fact, confidence can be labeled as an emotional "state." Even people with terribly low self-esteems can experience states of confidence in sports, in school, or even with the opposite sex. Therefore, lumping these all together might be a bit of a generalization. Let me show you two other areas where we can get a clue to someone's overall ego strength and sense of confidence. The good news is that by

Helen
Hunt

raising the t-bar, all areas of self-esteem seem to be affected.

The size of the personal pronoun "I" indicates your sense of ego and ego strength. The larger the capital "I", the less crap you tend to take from others. The smaller the personal pronoun "I", the more someone gets walked on or allows themselves to be treated poorly. The stand-alone capital "I" reveals a person's ego strength relative to the people in their world.

In a similar vein, a person's signature reveals their ego in a more public venue. Because people are aware their signatures will be judged as an extension of themselves, people often "doctor up" their signatures trying to make some kind of state-ment. It is for this reason that I rarely rely on just a signature alone to make an accurate assessment about a celebrity. Our

Harry Hamlin

public persona is usually a bit different than our private persona.

The size of your signature does reveal your ego strength. Contrary to popular opinion, ego strength is valuable to achieving

Jane Seymour

success. You might consider someone's ego as being bad and self-serving. I don't think that's always true. I think that if the ego is too large, it begins to take over the spotlight for self-serving needs. But, likewise, an ego that is very tiny doesn't have the strength to draw a line in the sand and stand for what it believes in.

One trait I do see in many leaders is an underline of their name. This is a bit of an explanation mark signifying our own importance. This doesn't bother me as a grapho-therapist. As long as we don't have arrogance, I think ego is a healthy function of a balanced per- son.

"The"　　　*the*　"the"

GRAPHO-THERAPY SUGGESTIONS:

If you can practice handwriting changes daily for at least thirty days, you will form a habit at the phsysiological level. This habit will serve you well for the rest of your life.

1. Cross your t-bar near the top of the stem on the lower case "t".

(Exception. If you tend to cross the letter "t" using the t-cross-bar as an entry into the next letter, you can keep it in the middle. This "connectedness" is labeled fluidity of thinking. This is a positive trait that supercedes the evidence of esteem in this letter.)

2. Write the personal pronoun capital "I" with well-proportioned loops. And if it's tiny, make it bigger. But not too big or you'll have

an inflated ego.

3. Make the first letters of you signature a size that gets noticed. If you have aspirations of leadership, consider underlining your name (always end the stroke toward the right side of the page on an underline.) Naturally, the size of these first letters is in direct proportion to the size of your overall writing. As a guide, I recommend making your beginning letters of your signature about 3-4 times as tall as the size of your middle zone.

FEAR OF SUCCESS

With all this discussion of success, how could anyone actually fear it? This doesn't make any sense, does it? Why would anyone not want to rake in the rewards of succeeding? There are two reasons people might sabotage their own success or have a strong fear of succeeding.

1. This person links severe pain to the changes that will occur if they succeed.

2. This person links tremendous emotional pleasure to the act of failing or coming up short.

Either model of their brain results in an unconscious effort to botch the best laid plans and self-sabotage their career or love life.

People with fear of success get close to the finish line and then find an excuse not to cross it. Those of you who have it will be glued to every word in this section. Those of you who don't might be scratching your head as to how fear of success occurs. But, trust me, it is a very significant and common roadblock.

This is the one "hell trait" that I will base a hiring decision upon without seeing the rest of the writing. If the "y" turns down, I turn down the application. This is not a trait that makes you a horrible employee. It makes you an unpredictable employee. When you get ready for that promotion, something happens to sabotage it. It's not that you just decide, "I don't want it." Sometimes something just happens. Magically somebody messes it up for you. You have an accident. You get sick. Well unconsciously, it's sabotage.

The fear of success trait shows up in the letter "y". If the last stroke heads up to the baseline and then turns away ... that's the fear of success.

Here's a metaphor to make it really easy for you to memorize.

Imagine the stroke of the letter "y" as the path of a racecar heading for the finish line. The finish line is the imaginary "baseline" in which each letter starts or stops at. If you don't actually write on lined paper, you might have to imagine where that line would be.

If the car makes its turn at the bottom of the "y", it is driving on the home stretch going towards the finish line. Imagine that car suddenly slams on the brakes and makes a u-turn to the right. Now, it didn't cross the finish line.

That's what the self-sabotage "y" does.

If you have this trait, pay attention. Although it might not affect all areas of your life equally, it'll affect some areas in very painful ways.

YOU WILL WANT TO CHANGE THIS TRAIT.

I met a girl who had this trait in every "y". She had been to the altar twice and the groom stood her up, both times. Now you could say, "Bad choice in grooms." True. But why did she choose those men? Remember, successful and happy people take total responsibility for their own lives. If it happens once, take notice. If it happens twice, it's a pattern. At some subconscious level, this bride wanted to fail. She wanted to sabotage her own success. I couldn't 't imagine why until I heard her mother's response. After the second groom stood her up at the alter, her parents took her on an "all expense paid trip to Europe."

Her parents said, "It's okay honey. Let's go to Europe. It will be all right. We love you no matter what. A couple of first class tickets to France and a day at the Hotel Spa will heal your pain." They embarked on the trip, and my friend got rewarded with love and pleasure for screwing up her wedding.

This is an example of how the rewards of failing can be more pleasurable than the rewards of succeeding. It is my opinion that many parents inadvertently reward their kids when they fail and set the seeds for the fear of success. The brain is constantly learning by linking pleasure and pain to different behaviors. This trait is a direct result of more pleasure (love, attention, connection, respect, comfort, etc) to failing than succeeding.

SUCCESS STORY: JENNY HATHAWAY

In 1994, I was promoting seminars from my hometown in Dallas, Texas. My brother owned a small bookstore that specialized in self-improvement merchandise. We received a resume from a lady named Jenny Hathaway who was moving to Texas from Boston. She made it very clear that she would like to work for the bookstore or my seminar company. Her resume was very impressive. She had great knowledge of all the various books, tapes, and self-improvement seminars. Plus, she was about as nice as anyone could be.

I said, "Fax me your handwriting." I don't do any hiring without looking at their handwriting. Absolutely not. I've been more strict about hiring based on handwriting than I have been about dating!

Jenny faxed me two pages of her penmanship. I was very impressed with 99% of what it revealed. She had enthusiasm, great self-esteem, unshakable integrity, energy, and a keen intellect. But she had the down turned "y". She had everything else going for her.

She had everything I wanted in an employee, but that singe trait scares me. So I explained to her why I couldn't extend the invitation, "Jenny, you have so many great qualities I look for. However, you have a trait that is a deal-breaker. I'm going to ask you about this and tell me if this is true. Do you have any self-sabotage or fear of success? I have found that people with the self-sabotage trait end up not working out for some reason. Something always happens. Does that ring a bell?"

She said contemplating my statement, "Bart, that's the strangest comment. In my personal life, I always finish what I start. But … of the last three companies I've worked for, all three went bankrupt." Oh, come work for me. Yeah, when can you start? I thought sarcastically!

She immediately saw the connection. Even though she didn't cause these companies to go bankrupt, she selected companies that had a pretty good chance of failing. And why? Because she was afraid of too much success.

Jenny said to me, "I'll tell you what, Bart. I will change my handwriting, and in 30 days, if my 'y' isn't changed you don't have to pay me! Let me do a test run for you. "

I said, "Okay. What do I have to lose?" Jenny literally wrote me three or four pages a day of "y's" going straight up through the baseline. She was serious about making the change. Jenny ended up being our most dependable employee and one of my best friends during that time of my life.

In fact, the changes in her own personality were so pervasive, I wasn't the only one who noticed. Within a year of completing her handwriting changes, Deepak Chopra offered her a job with his seminar company. Jenny had been volunteering for many years at Deepak's events, but she was never part of the paid staff. But, once Jenny cleared her roadblocks, she manifested an ideal job with an ideal salary. Within the year, Jenny had packed up and hit the road managing Deepak Chopra's seminars worldwide. In fact, Jenny has been happily employed by Deepak's company for many years now. I am so happy for her. She is now living her dreams. She travels the world helping others transform their lives through spirituality.

She told me, "Bart, your advice is what changed my life. Before I changed my writing, I had never attracted this type of opportunity. And if they did come my way, I had always sabotaged them before they came to fruition. Thanks for making me change my "y".

I know it sounds a bit bizarre that changing the loop on your "y" can make such a difference, but it is true.

HOW TO CHANGE EVEN FASTER

As you learned in a previous chapter there actually is a synaptic pathway that is formed with each thought. Handwriting is a visual representation of that thought process.

What happens if you begin finishing the stroke on this "y"? You create a new neuro pathway. If you do this every day, you end up creating a lot of neuro pathways. You can even increase the growth of those little neuro pathways by adding emotion to this learning experience. You add emotion by playing with your internal pictures, voices, or feelings.

You are welcome to doodle a page full of "y's" while you are

*Fear is the main source of superstition,
and one of the main sources of cruelty.
To conquer fear is the beginning of wisdom.*

— Bertrand Russell

*You gain strength, courage and confidence by every experi-
ence in which you really stop to look fear in the face.
You are able to say to yourself, "I've lived through this
horror. I can take the next thing that comes along."
You must do the thing you think you cannot do.*

— Eleanor Roosevelt

bored at work. However, you would experience faster change if you doodled "y's" during the fourth quarter of your favorite football teams comeback march to victory. You would build stronger muscle memory if you doodled "y's" while listening to the theme to *Rocky* or *Chariots of Fire* and imagining yourself as the champion!

If you add emotions to anything you do, you increase the number of neuro-pathways you create. When you add neuro pathways, the likelihood of this behavior becoming a habit increases. Handwriting is the same way. If you change it, and you do it consistently every day, you're changing from one neuro pathway that's bad and giving it a new and better one (one that says you're going to accomplish successful things). Now your brain has a choice. It has two highways to go down.

If a person has the fear of success, their internal mind might think: "If I work hard this week, I'll most likely win the award for top salesman of the month." Then, because the self-sabotage is such an ingrained pattern, their mind will move forward to create scenarios in which he doesn't win the top award. If the person changes their writing, they may still think those thoughts occasionally, but the conclusion will be different. Your brain will no longer tell itself the old self-sabotaging mantras. You will have two neuro pathways to choose from. You can choose a freshly paved "success road" or an old self-sabotaging road filled with potholes. Life is a bunch of choices.

IT'S MORE COMMON IN WOMEN THAN MEN

It's interesting that the fear of success trait is more common in women's writing than men's. I find it about three times in women for every one time in men. It's significantly noticeable.

My theory as to why this is the case relates to the difference in the way boys and girls are raised. When men were little boys, the culture emphasizes winning and achieving. There isn't much reward for second place.

Boys are much more competitive than girls. This might be one reason women grow up to be better team players than men. I have found that with women who have this "fear of success", there is a trend in the way their parents rewarded them. Their parents gave them love and affection if they came in second, third or fourth. Sometimes women and little girls actually got more affection for failing. "Oh, it's okay, honey. Let's get some ice cream." One sure can't point fingers at a parent for being loving. But, since we learn based on pleasure vs. pain, winning must hold more pleasure than losing. Otherwise our brain gets wired to choose losing over winning.

FEAR OF RIDICULE / REJECTION

(SELF-CONSCIOUSNESS)

As humans, the need for love and connection sits at the core of our being. The fear illustrated by this "emotional roadblock" is different than our basic emptiness when we are not loved. The fear of rejection or ridicule is a response to the social conditioning that occurs when we are children. Our brains are great learning machines. So effective that even just one strong emotional event can affect our behavior the rest of our lives. When a six year old stands up in class to answer a question, her brain makes a connection. If she gets the answer correct and the teacher praises her, her brain connects standing up in class with a good feeling of approval.

If she misses the question and the whole class laughs at her, her brain learns that standing up in class to answer a question equals humiliation and embarrassment. If this negative event is deeply emotional or occurs repeatedly, a fear of ridicule is developed. If you happen to be one of the millions of people who rank the fear of public speaking higher than the fear of death, you might have some self-consciousness.

In handwriting, a severe fear of ridicule is signified by the humps on the letters "m" or "n".

This self-consciousness in their handwriting is shown when the second hump is higher than the first hump. It's interesting, because in handwriting analysis, the opposite of a stroke is not always the opposite meaning. In the letter "t", the low t-bar and high t-bar have reciprocal meanings. However, in the "m" and "n", it isn't the case.

For instance, the opposite of the fear of ridicule does not mean you enjoy ridicule. You also can't say, "Just because I don't have a loop in my d-stem, I'm never sensitive to criticism." It doesn't work that way. This is why it may take a little bit of study with more advanced material to be 100% accurate when analyzing handwriting. In this example, the "m's" that go downhill indicate diplomacy. Diplomacy means you have the ability to say things in a very kind way and be diplomatic.

Diplomacy is a very positive trait. Self-consciousness has no redeeming factors. Therefore, the decision to exchange one for the other is a no-brainer. If your humps go uphill, it doesn't mean you can't be diplomatic. But it does mean that you have a little bit more self-consciousness than you have diplomacy. In handwriting, the stronger trait will occur in any letter where two or more traits might occur. Often, the letters will alternate one shape to the other shape. This indicates both traits are a significant portion of the personality.

In a sales career, this trait is very detrimental to success. If you can't make cold calls because you're afraid they might say "no", you have a big hurdle to overcome. If you give me a stack of sales-men's handwriting, the one writing with self-consciousness is invariably the sales manager. Why? Because he has chosen to train and administer rather than deal with rejection on a daily basis.

If you are single, you might experience self-consciousness when you meet someone new. If you feel nervous to speak or a bit uncomfortable about doing things wrong, you are feeling the fear of rejection. Here is a test. The next time you are in a social situation, pick someone across the room that you do not know. Walk right up to them and strike up a conversation. In many people, the level of anxiety in this scenario is in direct proportion with the level of self-consciousness you have.

I guarantee you that by changing this trait you will feel positive results.

There's one way to find out if a man is honest- ask him.
If he says, "Yes," you know he's a crook.
-Groucho Marx

LACK OF HONESTY OR LACK OF INTEGRITY

I wish I could point out one letter that indicates integrity and one letter that shows a big fat liar. However, integrity is not a per-sonality function that can be pinned down to just one trait or just one letter. Actually, a trained analyst can spot integrity and honesty in a person's handwriting. In spite of the complexity of that task, I will share with you one letter that is an essential component to that evaluation. I'm not holding back on you ... it really can get complicated. I have found an interesting fact. Handwriting that indicates integrity is as much a function of noticing which traits are NOT present as a function of looking for specific strokes. Some of these roadblocks to success are exactly those "negative traits" and there are many more not discussed in this book.

For this discussion, simply focus on the oval shaped letters such as the letters "a" and "o". I tend to use the "o" because it has proven to be more accurate. The way people write the letter "o" indicates how open they are with their communication toward others.

Is your "o" clear and clean, like you could put your eye up to it

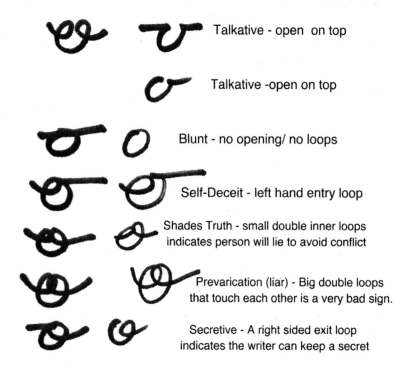

Talkative - open on top

Talkative - open on top

Blunt - no opening/ no loops

Self-Deceit - left hand entry loop

Shades Truth - small double inner loops indicates person will lie to avoid conflict

Prevarication (liar) - Big double loops that touch each other is a very bad sign.

Secretive - A right sided exit loop indicates the writer can keep a secret

Fear is the opposite of love.

Anger, guilt, and judgment are all based in fear and they are not loving. Unconditional love is the absence of fear. Practice unconditional love.

and see through it? Does it contain loops and circles? Is it narrow and closed? All the variety speaks volumes about your level of candidness. Even a secretive person can seem like a liar because he tends to withhold information, instead of offering it. If the truth carries pain and dire consequences, even a basically honet person can be persuaded to hold back total truth. It can get complex.

I've made a simple o-chart for you to learn the various ways to make an "o".

In summary, to live in the highest level of integrity, you do not want to have double loops in your "o". You will want to have some open space inside the oval. Being secretive is not a bad thing. It's up to you whether you want to be very blunt, talkative, or keep some things private. If you happen to be a person with a high degree of sarcasm, you might opt to keep some things to yourself. (Sarcasm is

revealed by a sharp needlepoint ending on the letter "t".)

ANGER OR RESENTMENT

A very important trait to eliminate right now is anger from your past. Clearly, the emotion of anger is in direct opposition to the emotion of happiness. Naturally, many people have issues from the past that are unresolved. Those issues can show up in a variety of ways in someone's personality. If you feel you have unresolved anger, then you must resolve it in order to be truly at peace with now and the future. Anger affects the way you interact with your

January 20, 1985.

Dear Poley,

Christmas, New Years and the 12 days of Christmas have come and gone. I felt reclusive during the holidays and couldn't bring myself to send season's greetings to anyone. So it goes. But I got over it.

Resentment Strokes

So please accept my heartfelt thanks for all you have done and be my wishes that the coming year will give you much Peace and Joy

Ted

Handwriting of
Ted Bundy

Resentment shown in a serial killer's handwriting.

lover, your family, and even small things like traffic.

The following stroke does indicate anger. However, handwriting analysis does offer other indicators of such anger, but they are more advanced than I choose to describe in this book. So, if you have symptoms of anger, but don't have the stroke, don't be surprised. Thankfully the following stroke I do not find in high number of people.

When I see a hard straight beginning stroke that starts below the baseline, I realize this person is hanging on to anger that has its source in the past. If the stroke starts within the middle zone, then the anger is more likely to be caused from a current situation. This stroke is usually very heavy and is straight and rigid like small metal ruler leaning toward the letters.

I have only personally met a few people with a severe case of this anger and resentment stroke. One was an older bitter man who ran a Poker room in Las Vegas. He was always rude to the staff and customers. Rumor had it the only reason he had the job was he pleaded guilty to a crime he didn't commit and spent time in jail in place of the casino owner. All I know for sure is he was one pissed off guy. He might have had some money in his pocket, but he sure wasn't happy.

Another person was a man who faxed in his handwriting while I was on a radio show. He was actually a well-known politician in the Boston area. He had this resentment and anger stroke. Although he was pleasant during the interview and denied being angry, I think the handwriting was accurate. He was the state-wide tax enforcer for Massachusetts. I guess he found an outlet to express his anger - destroy people and their businesses if they didn't pay their taxes. I can think of more loving jobs on the planet.

Earlier in the book, I asked you: who would you allow to baby-sit your daughter? The handwriting sample I used was a man serving a life sentence in an Arizona prison. Look again at the handwriting sample in chapter five and notice the resentment stroke. In fact, he's got every bad stroke I've ever taught and a few I've never thought of. He is a mess.

Here is an interesting fact that might motivate you to find a way to rid yourself of all anger. Of the dozen or so handwriting samples I've taken from convicted serial killers, severe anger and resentment were the common traits found in all of them. This emotion doesn't make people violent or homicidal. This trait does fuel the fire if these traits are present.

The most pervasive example of resentment is shown in the convicted and executed serial killer named Ted Bundy's penmanship. His handwriting is shown in the next diagram. Notice the long firm beginning strokes indicating resentment from the past.

Your assignment is to stop making any type of hard upstroke to begin a letter. In addition, you might take up meditation and investigate therapeutic techniques to let go of the past. Many of my clients and friends have had great success clearing up issues from the past using the techniques of NLP or Time Line Therapy. See the appendix for recommended resources, seminars, or practitioners.

FEAR OF CRITICISM / SENSITIVITY TO CRITICISM SENSITIVE D-LOOP

The tendency to be too sensitive to criticism is often confused with a fear of rejection. It is not the same. The fear of rejection is based on the fear of what might happen in the future. The sensitivity to criticism is a response to what is happening in the present. Naturally, if you feel pain each and every time you do something, you begin to expect the pain and adjust your behavior.

In a phrase: words hurt. What people say or what we think they think can hurt worse than sticks or stones. This is one of the most common of emotional roadblocks.

The analogy I like to use is this. Imagine you have an open wound on your arm. You would most likely create a bandage, a sling, or simply be very careful not to expose it to any of the ele-

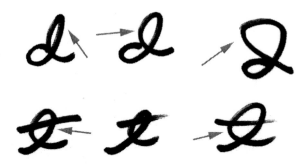

ments. One grain of salt could really cause a lot of pain. People's negative thoughts or negative comments are like grains of salt being shoved into that open wound. When this occurs, you can't help but react. People react by running away or fighting back.

People with large loops in their lower case d-stem are very sensitive. You must watch these people carefully, as they are often irrational in their assessments of criticism.

Think about the ladder and the blue prize game. Why would this trait stop me from climbing the ladder?

What if I get to step two and you laugh at my butt? What if you tell me I am uncoordinated and walk funny? I might stop in my tracks and come down off the ladder. At the very least, I would withdrawal from you. Or, I will use sarcasm to criticize you back and defend my ego. And if you have a major fear of criticism, you just might not take any action that gets you criticized.

The best-case scenario is that I don't have a loop in my "d". It doesn't bother me if you laugh at my butt or tell me I walk funny. What if the wound on your arm spontaneously healed? No matter how much salt I threw at you, you would feel no pain.

Re-tracing the d-loop is like healing an open wound.

Does fear of criticism make a person bad? No. Does it make for a bad employee? Not necessarily. It does make us have strained relationships with those around us. Other people have to walk on eggshells around a d-loop person's sensitive feelings.

I would go as far as saying a very large balloon shaped d-loop is usually a big negative. A large fear of criticism usually causes the person to lean on his defense mechanisms to handle the imaginary pain he feels.

Do you have a loop in the lowercase "d"? A totally retraced short d-stem means that you don't give a hoot about what people think about you. You can still have compassion without being irrational and without feeling the emotional pain. Wouldn't that be a nice way to relate to people?

VANITY D-STEM

The height of the "d" also has significance. A short d-stem height means you're very independent in the way you think and in the way you make decisions. If it's really, really tall, it means you have a high dose of pride, dignity, self-respect, or even vanity. People with tall skinny d-stems tend to dress very sharp. Tall skinny d-stems indicate a preoccupation with their "image." Yet the same person often doesn't give a flip about the criticism from just one individual.

So if you have too much pride, it could end up as vanity. Arrogance is usually thought of as a negative trait. Pride is a good trait, but arrogance is a negative trait. These two traits are just a centimeter in difference.

STUBBORN D-STEM

One last trait I want you to look for in the d-stem is stubbornness. This is depicted as a d-stem that looks like a teepee or a person's legs spread wide like and upside down "v". A person who writes their d-stem like this will be very stubborn. In other words, they don't like to be confused with the facts once they've made up their mind. They will argue a point even when they're wrong. These people are hard to get to budge once they've made a decision about

Braced t or d stem.

something. You may know someone just like this. I would suggest that stubbornness is not a useful trait in most cases, because it means these people lack the flexibility to admit when they're wrong and learn from their mistakes. Also, these people challenge relationships, because they have difficulty compromising when necessary or meeting people half way. If you notice this teepee-shaped d-stem in your handwriting, I would suggest you retrace the d-stem until the teepee closes. You'll find that after you do this, people are much easier to work with, because now you are.

STUBBORN D-STEMS / T-STEMS:

The reason I have elaborated on the variety of shapes of the d stem is ... I want to make sure if you de-program one negative trait, you don't accidentally program another one.

So, remove the loop from you d-stem or make it smaller. But don't make the stem any taller than it already is. And retrace the d-

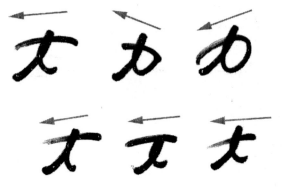

stem, so that stubbornness doesn't creep into your personality as well.

You'll find that by closing that d-loop, you'll quickly become less sensitive to what

people say about you. And coming from a person who has successfully eliminated that trait, life is so much more enjoyable now that I can handle criticism constructively instead of feeling pain from it.

SELF-CASTIGATION

The trait of self-castigation is a sister trait to living in the past. In handwriting analysis, any stroke that consistently ends toward the left side of the page has something to do with the past or internal thoughts. Self-castigation is the need to be punished. It is the combination of two traits:

1. Thinking about the past is indicated by someone crossing the t-bar right toward left.

2. Crossing the t-bar toward the left and ending it with a sharp point means sarcastic toward self.

So, the person is using their favorite defense mechanism, sarcasm, to punish themselves. This is the person who puts himself down all the time. There are many comedians who use this trait by making fun of themselves to be funny.

By the way, this trait is accurate even if you are left-handed. Handwriting analysis does not care if you are right or left-handed. It also can't determine if you are male or female, black or white, Asian or American. Left-handed people tend to have the hardest time re-training themselves to cross the t-bar from left to right. But, it can be done.

An example of how this simple change can affect your thinking is the story of Joe Lester. Joe was one of the first people I met as a freshman at Pepperdine University. We have been friends ever since. Because I knew how to analyze handwriting even as a freshman in college, I offered my advice to my friends there. Joe is the only one I can remember who actually took my advice to change his handwriting.

Even though Joe was left-handed and tended to print everything, he noticed he crossed the "t" backwards (right to left) and very low. So he made a conscious effort to change his t-bar. He gives me a lot of credit for his current successes, but I can only take credit for understanding the power of Grapho-therapy.

When we were freshman, Joe drove an old 1979 brown Toyota Celica with the paint peeling off and no air conditioning. It was truly ugly. But, like most kids, we didn't have much budget for a new car.

Joe drove his ugly Celica past the Ford dealership every day for almost two years. As he drove by, he would always stare at the super fast Mustang GT and think to himself "some day." Joe had been reading some self-improvement books and practicing his t-bars earlier that day. This bright and sunny California afternoon, Joe turned the corner headed toward the Ford dealership. But, instead of saying "some day" Joe had a different thought. He said "I wonder if I can afford it today?" Within a few hours, Joe was driving a brand new white Mustang GT. As it turned out, Joe could have afforded to drive that car anytime over the past twelve months. But his belief system didn't even allow him to conceive it. When he did think about having something that nice, his inner voice told him he need-

ed to suffer in order to pay for school. (Self-punishment) To this day, Joe swears that the change he made in his letter "t" (crossing the t-bar left to right) made the difference in the shifts in his thought pattern.

Joe has continued his pattern of getting what he wants. After ten years working in the shadow of Hollywood and the California stars,

Joe and his band signed a deal with a major record label. (The band is called California.) Most musicians usually give up before they ever reach their dream of making it big. But Joe did what it took to get up that ladder of success. First, he removed his own internal roadblocks. Then, he adjusted his plan until he found a way to succeed. Naturally, Joe's handwriting reveals many of the success traits we discussed in the previous chapter.

GUILT AND OR LIVING IN PAST

Too many strokes that end to the left can be destructive. Because all goals are in the future, spending too much time dwelling on the past can be detrimental to a healthy attitude.

Here is an example of some letters that reveal a tendency to dwell on the past or show a guilt-complex.

People who write like this will often have the martyr complex. Working harder than they have to or just creating a situation that causes them pain. For some reason, they think feeling the pain gives them a sense of completion.

It reminds me of the Catholic guilt syndrome. Most people who are not happy with the Catholic Church's use of guilt as a mechanism for control find that the emotion of guilt can only be handled if they do something to suffer a while. Usually the emotion of guilt is painful enough to count as suffering. Other times, people attract relationships and even physical disease to keep themselves in a state of suffering.

So, when Catholics conduct themselves in a behavior they were taught was wrong, they automatically feel bad. Remember our brain is an efficient learning machine. If you grew up Catholic, you may want to spend some time de-connecting the emotion of guilt from certain loving and pleasure-filled activities (like sex). I have no intention of picking on the Catholic Church. The same guilt feelings can come from an over protective mother or a number of strict dogma based religions. Catholic parents are infamous for using guilt and punishment as a means of trying to control their children. As you know, pain is an effective motivational strategy. Unfortunately, this strategy leaves scars.

Remove the excessive backward strokes. You will be much happier.

CONCLUSION

When you remove these bags of cement from your path you can easily navigate up the ladder. By changing your handwriting, you have a direct channel to program you unconscious mind. Once you remove the roadblocks, programming the success traits will be a piece of cake.

Now, let's go back into that gymnasium in your mind. Imagine walking firmly up the ladder and grabbing the blue gift. Open it and realize it took a few simple steps. Those steps are summarized here:

1. Choose what you want.

2. Create a plan.

3. Remove the roadblocks from your path.

4. Start the plan.

5. Take feedback and adjust the plan accordingly.

6. Get your outcome.

7. Celebrate.

Oh, don't forget the last step. Always remember to celebrate. Give yourself the emotional reward of celebration when you accomplish things. There is a very practical reason for this. If you do not reward yourself with a significant emotional event upon achieving success - you will be training your brain that success = no pleasure. Then, your next accomplishment will not be as automatically motivating.

Train your brain to link massive pleasure to getting what you want. In order to do that, you must reward success. Give no emotion to failure.

Other Resources:

www.bartbaggett.com/timeline

www.bartbaggett.com/change

Change Your Life in 30 Days Workbook for Adults (Change Your Handwriting, Change Your Life)

Change Your Life in 30 Days Workbook for Kids (Change Your Handwriting, Change Your Life)

PART THREE:

THE SECRETS TO BEING HAPPY NOW

Universal Truth #9

A balanced life is a happy life.

Live your life doing what is important, not urgent. Urgency creates drama. Drama throws you out of balance. Invest your time and energy into what you truly know is most important. Only then can you live in a drama-free zone and experience deep effortless fulfillment on a daily basis.

Chapter 8

The Secret Sport of Life-Boarding

I have talked about the power of the unconscious mind throughout this book. The concept I am going to present to you now is directly from a higher source. As I was preparing the material in this book, my mind was swimming with useful ideas from hundreds of sources. One of my unique talents is the ability to research, synthesize and present very complex ideas in a simple format. However, when I started thinking about the question of "how to have a happy life" it seemed overwhelming.

I was meditating on this idea of how to best illustrate the art of maintaining happiness in one simple visual diagram. I sat in a quiet place and took inventory on my own life. I was happy, very happy. I thought about why my life was happy. I contemplated many models of psychology. I thought about Abraham Maslow's idea that we work up the pyramid of our own needs toward enlightenment (more on this in Chapter 10). I remembered Steven Covey's concept of categorizing your time into quadrants in which you stay out of urgency and focus on what is truly important. I analyzed my own satisfaction in the six human needs that will be covered in chapter 10, as well. Also, I remembered the very useful vocabulary words "story" and "drama" as originally coined from the 1970's EST seminars.

During my meditation, I had an intuition that there has to be a way to tie these useful life models together in a single, easy to utilize, dynamic diagram. But as I thought, no answers came to me. In fact, the more I thought, the more confused I became. So I practiced detachment. I set an intention of creating a useful model that I can use to guide myself daily toward maintaining a sense of balance and happiness. I asked my unconscious mind to take over. I left it to my inner source to figure it out, because at a conscious level I was coming up empty. Then I slept on it for several nights.

Sometime within the following week, I woke up from a dead sleep with a vision. I scrambled for a pen and some paper on the bedside table. I started writing. I had a sense of what was in my inner mind, but I couldn't see it quite yet. As I drew the circle and imagined myself there, it became clear.

I had created a model that makes keeping it all together as just a simple exercise in balance. The model even became more useful as I shared it with some of my more kinesthetic (feeling based) friends. It works.

Here's what I came up with. I call this the "Life Board." The purpose of the Life Board is to use it as a dynamic working metaphor for all areas of your life. The sport in which you pretend to play is "Life-Boarding." Life-Boarding is an adventure sport that has its joy in "being" not "accomplishing." There is no specific goal in mind. You just thoroughly enjoy the "Zen" of boarding. Plus, you make your own rules, choose your own path, and create as many or as few objectives as you want as you "Zen" down the mountain.

It has become one of my favorite models of how I interact in the world. It also helps me be happy in the moment. Before I present this model to you, you must be on the same page with me in two vocabulary definitions: *story* and *drama*.

YOUR "STORY" AND YOUR "DRAMA"

First, the word "story" is defined as a person's interpretation of what happened in the real world. This is based on a simple premise that no one knows what really happens in the world. We are only privy to our version of what happened through the filters of our own perspective, beliefs, biases and internal wiring. So, in a nutshell, there is what actually occurs and people's interpretation of what occurs. The interpretation is our "story" of what we think happened. The most popular example is our own version of our story of our childhood. Don't misinterpret the word story for imagining that you don't think it is reality. Oh, my friend. You have bought hook-line-and-sinker your story an absolute truth. That's the point. It may not be the truth, but it is a story you have chosen to believe.

Imagine if you will that you are a screenwriter penning the next blockbuster movie. You come up with a very moving storyline of a kid growing up not getting the love or attention she needs from her parents. You think, "Hmmm. The facts are the father worked too much and the mother was an alcoholic. That's just the facts. It needs something to make it compelling. The story needs an important element to make it exciting. And, like a good storyteller, you start writing in the "drama." You begin making the story more interesting by having the heroin skip school, get hooked on drugs, fall in love with the bad boy, etc. Now you've got some excitement.

Most of you reading this could be great screenwriters if you only realized you are already doing it. You create drama all the time out of insignificant events, and you make up stories everyday about what really happened.

Now, do you know anyone who has a really big story about why their life is so screwed up right now? Think of a specific person. Think about the father who did this, the mother who did that, the ex-wife, the sister, the jerk boss, etc. It gives people peace at night to blame their problems on others. Their story serves them. Even you have a good story or two, don't you?

Why did your last relationship fail? Do you have a story of why it was your partner's fault? How about your story of why you don't have enough money? You've got to have a story about that. Now, I don't know whether your "story" is reality or fiction. I have talked to marriage counselors about this concept. Invariably, a husband and wife have two completely different stories about the exact same event. It's all based on their point of view. The point is our version of reality is all a story. You can choose to believe it or choose to not believe it. The question is do you create drama in your story or do you create peace, fun, laughter, and joy in your stories?

 Grab a pen and paper and play along as we create a visual for your life. Draw a large circle and divide this circle into four quadrants. Label each of these four quadrants as you see in the diagram below. Health, Family, Love, Money.

In each quadrant, make a notation of the top three stories or dramas that you deal with in relationship to each category. For example, if you have a disease, list that disease in the health category. If you have a bad back, list it in the health category. If you've had a divorce, put your ex-spouse's name in the "love " category. If you think your father is a jerk, put his name in the Family/Friends category. If you struggle to pay your bills each month, list bills in the

money quadrant. By the way, you are not limited to just four categories. Some people have added their own categories such as "spirit/religion" or "hobbies/creative", etc. But, for the simplicity of the instruction, use just four quadrants for the demonstration.

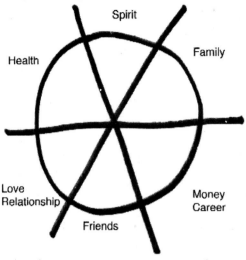

The first step is listing what your stories currently are. Again, there is no judgment whether these stories are true or not. They just are your perception. What is happening right now in your life regarding your health that is unintentional? List any events you are dealing with: depression, cancer, the flu, a broken leg, a friend's health challenge, etc. What is happening in your love life right now? Make a list. Do the same with money and family.

Now when you have completed writing down a few of your favorite stories, draw an inner circle and an outer circle. Label the inner circle "Intentional Excitement" and label the outer ring "External Drama."

The Life-Board.

Can you keep balanced?

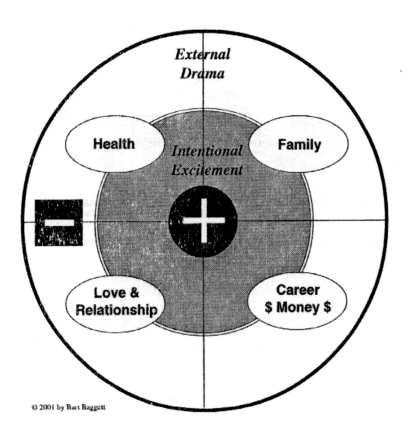

© 2001 by Bart Baggett

Look at all your stories and make a note of which ones are created by the "world" and which ones you created yourself because they bring you joy and fulfillment.

The next diagram shows the handwritten notes of a diagram of a woman named Nicole. You might notice that Nicole's martial arts training is an intentional excitement. Her lower back pain is an external drama that she didn't choose consciously. Nicole also has a job she loves, but it doesn't pay her enough money. Thus, she struggles with the house payment and then has no savings. She gets along great with her mother, but dislikes her stepfather. Etc. etc.

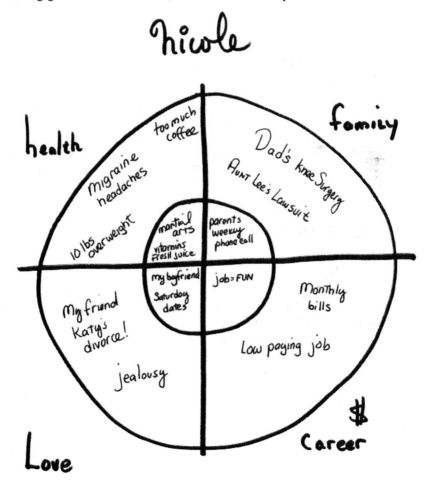

I have asked you to label the outside of the circle as External Drama. This is the "default" zone that most events occur in life if you don't set clear intentions.

Now, in your mind, put that disk on the floor and make that circular disk about six feet in diameter. Imagine yourself standing in the center of that inner circle.

Look around you. Are the areas balanced? Are there more stories and events in your love life than in your health area? Are you spending much more time in your money / career section and ignoring your love life? Once you have a clear image of you standing in the center of the disk, close your eyes. Imagine having to use your internal sense of balance to stay centered.

Well, this should be pretty easy if the board is sitting in the middle of your living room. So, let's add an element of risk to the game. Imagine you are standing on your Life Board and the board was atop a four-foot rubber ball. Now, keep your balance. Focus. Sure, it's easy to keep your balance as long as someone doesn't jump up into your "love" area and have an emotional breakdown. Hmmm. The weight of that person's drama sure takes the focus off of the other three quadrants. Isn't it interesting that other people's drama can throw you off your own balance?

Occasionally, no matter how balanced you are, life throws you a curve ball. If you are firmly centered, you can adjust to handle the unexpected external event and get back on track. However, I have found that if you don't consciously set out to create intentional excitement in each category, life will hand you some excitement in the form of drama. For some reason, your unconscious mind doesn't want you to be bored.

If you don't eat healthy, the disease finds you and creates some excitement in your health zone. If you don't choose your friends carefully, then you end up hanging out with losers who bring all types of drama right to your doorstep.

Most people spend their life in the outer circle. They are "reac-tors" not "creators." They let outside influences (people, things, events) dictate to them how they're going to spend their time and energy. They let events dictate their moods. Rather than being at cause in their life, they live at the effect of everyone and everything around them.

NO DRAMA ZONE

Recently a 23-year-old girl stopped by my office on a 100-degree hot Texas day. As she was talking to someone, she started telling him she was very angry. When the compassionate person asked what was wrong, she sobbed, "I'm so mad. It's just so hot out-side and I have to walk all the way home."

When I overhead this I simply shook my head in disbelief. First, I knew the girl lived about four blocks away. Secondly, I found her poor attempt at getting attention humorous. Third, I saw a vivid example of someone allowing an event as impersonal as the weather control her emotions! The temperature of the air actually had more control of her emotions than she did. Wow. How unfortu-nate.

Perhaps the saddest part of this story is that this girl was really angry. She wasn't pretending to be upset. She actually felt the emotions of anger and frustration. What a hard life she has chosen, because she has not figured out how to "Just say No to Drama!"

No Drama Zone   Drama Queen

The secrets to living in a "No Drama Zone" is to simply set new rules about who you allow in your personal space and what you allow them to talk about. I'm very serious when I tell you I will cut people off in mid-sentence if they start telling me a whiney self-serving dramatic story about some event. I simply hold up my hand and say, "Nope. You are standing in my No Drama Zone. If you want to tell a story about why your life isn't working, go somewhere else. If you want my help, just tell me the facts." In most cases, the speaker doesn't want you to know the facts, and they don't want an easy solution. The story is providing them comfort and a good excuse for them feeling the way they do. If they said no to the drama, they would half to give up the benefit of the tragic story. (Attention, love, sympathy, etc.)

The "no drama" diagram was inspired by my friend Amber and her high drama family. I learned a lot by watching her learn to the tools to set new "no drama zone" boundaries in her own life. Thanks!

THERE ARE TWO KEYS AVOIDING THE DRAMA ZONE:

1. **Create new rules** and inform your friends about the no drama zone. You make it, you enforce it.

2. **Learn to say "no."** People tend to have a hard time saying no to requests. Once you learn the value of your time, you will have to say no to various random tasks. You must learn to say no to invitations to parties, to meaningless TV shows, and especially to your high-drama friends.

Why is it so hard to say, "No, I won't bail your son out of jail using my rent money." That does three things. First, it avoids putting you in a financial crisis. Two, it keeps you out of someone else's family drama. Three, it sends a signal to that drama queen that you are living your life in the "no drama zone" and he won't call you again. Saying no is a powerful lesson. The words drama queen applies to both male and female drama addicts. I find that labeling a man a drama queen is just insulting enough to get his attention! So if you catch yourself having dramatic episodes. Stop it. Stop whining and complaining and take responsibility for your life.

If you plan to run your life in a no drama zone, you must make daily conscious decisions to fill your life with intentional excitement. Otherwise, your brain will be bored and you will create your own drama. Your mission is to stay balanced in the inner circle.

HOW TO CHOOSE YOUR OWN MEANING TO ANY EVENT

The trick to evaluating any story is to find a meaning that creates a positive learning or a positive emotion. You do this by asking this question.

What does (some event) mean to me?

Then, turn it into a statement.

I will choose to believe that because (some event) happened it means _____.

Here is an example:

What does my boyfriend not coming home last night mean to me?

Then, turn it into a statement.

I will choose to believe that because my boyfriend did not come home last night means he was sleeping with another woman.

Or you could choose...

I will choose to believe that my boyfriend did not come home last night means he doesn't love me.

Or you could choose...

I will choose to believe that my boyfriend did not come home last night means he fell asleep again at his buddies and he is a bit irresponsible.

Now. In most situations, we don't know which of the chosen meaning will turn out to be true. In fact, we may never know. So, it is wise to pick the meaning that creates the least amount of drama and emotional pain. Again, we are choosing stories and meanings without all the facts. Choose empowering stories.

THE ART OF MAKING A DECISION

The sport of "life-boarding" is really just a sport of making good decisions.

Will you let the events of the outside world run your emotions or not?

My health is important to me. I realize that the more attention I put into my health quadrant, the less drama will come to me from the outside world. Therefore, I have chosen healthy habits such as juicing, lifting weights, and attending yoga weekly. I even attend seminars and watch TV shows to pro-actively create excitement about my health and fitness. Because of this, I have very few health challenges that create drama in my life. I will discuss the importance of living a healthy vital life in Chapter 12.

So here is the bottom line. If you're not intentionally creating health, you are unintentionally creating sickness. If you're not intentionally creating wealth, you are unintentionally creating financial struggle. Invest early.

THE FULL BLOWN LIFE-BOARD

In my version of the Life-Board, I have outlined four quadrants. Actually, I prefer the model with six quadrants when I am meditating on which areas need my "intentions." In my six-quadrant version, I added separate categories for friends and spirit. Naturally, some people feel spirit travels with them in every category. Also, since my family is also part of my circle of friends, I often group them together in my diagram. You may create quadrants in your balance board that I have not thought of.

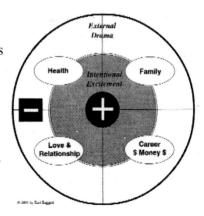

This is my most complete and professionally designed to Life-Board model. Turn back a few pages to see the enlarged version you can actually read.

Now, to add a degree of movement to the mental imagery, I imagine that I am not only balanced on a large rubber ball, but that that ball is rolling down the groove of life. From the past toward the future. It's like snow-boarding down a mountain. There might be bumps. There might be turns. It's all about handling what life hands you, and you come up standing anyway.

I Imagine myself on top of the disk. I'm standing there looking down on the different areas of my life. I'm in balance. I spend time at the gym, I spend time on my love life, I spend some time working on my long-term investments, and I call my Mom once a week. Everything is cool.

Then, somebody comes along and whack, you lost $50,000 in the stock market. Then whack, your dog got hit by a car. Or whack, your mother is in the hospital. How do you keep balance then? If you have created emotional, physical, or even financial savings in each quadrant ... then no problem. You can leave the center of the disk, handle the emergency, and return to the center. Your weight won't throw off the balance if you have invested time in each quadrant before you experience a crisis.

Most people do this: they spend the time on the outside of the circle running from quadrant to quadrant like a rat on a wheel. Running as fast as they can putting one fire out before another fire gets out of control. Steven Covey, author of *The Seven Habits of Highly Successful People,* calls this living in "urgency." Squeaky wheel does get the grease. But, if you invest time into emotional maintenance, the wheels don't get squeaky.

Focus on health, relationships, career, spirit, family, money. If you get too off-centered you end up falling off your Life Board. You get back on only to fall off at the next bump in the road. Life can get very frustrating if you can't maintain your balance.

And the way you stay balanced is very, very simple: make good decisions. Every moment of every day, you have a choice what thoughts you focus on inside your mind. Spend time daily asking yourself, "What can I do to create intentional excitement in each of these quadrants? How can I make an emotional deposit into my relationship, family and friends? You know that if people get their needs met from you in peacetime (daily life), there is no reason to create a war (drama) to get there needs met.

Imagine you are driving your car tomorrow. Some person cuts right into your lane and almost crashes into you. You have a choice of what goes through your mind, and what action you take next. That's called a decision. Choose happiness. Maintain balance.

It sounds so simple. It is simple.

Universal Truth #10

Rules are made to be broken.

CHAPTER 9

CREATE YOUR OWN RULES

Have you ever stopped to think about the rules you live by? Most of us just accept our rules as the right way to live. Then, as we age, we attract and select other people who have the same rules. The most obvious rules are the unwritten rules of what clothes are fashionable to wear. Perhaps you have to drive a certain brand of car to really fit in or live in a particular neighborhood. If you think about it, these are rules you have chosen to live by. This chapter is about more subtle rules you may not be aware of.

I met an interesting guy recently. As I was opening a new corporate bank account, this nice older man sat down and patiently waited while a new clerk typed in my banking information. The clerk acknowledged him, and I had the distinct impression that Herb was one of the bank's most valued customers. Herb and I exchanged a joke or two then we went on our way. About a month later, I saw Herb lifting weights at my gym at 7 am. I'm sure I would have run into him sooner, but I don't get to the gym at 7 am very often. As Herb and I became friends, I marveled at his energy, youthful attitude, and even physical strength. Herb told me he was now 83 years young and never felt better. I thought to myself, I'm talking to an 83-year-old man who is both rich and happy - research time! I have this novel habit of asking the most successful and happy people I meet, "What is your one secret of success or happiness?" This morning Herb told me it was an easy answer. Herb said, "Each morning that I wakeup and realize I'm still alive- I'm happy! A weekly dose of dancing and women doesn't hurt either!" Herb was my new 83-year-old hero. Herb didn't realize he was telling me his rules for being happy. Herb's rules for being happy were simple. If he was alive, he was happy. Hmmm. Perhaps that is why Herb was happy all the time.

I know another guy named Russell. He is an attorney who always appears to have just lost a big case. The brief time I visited with him, I asked him what was his secret to success. Russell answered without a smile, "I'm successful because I've paid my dues. Someday I won't have to work this hard. I will have earned the right to relax and be happy. Life is hard so I work hard. There ain't no easy way to the top." Wow. Can you see why Russell is miserable most of the time and Herb always has a new joke to tell? Not only is Russell's belief system totally toxic, but his rules for being happy include being successful first. And, he believes he can't be successful unless he works hard for many years. Hmmm. That sure seems like a long road to drive just to be happy. I guess nobody told Russell he didn't have to live by his father's rules. (Russell's dad was an attorney, too. I have to guess his dad shared this "success formula" and Russell bought it.)

I think it can be a revolutionary experience when we realize that many of our rules are actually keeping us from being happy. For most games we play, rules are designed to create order, structure, and perhaps fairness. In the game of chess, why can a Bishop move diagonal and a Rook only move horizontal? The answer is: that's the rule. In Soccer (European football), why must you use your feet only, but never your hands? The answer is: that's the rule. We simply accept rules as being fact without ever asking ourselves who made them or if they are the best possible rules to live by. As a society, we must have rules about traffic, ownership, real estate, sports, and the law. If we didn't have the commonly agreed upon rules, we might live in total chaos. Some people would certainly take advantage of one another, and there would be less fairness in the world.

What was the rule about talking back to your parents? Did you have a rule about staying out past midnight when you were in high school? Did you notice your friends not only had different curfews, but received different punishments for breaking them? What is your current rule for letting you know you deserve a vacation? What is the rule for allowing yourself to buy a new blouse or clothing item? Do you have to earn it? What is your own rule for letting your emotions show? (In other words, when is it appropriate or acceptable for you to cry, yell, scream, or laugh hysterically?) Does someone have to die before you allow yourself to cry?

I remember the funniest scene relayed in one of Richard Bandler's books. A hysterical woman came storming into his counseling office yelling, crying, and sobbing. "I can't take it anymore! I don't know what to do. I'm totally lost, etc." After about 20 seconds, Richard held up his hand in a stop position. He said calmly. "Miss, just stop. Your appointment has not started yet. You are early. Hold on one minute." He stood up and got himself a glass of water. Meanwhile, the previously hysterical client simply stopped the tears and shut up. She sat down and waited while her eyes watched Mr. Bandler pour the water. One minute later Richard raised his hand and said, "Now, continue." She started bawling and sobbing and resumed telling her story.

The point to this therapist story is that everyone has rules when it is okay to feel certain emotions and when it is not okay to feel or express them. For this woman, during her counseling time was the totally appropriate place to let it all go. However, she truly felt like she had no control. When in fact, she had total control. She just had certain rules about when it was okay to act that way.

Think about the real important emotions that you value so much. Love, freedom, security, adventure, etc. What are your rules about feeling each emotion? Are the rules you have set up to feel these key emotions strict or easy? Have you unconsciously set up

Great men are they who see that spiritual is stronger than any material force, that thoughts rule the world.
-Emerson

There are some days when I think I'm going to die from an overdose of satisfaction.
-Salvador Dali

What a wonderful life I've had! I only wish I'd realized it sooner.
-Colette

your life to win on a daily basis or lose every day?

What has to happen for you to feel loved? (Must your spouse bring you flowers, touch you in that certain way, kiss you?) What has to happen for you to feel successful? (Make $100,000 per year, be on the cover of *Biography Magazine*, win a gold medal?) What is your rule for allowing yourself the feelings of absolute joy and happiness? (Must you save the world, be debt-free, be married, or just be alive?)

Most people have rules that make it very hard to win at the game of life? In fact, some people design rules as if their life were a game at a carnival - almost impossible to win. Remember those carnival games along the Midway? The games looked easy, but there was always some catch that made it hard to win. The basketball hoops were much smaller than normal basketball hoops, the nickels were thrown onto a plate that has grease on it, and the guns didn't ever aim straight. And, if you were lucky enough to win a game, you never won the huge pink bear on display. You won a cheap plastic glow ring instead. Midway games were set up to lose most of the time. Are your rules for being happy set up against you?

I've seen boys play field hockey and intentionally make the goal smaller so it is harder to score in the name of competitiveness. Why? Well, they believe that if the goals are harder to achieve, the feeling of scoring will be that much more enjoyable. Perhaps they are right. The elation of a hockey goal seems to be a lot more exciting than a two-point basket in a typical basketball game. They have different rules based on different values. Some sports value lots of small repetitive emotional wins, while others value more difficult, patiently won scores that result in a higher emotional win.

I have a friend named Stephanie who ranks health as her highest value. She spends hours a week working on her physical fitness. She has a rock hard thin body that makes men walk into walls when she is laying by the pool. However, her rules state that she must have a 15% body fat in order to be fit. She even has stated that she doesn't even think she looks good if she doesn't have that 15% body fat percentage. When I asked her about this rather stringent "rule" to be healthy, she confessed she is much better than she used to be. She is now firmly focused on being healthy without much concern about avoiding fat. Her rule for being healthy is 15% body fat.

In fact, her younger sister suffers from Bulimia. More common among young women, Bulimia and Anorexia are diseases in which a person loses a tremendous amount of weight because she either refuses to eat or makes herself throw up after she eats. This is a case where the girl has extremely dysfunctional, irrational, and danger-ous rules about what her body must look like in order to be pretty. This family history may play a role in her particular rules.

I know people who have rules about money that seem just as sick. Some believe that in order to be virtuous, a person must be poor. Some believe a rich man can't get into heaven. Some believe that the only way to be happy is to have money first. Some believe that in order to feel successful, they have to hold a certain position or make a specific amount of money.

Most couples have conflicting rules about things in their rela-tionships. Until you recognize and negotiate these rules at a con-scious level, people get their feelings hurt. My family was taught that is was both economical and respectful to turn the lights off when you leave a room. This conserved electricity and showed respect for my dad's hard work. However, in one of my first rela-tionships where my lover spent the night frequently, I realized she didn't share the same rule. After being irritated for a week and get-ting up in the middle of the night to turn off the lights, I asked her about the lights. She told me that her mother taught her to leave the lights on, so that the other people in the house could see if they got up in the middle of the night. She thought she was showing respect. I thought she was showing disrespect. Same action. Different rules.

I changed my rules. Now I don't run into furniture in the middle of the night.

Would it benefit you to routinely inspect your own rules and challenge yourself to change them to make it easier to win? I guess you have to ask yourself what game you are playing. Are you playing to be competitive? To get stronger? To build toughness? To see how much you can suffer through? Are you playing to experience love and joy every waking moment? Is that the purpose of this game called life? Or, do you believe what the Dalai Llama says is the purpose of our life? Be happy.

I'm not a saint, not a channeled spirit of a dead guru, or even a current master of philosophy. But, if I were to choose the rules of the game of life, I think I would make the rules easy, so I could experience lots of success, joy and happiness instead of making them so hard I would experience frustration, confusion and pain. Call me crazy! If I were making the rules of life, I would set the rules up so I could win ... all the time.

Oh. I just had a breakthrough. I am in charge of creating the rules of life. My life.

Who is in charge of creating your rules?

Universal Truth # 10

You may not always get what you want.
But, you can always find a
way to get what you need.

CHAPTER 10

SIX HUMAN NEEDS

I was recently presenting a workshop to a group of sales people. During the program, I was repeatedly interrupted by a rather obnoxious but well-meaning man named Bill. He would ask questions at inappropriate times, make sarcastic jokes, and generally tried to get attention from the group. It didn't really bother me, because his intentions were positive and his jokes were funny. Afterwards, I was visiting with one of his coworkers who made an interesting comment. She said, "Sorry about Bill's obnoxious behavior. He gets a lot of his needs met by acting that way."

I thought that was an interesting way of understanding someone's behavior. We do certain things because they meet some need. I would have to speculate we also don't do certain things because they don't meet any of our needs. If human beings have some basic predictable needs, then it would make sense that based on our individual history, we might see different options for meeting those needs. So, instead of focusing on the behavior we would like to change, perhaps we could ask what need the behavior fulfills and then simply find another action that could satisfy this need. Take Bill for example. If Bill was getting a sense of "significance" by drawing attention via his obnoxious behavior, you would ask what other actions could Bill take in order to feel a sense of significance? You can't expect to erase a negative behavior without first finding a substitute to get the need fulfilled.

If you ground your sixteen-year-old son from driving his car, you also have to provide a solution for him to get to and from work each day. The need of transportation still exists, so it must be dealt with. If you don't provide an alternative vehicle, you might not like the results. Find him a ride.

If you are discussing the action of saving money vs. blowing all your money on clothes, ask yourself what needs are being fulfilled by each action. For some people, having a large cash savings is essential to feeling the need of security or certainty. However, for others, they already feel a sense of certainty from their weekly pay-check. For them, the option of having new clothes fulfills the more pressing need for variety and perhaps even significance by wearing the right name brand of clothes.

It is my opinion that if you can get your needs fulfilled in a healthy way, you experience ultimate fulfillment. Personally, ultimate fulfillment sounds like a very good outcome to aim for.

The first time I learned about the concept of human needs was from the works of Psychologist Abraham Maslow. Abraham Maslow was a pioneer in the field of psychology. He was one of the first psychologists to study healthy people instead of sick people. His life work was devoted to investigating the inner workings of a "self-actualized" person and assisting others to achieving this peace-ful, happy, evolved state of being. Maslow believed that people already have the inner resources for their own growth and healing.

Maslow is one of the founders and leaders of the humanistic school of psychology. He is most well known for his concept com-monly called, "Maslow's Hierarchy of Needs." The top rung of this Hierarchy is becoming self-actualized. He states, "self-actualizing people tend to focus on problems outside of themselves, have a clear sense of what is true and what is phony, are spontaneous and creative, and are not bound too strictly by social conventions." He also coined the term "peak experiences." These are profound moments of love, understanding, happiness or rapture. It is when a person feels more whole, alive, self-sufficient and yet a part of the world, more aware of truth, justice, harmony, goodness, and so on. Self-actualizing people have many such peak experiences.

In Maslow's hierarchy of needs, a person must first satisfy his simple life needs before he can progress to more spiritual "human" needs. He states that a person will be very motivated by thirst, but quickly forget about their thirst when they can't get oxygen from the air. Breathing is a more fundamental need than drinking. Shelter is a security need which is more fundamental than experiencing love. His hypothesis is you must satisfy all the base needs before you can begin to experience the higher, Psychological needs. Here is Maslow's famous Hierarchy of Needs chart:

Beyond the details of air, water, food, and sex, he laid out five broader layers: the physiological needs, the needs for safety and security, the needs for love and belonging, the needs for esteem, and the need to actualize the self, in that order. You might notice that the need for self-esteem is just one step away from self-actualization. In my research self-esteem is also the key element in the personality profiles of rich and happy people.

1. The physiological needs. These include the needs we have for oxygen, water, and nutrition. Also, this includes the needs to sleep, be active, heal, avoid physical pain and have sex.

Maslow believed, and research supports him, that if a person lacks a specific vitamin, the body will crave a food that contains that vitamin. Some people crave orange juice not knowing consciously that they are deficient in vitamin C. This "craving" theory is important to understand that your nature as a human is to get your needs met.

2. The safety and security needs. When the physiological needs are largely taken care of, a person will become increasingly focused on creating a safe place to live and feel secure. In the ordinary American adult, this set of needs manifest themselves in the form of urges to have a home in a safe neighborhood, a job security and a financial nest egg. Fears and anxiety can occur when we fear losing this level of security.

3. The love and belonging needs. Once a person feels secure and fed, he might begin to feel the need to satisfy the emotional needs of being human. The person attracts friends, a lover, children, affectionate relationships, even a sense of community. Looked at negatively, he becomes increasing susceptible to loneliness and social anxieties.

4. The esteem needs. After the first three levels, Maslow says we begin to focus on self-esteem needs. Maslow noted two versions of esteem needs, a lower one and a higher one. The lower one is the need for the respect of others, the need for status, fame, glory, recognition, attention, reputation, appreciation, dignity, even dominance. The higher form involves the need for self-respect, including such feelings as confidence, competence, achievement, mastery, independence and freedom.

The negative version of these needs is low self-esteem and inferiority complexes. Maslow felt that psychologist Alfred Adler was really onto something when he proposed that self-esteem issues were at the roots of many, if not most, of our psychological problems. In modern countries, most of us have what we need in regard to our physiological and safety needs. It seems to be the self-esteem needs and the loving needs that keep us from experiencing the benefits of Maslow's self-actualization.

All of the preceding four levels Maslow labels deficit needs. Which means if you do not satisfy them, your body craves you to do something to satisfy them. But once you satiate the need, you feel no craving at all. In other words, these needs cease to be motivating. As the old saying goes, "You don't miss your water till your well runs dry!"

I think Maslow's version of the human needs is a very useful model. If nothing else, Maslow has given us a reason for walking this planet. He believes we are here to evolve through the stages into enlightenment, or as he calls it "self-actualization." In fact, this short summary doesn't really do the concept of his contributions justice. However, I don't think his ladder theory really covers the spectrum of all the needs and has a few notable exceptions. Viktor Frankl formed the basis of his book *Man's Search for Meaning* while suffering tremendous physical and emotional hardship in a Nazi concentration camp. Many artists could barely keep food on the table while they created their most outstanding work. Rembrandt and Van Gogh are great examples. So, it is clear humans can experience self-actualized thinking while experiencing deficits in the lower rungs of the ladder.

All this theory on the human needs didn't fully explain why Bill chose to be obnoxious in my seminar or why a thirteen-year-old boy joins a gang in East L.A. It also doesn't explain why someone would spend four nights a week in a bowling league while his co-worker at the same day job works a second job in order to achieve

*If the essential core of the person is
denied or suppressed, he gets sick
sometimes in obvious ways, sometimes
in subtle ways, sometimes immediately,
sometimes later.*

-Abraham Maslow

financial and emotional freedom. Are there other needs that motivate us? I think there are.

SIX HUMAN NEEDS

I first learned about this model of the "Six Human Needs" from author and motivational speaker Anthony Robbins. He discovered that people all over the world seemed to display a pattern of the same life challenges. From his seminars and coaching practice, he noticed people were being pulled into different directions by needs that seem to be paradoxical. However, consistently across cultures, people always found a way to satisfy these needs. The problem was that these needs could be satisfied in a destructive or a healthy way. Your brain wants you to find a healthy (no-drama way) to get its needs met. But, if you won't comply, you might find yourself smack dab in the middle of a destructive method of getting these six basic needs met. Let's take a look at these six basic needs and evaluate how you are getting them met in your life.

The interesting thing about this version of the human needs theory is that you don't ever become completely satiated. We simply fill up our tank for a while and have to fill up our tank again later. It is also a bit frustrating to realize that as we get one need really satiated, it pulls us farther way from another need. So we spend a lot of our life balancing these paradoxical needs. Realize that humans yearn to satisfy all six of these needs. You are already finding ways to satisfy these needs. However, sometimes the method that you have chosen is filled with drama, crises and toxic thinking.

I have arranged these six human needs in the form of a triangle. Naturally, you can exist while craving one or more needs, but it becomes increasingly difficult to maintain balance and avoid drama if you crave these unmet needs for too long. Remember that the needs described here are natural and necessary. The method you choose to satisfy these needs are a choice.

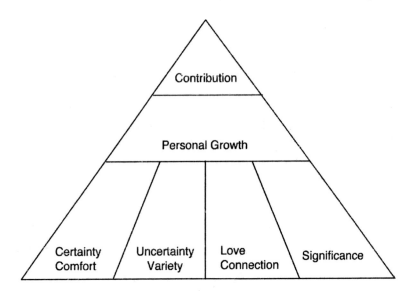

CERTAINTY / COMFORT

The need for certainty goes much deeper than having a few dollars in your pocket or a roof over your head. The need for certainty is a deep-seated desire to have some predictable outcome, comfort, rules, or patterns in our life. The need relates to the basic motivation I discussed in chapter two: pain vs. pleasure. Certainty is the desire to avoid pain and gain pleasure. A high degree of certainty gives us comfort. Maslow's lower needs such as food, air, shelter, and basic security would be considered a need for certainty.

The opposite of certainty is total chaos. Earthquakes, war, and emergencies send our emotions stirring with anxiety. People will go as far as to give up their freedom to regain a sense of certainty. Germany elected Hitler in 1937 to regain some economic certainty. How many women have you known who stayed in a physically abusive relationship because they prefer the known pain vs. the unknown events that might occur if they leave?

There are many positive examples of certainty. People get married because they want certainty in their relationships. Getting married often provides a feeling of consistent love and connection, improved financial security and sexual expression. This is a very healthy way to get this need met on a daily basis.

The method you might be choosing to give you a sense of certainty or comfort might also be the one thing that is holding you back from obtaining financial freedom. Many actions you could take to gain wealth require you let go of security long enough to develop another, more lucrative source of income. I would not suggest you quit your job without a logical way to pay your rent. However, if the job you are currently working in takes up all your spare time and you are not getting any closer to your financial goals, you must find a better way. It isn't just fear of failure that might be holding you back. It is a basic human need to feel a sense of certainty in your world.

Some potential vehicles for obtaining certainty are: religious faith, property ownership, control, dominating behavior, learned helplessness, stockpiling food, a storm shelter, life insurance, money in the bank, etc.

For most people, the need for certainty comes down to one word: control. People try and control their world and the people in their world to create a feeling of certainty. If you think back to the life-boarding diagram, you realize you can't really control all the events in your world. (I would argue that you have an influence in what events you attract, but that really is a more philosophical discussion.) The one thing I know for sure is you do have total control of your decisions about what each event means. In other words, the only thing you can control is what something means. Once you decide to control the meanings of everything in your life, you can stop trying to control the events.

Certainty is the feeling that an event will be as you expect it to be. Too many surprises make us feel unstable, insecure, in danger. It is akin to the comfortable feeling of coming home after a long vacation with tons of adventure. There is a special comfort about some place that is familiar to you. This is true even if every moment of that vacation was filled with luxury, silk sheets, milk & honey. You still have a warm feeling to coming home to a house with a familiar smell.

Until I fully grasped the concept of the six human needs, I would confuse this need with other values such as "belonging, comfort, familiarity, and security." After all, Maslow says security is a basic human need. I don't argue that. However, I think that people unconsciously decide what has to happen in their world to make them feel secure. But, security implies a "protection from danger." The word "certainty" broadens this need into other areas of our life that include non-dangerous elements.

I had a slightly scary event happen to me this year that illus-

trates the need for certainty clearer than any metaphor I could create. Because I live in an urban setting, I see many homeless people
on a daily basis. I often pay them a few dollars to move boxes, take
out the trash or sweep up the driveway. One summer day, I hired a
transient named Dwayne to do some odd jobs around the office.
Over the next few months, I hired Dwayne a number of times, and
we began to form a mutual respect for each other. It was clear
Dwayne had never been exposed to a lifestyle of abundance, kindness, and fairness. One day while taking a break, Dwayne confessed
to me that he had lied. He hadn't worked in South Carolina for his
sister. He had actually been in Federal Prison since he was 15 years
old in Connecticut. I was one of the first people Dwayne met after
he was released. He told me I was the only person who extended a
kind hand to treat him with respect, offer him a job or give some
cash when he needed it.

I was honored by the compliment, but I must say I was very sad
to imagine that my fifteen minutes of combined kindness to a
stranger was a "peak experience" for this man. Wow. I'm sure I
couldn't even imagine the pain he had experienced throughout his
twenty-year prison sentence. To make a long story short, here is
how my short friendship with Dwayne ended. As we were taping
boxes of books to be shipped, something strange happened. Dwayne
had loaded some boxes into the truck and returned. I felt him walk
up behind me and slowly put his right hand around my neck. At
first, I thought he was hugging me with appreciation. (He had needed some hugs the night his mother died.) It wasn't until his voice
said with fear and regret, "I'm so sorry I have to do this, Bart." It
was only then did I feel the knife blade slightly touching my juggler
vein on the left side of my neck. Dwayne was at least 6 foot 5 with
hands the size of an NBA basketball player. He held the small
kitchen knife in the palm of his hand – like I've seen people hold
sharp objects in the prison movies. I knew he had held a knife like
that before.

Riches are not from an abundance of worldly goods,
but from a contented mind.

-

Mohammed

I said jokingly "You're kidding me, Dwayne. You're just fooling around, right? Tell me your kidding."

"I'm sorry, but I've got to do this."

"Dwayne, you know you aren't going to hurt me. I'm the nicest guy you ever met - you told me that. What are doing? What do you want? You can have whatever I have."

His voice cracked, "I just need some money. Give me your money."

I kept my cool. I acted as if I were talking face to face with an employee, firm and compassionate.

"You also don't have do this for money. I've given you money before. All you have to do is ask. Now let me go and put down the knife."

His grip tightened. Again, I felt the blade. "Sorry, just give me your money first. Give me the money."

He slid the black leather wallet from my back pocket and opened it with the knifeless hand.

"Dwayne, have you lost your mind? I've only got $20 in my wallet. I would have given you fifty if you just asked."

Upon realizing his ruse to rob me was a financial failure and realizing he actually couldn't hurt me, he loosened his grip. He backed away with tears in his eyes. He said with the most startling level of pain, "I just want to go back to jail. I wanted to hurt you so you would send me back to jail. It's too hard. I can't make it out here. I'm sorry. I've got AIDS. I can't get a job. I don't have a home. My Mom is gone and I can't make it out here. I'm so sorry. I just want to go back to jail ... it's all I know. "

He was so emotional he didn't realize he still was clutching the knife in his hand. I sat him down in a chair. I discreetly lifted the knife and let him cry for few moments. He tried to just leave into the night. I stopped him and offered a ride to the bus station. I bought him a ticket to Houston, and I've never seen him since.

Can you imagine a man needing a sense of "certainty" so bad that he would choose going back to federal prison where he had been raped and beaten? Clearly the need for a sense of "certainty" was stronger than his need for freedom, love, sex, creativity, fun, etc.

Thanks to my encounter with Dwayne I understand the need for "certainty" at a much deeper level than I ever could have before. Also, my own survival needs were tested. As strong and physically fit as I am, my life was in danger. My sense of certainty was compromised. I haven't hired a homeless man since. Because of that emotional encounter, my decision process about my own personal safety has changed. That was a minor incident in the scope of my life. But, I'm sure you have had major incidents in your life that have created an unconscious pattern for getting your "certainty" needs met. You have to periodically go back and reevaluate those patterns. If you made the decision when you were 16 years old to never trust another person, then that system might not be the best choice to get your needs met as a 36 year old.

Certainty/ Comfort   <----------- *paradox* ----------->   *Uncertainty / Variety*

UNCERTAINTY / VARIETY

The need for uncertainty is the paradoxical brother to certainty. Have you ever wondered why men get married and then cheat on their wives that they love? One reason is they have not found a healthy way to satisfy this need for variety. Specifically in a relationship, the couple must work together to keep it fresh and new. Too much predictability will make each partner restless.

Predictability satisfies the need for certainty and leaves a craving for some variety.

Uncertainty shows up in our love for surprises, adventure sports, movies, TV, competition, diversity, and all forms of excitement. Have you heard the phrase "variety is the spice of life?" How do you get a sense of variety into your life? Some potential vehicles for this are: new relationships, learning, accepting more responsibility, taking on new challenges, sports, picking a fight, getting into trouble, breaking the law, drugs and alcohol. Take a moment and list your methods for creating variety in your life. Just like the lifeboard game says, "If you don't intentionally create what you need, life will create it for you in the form of drama."

This may sound strange, but some people actually put themselves into financial crisis, because it satisfies this need for uncertainty. Clearly not many people would admit to this at a conscious level. But how many times have people you know waited until the last possible minute to pay a bill or earn some cash. Procrastination is obviously a personality trait they might want to improve upon. They are also clearly more motivated by a deadline than the comfort they would feel if they just worked extra hard at the first of the month and relaxed having all their bills paid at the end of the month. As we learned from the life-boarding diagram, people often create drama because they despise boredom. I think the need for a bit of uncertainty or variety is also being satisfied by allowing drama to take over in financial situations.

SIGNIFICANCE

The need for significance can include a sense of being needed, important, different, famous, unique, making a difference and having clear sense of purpose. The need for significance is the need that I recognized most in myself. I spent a large part of the first few years of my career creating press clippings and television appear-

Nine-tenths of our suffering is caused by others not thinking so much of us as we think they ought.
-Mary Lyon

It's a great satisfaction knowing that for a brief point in time you made a difference.
-Irene Natividad

ances. On the surface, I told myself it was for marketing. But at the core level, my need for fame was an overblown desire for recognition. As I analyzed my own past, I recognized I had the "not popular" emotions still hanging around from childhood. In my subconscious mind, I thought fame would make me feel significant. Well, it actually was a very effective tool to make me feel significant. However, like any potential vehicle that you use to get your needs met, you have to ask what is the cost of getting this need in this way. My need to be famous was like a drug in which the same dose no longer had the same emotional response. For example, if I do a radio show these days or a local newspaper interview, my pulse doesn't race a bit. It has lost its sense of uniqueness. After about the 1000th interview, it felt like a natural extension of my career. So, I recognized that if I didn't find other ways to feel significant, I would be chasing higher degrees of fame all my life. I've watched celebrities play that game - I chose to find other solutions.

For me, publicity is now simply a vehicle to contribute my ideas to other people. When I changed my perspective and intent, I found a rejuvenated motivation to hit the media circuit. I think I noticed the paradox most clearly at my high school ten-year reunion. I thought my recognition would make me more likable to my old friends. I have to assume they were either intrigued, curious or impressed. But my accomplishments did not create any more rapport, love, or connection. In fact, with many kids it had the opposite effect. The child inside of me really wanted to connect or gain approval from this set of peers. The real emotion I was looking for was love and connection - I had wanted it through the vehicle of fame. That night, my sense of connection only came from the art of "connecting" on a humble compassionate level. I learned that the sense of significance and love / connection are two different needs that tend to have polarity. One pulls away from the other.

There are hundreds of ways to gain a sense of significance. The obvious ones include winning a gold medal, being elected president or getting promoted. Other healthy avenues include taking on responsibility in clubs or churches, being the smartest kid in class, knowing the answer, being the class clown, having a different style, education, being a parent, owning certain possessions like original art. These ways do make us feel a bit unique.

However, some people use destructive means to feel significant: schoolyard bully, violence, sarcasm and tearing down others, attracting a disease or physical disorder, or using scarcity as a means to get attention and recognition. Let's face it. If you are always the person who is "down and out" and the family is always coming to your rescue - you feel significant. In the therapeutic practice called Time-Line Therapy, Dr. Tad James frequently discusses how all people with a major disease have some emotional benefit associated with having that disease. Usually in hypnosis, Dr. James can discover the hidden emotional benefit they are receiving. In most cases, the needs of "significance" and "love and connection" are being met as a direct result of this physical crisis. It makes sense. If someone is having a tremendous craving for love, one of the fastest ways to spark their family to give it to them is to get really, really sick.

Dr. Tad James and other time-line practitioners have had seemingly miraculous success assisting patients in spontaneous remission of life threatening diseases. The therapist's job is to assist the patient in first locating and changing the original unconscious decision that started the disease process. Secondly, they work with the patient in creating another, healthier way to meet these needs. The largest roadblock to recovery is finding a replacement method for obtaining the "hidden benefit." Very few patients will admit at a conscious level that contracting a life threatening disease has some hidden benefit. But, in James' experience it always does.

As I stated before, your mind is a very powerful creator. If you aren't going to put in the time to meet your life needs, your unconscious mind will go to work doing it for you in the best way it knows how. You may not like the solution it comes up with.

Significance   <----------- paradox -----------> Love & Connection

LOVE & CONNECTION

Many would argue that the emotion of love is the most power-ful emotion in the Universe. Many metaphysical and Eastern reli-gions believe that pure unconditional love and God are one in the same. It is clear that love and connection are basic human needs that we all must fulfill. You can get the feeling of love and connec-tion in many healthy ways: bonding, oneness, sharing, intimacy, teams, marriage, sex, family, etc.

I've heard of people getting this need met in very destructive ways. A friend's sister routinely smokes crack cocaine with her own mother. When asked why she does that, she simply stated, "I didn't want to do it, but it seems to be the only way my mother and I con-nect." (And you thought your mother was dysfunctional! Wow.) Kids around the country get a feeling of connection and love from joining gangs. They feel connected and a sense of belonging that was often missing from their own family. It is often common for young girls to engage in sexual activity long before they are emo-tionally ready. So, they have sex with boys in an effort to get the love and connection they need. Sometimes it works. Sometimes it backfires.

One of the paradoxes in the Six Human Needs theory is that the more significance you gain, the less love and connection is experi-enced. Because significance is also seen as uniqueness - most sig-nificance requires an elevated position or separation from the group. If you separate to be noticed, the ability to connect is weakened. I noticed it almost immediately in my early days as a handwriting expert. The more famous I became, the more of a target I became for other, less recognized, handwriting experts. If people have low self-esteems, then someone else's success often makes them feel like a failure. The easiest way to erase that jealous feeling is to criticize the person succeeding. You see this in every corporation and political party in the world.

For me, it was confusing. I personally introduced more than 5 million people to the incredible science of handwriting analysis during the 1990's. That exposure and credibility had to assist in other handwriting experts selling more books, getting more business, and generally being more respected. However, because I was the one receiving the "fame," I was getting less connection (and no love) from my peers in the industry.

On a personal level, I also noticed the more I did things to make me feel significant, the more it alienated many of my friends. If you go through a period of sudden financial windfall, many of your friends will treat you differently. In fact, many studies of Lottery winners who win a million dollars or more reveal most of them believe their life was more fulfilled before they won the money. How can that be? Because they didn't have the wisdom to maintain the connection and love that was there before the money.

Imagine a circle of blue-collar workers who get together weekly to drink beer and criticize the "suits" at the factory and complain about taxes. For these guys, part of the basis of their sense of connection is this sense of scarcity, anger, and feeling of being an underdog. If one of those guys wins a million dollars and quits his job - he has lost rapport.

Most people find that as they increase their income and improve their financial status, they are forced to make new friends. Because rapport is based on a perceived sameness - people lose rapport when one of their group members outperforms them. You should be aware that this might happen to you when you decide to become rich. Your newfound success might chase away a few friends. Be ready for it.

The first book I wrote is called *The Secrets to Making Love Happen*. It is a 304-page book about the art of creating and attracting love into your life. If you do not have a lover in your life that assists you in getting your love and connection needs met on a daily basis, I suggest you read it. This book also teaches the science of handwriting analysis in detail. If the handwriting analysis portion of this book intrigued you, this "relationships" book will be very valuable for you. In summary, find a way to get your sense of love and connection in a healthy way. If you don't ... drama will step in to create it for you.

GROWTH

For me, personal growth has been the background fabric of my life. I can track the level of my success by the amount of time and money I have invested into my own personal growth. I routinely meet people who have never read a self-improvement book. I scratch my head in disbelief. They claim they want to be rich, but never read a book on investing. They complain about being lonely, but never attend one seminar on relationships. Even the people with weight and health problems do try various diets, but few actually ever learn the fundamentals of being healthy. They are just focused on not being fat. It is my personal belief, that if you do not make an intentional effort to constantly progress in your personal and spiritual growth, life will create its own, harder, curriculum for you to learn things.

The purpose of investing in personal growth is to discover ways to experience more life fulfillment. Perhaps this is a more spiritual idea than a psychological idea. I have a belief that we choose and attract people into our lives to learn lessons. I would go as far as to say our entire mission on this planet is to learn lessons. The Hindus in India believe that the purpose of reincarnation is to give the soul

*The growth of the human mind is still high
adventure, in many ways the
highest adventure on earth.*

— Norman Cousins

an opportunity for growth in each lifetime. Eventually, one would achieve nirvana and not have to return to this earth plane for more lessons. The Buddhists use the word enlightenment to describe this state of spiritual awakening. Abraham Maslow describes this state of mind as "self-actualized." All of these different terms refer to the end result of a lifetime of personal growth.

If you don't make an intentional effort to read books, attend seminars, or constantly find ways to stretch yourself and grow, then you will be forced to learn the lessons and have growth the hard way. Well-taught, interactive seminars are like "boot camp." They set up situations that don't have dire consequences so your brain can learn new behaviors. If you learn it in a controlled, intentional environment, your brain starts to make new neuro-pathway connections to assist you in changing. If you really get the lesson, you will most likely not need to experience it again out in the real world. I remember after taking three years of Kung Fu, people treated me differently. Street people stopped even talking to me. Usually a Martial Artist is the last person to get drawn into a fight. Once you learn your lesson, life doesn't keep testing you over and over. Make personal growth a priority.

CONTRIBUTION

Very few people will argue that contributing to others isn't a good decision. However, it may not seem like a primary life-long need. I do find that the this need to contribute is more commonly obtained on a daily basis by those people who are skilled at getting the other five needs met in a healthy and ecological way. This might be because inherent in the spirituality of contribution is that the other needs get fulfilled. When you are contributing, people respond to you in a way that meets many of the other needs automatically. This is why I positioned this need at the top of the pyramid diagram. Scheduling contribution as part of your life might be one of the most important "success secrets" that most people overlook.

You don't have to look any further than India's Mahatma Gandhi. If you haven't watched the amazing movie starring Ben Kingsley, I encourage you to go rent it. There are so many incredible pieces of life wisdom illustrated in the life and teachings of Gandhi. In the context of this discussion of needs, Gandhi's primary mission was contribution. He dedicated his entire life to the seemingly impossible mission of freeing India from British rule through his policy of non-violence. An interesting thing happened to Gandhi when he made his sole focus on contributing to the welfare and happiness of his country. All his other needs automatically became fulfilled. The world held him up as a national hero in his lifetime (significance). He had unending opportunities to travel, meet millions of people and create change (variety). He was loved and adored by his family, friends, and his country (love and connection). And, as a result of his work, people always surrounded him to provide his basic needs of food, clothes, security and comfort (certainty). Actually, he was famous for making his own clothes by hand using Indian yarn. Truthfully, his incredible faith gave him a higher sense of certainty than most people ever experience. If you want to model some very useful and powerful belief systems, study some of Gandhi's teachings.

Are you willing to sacrifice your needs to get your dreams?

Have you ever seen amazingly talented people living mediocre lives? It is very common.

Billy Joel sings about this in his hit song *Piano Man*. His lyrics go like this, "They sit at the bar and put bread in my jar and say, 'Man, what are you doin' here?'" Just because you have talent does not guarantee you will become rich or happy. And talent definitely does not guarantee a life of total fulfillment.

I have a friend who has lived this truth for many years now. His name is Greg Wilson. And, I hope that by the time you read this, he is the most famous comedian in the United States. However, I've known him for five years and for the last four years, he has been stuck in second gear. His goal is to be a cast member of the TV show *Saturday Night Live,* and go on to be a famous comedy actor. He could easily be the next Robin Williams or Eddie Murphy. But first, he has to make some shifts in his own thinking. He must be willing to take more risk. His struggle for success relates perfectly to the concept of "needs."

Before I explain, let me tell you that Greg is one of the funniest guys I have ever met. My sides hurt from laughing so hard even if we just have lunch together. Imagine how hard I laugh when he is on stage. Secondly, I really want Greg to succeed. I hope writing about this insight helps both you and Greg achieve success faster.

I discussed the concept of the "Six Human Needs" with Greg on the set of *The Process of Creative Deception* (a recent independent movie we appeared in together). I quickly discovered the real reasons he has made very slow progress in his career. Greg thought his roadblock to success was merely a question of location. If you want to break into comedy and acting, it is commonly accepted that you must live in New York or Los Angeles while you get started in your career. (That may be a limiting belief ... but it is a belief with lots of statistics that support it. Be where the action is.)

Greg needs to move to New York City. He has known this for years. When I asked him, "When are you moving," his answer was he didn't know. Upon probing, the first excuse was one that many of us use: "I don't have the money." In Greg's case, he had spent his early 20's hopping from temp job to temp job earning wages and not saving a penny. So, the thought of moving to New York City to become an actor was frightening. New York living expenses are about three times more expensive than Dallas, Texas. He "believed" he simply couldn't afford it. (Once a belief is set ... action or lack of action follows.)

Hmmm ... I found myself thinking, what's the difference? He

Common sense is not so common.
-Voltaire

can be poor in New York just as easily as he can be poor in Dallas. Why not be poor where he could be "discovered?"

So Greg's lack of financial abundance and his unwillingness to "learn" what it takes to become financially wealthy has kept him stuck. Yep, having no money really sucks. Ask Greg. I know this because I had repeatedly offered Greg advice on writing books, doing odd jobs, getting into radio, or other money making deals over the past few years. Greg always had resistance to any opportunity. Excuses varied - results were the same.

For a long time he would never get a real job. He just took temp jobs.

One day I asked, "Why aren't you at a real job that pays well?"

He said, "Because I'm going to go to New York City and I'm going to make it big. I don't want to be tied down when that call comes."

I said, "If the call comes, you could just quit."

He put himself in a state of uncertainty about both his finances and his moving to New York. In fact, if you want to analyze it even more, one could say he found lots of benefit from living in scarcity. Much of his standup stage act focused on his lack of money. "I'm so poor ..." This is a good comedy tip: get rapport with most of your audience. Since most of America can relate to scarcity thinking, they loved Greg on stage.

As I talked to Greg this time, I quickly discovered that there was another reason he didn't just pack his bags, move to New York, and audition for the *Saturday Night Live* cast. In Dallas, he was already getting most of his needs met. This was the key piece of information that really explained his lack of action. How could he be getting his needs met when he was financially struggling and his dreams were unfulfilled? First, think about the pain vs. pleasure principal. If there was no immediate pain in his life today, his motivation to make a change is less. Further more, if he was experiencing pleasure, he had incentive to stay.

If he moved to New York, what happens to his needs? He is no longer significant. He is insignificant. He is a "nobody" in a town of greatness. He knows nobody there, so he would be lonely. There is a lot of uncertainty in both the financial and emotional arenas. So, the first few months of his New York experience, he would be craving certainty, significance and love.

Let's evaluate his life in Dallas, Texas. He performs in Dallas' top rated Improvisational Comedy Troupe each weekend to a packed house of fans who scream his name. In fact, he is a local celebrity. People stop him on the street and recognize him. (Need fulfilled = significance.) Cute, young, single, sexy women come to his shows and treat him like a celebrity. (Needs fulfilled = significance, variety, love, and connection; and one more not on the list: Sex ... lots of sex.) Furthermore, his three brothers also live in Dallas. (Need fulfilled = love and connection.) If sense of family is an important value to you, you can see how this is fulfilling. Family that lives in the same town gives people an added sense of security. The guys in his comedy troupe are his best friends. (Needs fulfilled = certainty / belonging/ connection.) In summary, he's got a fun-filled life of local celebrity status, lots of young sexy girls throwing themselves at him and best friends. So why would he want more?

Well, he has a dream. A dream that is bigger than a part-time comedy troupe in Dallas, Texas. He thinks he is talented enough to be a top rated stand-up comedian, star in a sitcom and even work in movies. He wants to be a bigger fish in a bigger pond. So how does he get from point A to point B?

First, he has to be willing to let go of the things that are keeping him here and find a way to fulfill those same needs in New York or Los Angeles. So, according to this model of human needs, the reason Greg has not achieved more steps toward his goal is he has been getting so many of his needs met here, he isn't properly motivated to go for it. Greg needs some leverage - some hardcore motivation.

He has to create for himself a strong enough "reason" to leave this all behind and go for his dream.

JEWEL

A great example of a star who had this leverage comes to mind. In 1998, a new pop music sensation hit the American music scene named Jewel. She was just 15 when she talked her mother into packing up their station wagon and moving to Los Angeles to break into the music business. They drove all the way from Alaska to Los Angeles and spent every last dime of their savings. The first month in Los Angeles, they both slept in the car and showered at the public showers on Venice Beach. Jewel had talent-o-plenty. She took her guitar and performed at every restaurant, bar and club she could. Sure enough, an agent heard her angelic voice one night and signed her to a record contract.

Some would say she was lucky to be in the right place at the right time. I say luck is timing meeting preparedness. If it weren't that producer, it would have been another one. Jewel is very talented. But, her unyielding persistence and commitment to her dream is why she is a star today. After all, it is unlikely she would have been discovered by a record producer if she stayed in Alaska.

What do you think would have happened to Jewel had stayed at home and became a big star in her small town? What would happen if she were getting most of her needs met from her close family and friends and performed at church on Sundays? What would have happened if she had six brothers and sisters begging her not to move out away from town. I don't know the answer to that, she might have moved anyway. But, I suspect Jewel wasn't getting many of her needs met in the small town in Alaska. If she was experiencing pain or getting none of her needs met, then she had a lot of leverage for her to "get out of town" and follow her dream. If you have a dream, you have to find a way to create some leverage on yourself to take action.

There is an ancient legend in Greek mythology of a General burning his own ships after he landed in the harbor. He was telling his men that there was no turning back - that is leverage to do it, now.

In Greg Wilson's situation, his local success might just be what was holding him back from his destiny. Sounds weird. The experiences on stage at Ad-Libs absolutely gave him the experience and talent to live his dreams. But at what point do you walk away from a "good thing" to go for a "great thing?"

This same question could apply to your own current job or relationship. If you aren't getting ALL of your needs met, do you leave or do you stay? I've had to make that same decision in more than one "good relationship." It is easy to break it off with someone who is a horrible, mean person. But when your lover is kind, gentle, attractive, etc., that's the tough one. What needs are you willing to live without? Or, to use a poker player analogy, are you willing to take a risk, turn in your cards, and draw another hand?

The enemy of the great isn't the bad — it's the good.

I asked Greg a simple question, "If Ad-Libs were to close down tomorrow. Would you be on the next flight to New York City?" Without hesitation, he said, "Yes." In my opinion, he has the talent to make it. But, Greg has to be willing to forsake some needs now in order to get all his needs met and fulfill his dreams.

What in your life is "comfortable," but not outstanding?"

Assignment: This exercise is best performed in a quiet place when you can be focused and not distracted. Give yourself about 30 minutes. Write down your answers.

ASK YOURSELF THESE QUESTIONS:

If I were 100-years-old, looking back on my entire life ... is right now the best time of my life?

If not, what has to change to make it better?

What mediocrity did I settle for?

What dream did I not pursue because I was too scared, lazy, or comfortable?

And, finally, what action do I have to take in order to NOT have any regrets?

If your life isn't satisfying you at every level yet, you've got some exciting, adventurous, uncomfortable times ahead of you. But hey — it beats looking back on a life filled with mediocrity. And, the rewards might just be huge - you could just get all of your needs fulfilled and accomplish all your dreams. If you are going to spend a few years on this spinning rock anyway, why not do what it takes to live a totally fulfilling life of joy, happiness, and wealth why you are here?

(* Since I wrote this chapter in the spring of 2000, Greg has already made the big leap to New York City! Go Greg! You can get an update on Greg's career at www.thegregwilson.com.)

Universal Truth # 13

Happiness is a Choice

CHAPTER 11

THE SECRET TO STATE MANAGEMENT
HOW TO CREATE ANY EMOTION IN UNDER 60 SECONDS

Can you make yourself really sad right now? Think about how you would do that? What would you do? Don't do it just yet. Think about the internal process that you would have to take yourself through in order to create sadness instantly. Now, take a moment and see how fast you can make yourself feel really really sad. When you have successfully put yourself into a state of "sadness," keep reading.

What would you do with your body? Would you slump down or stand up a little bit? Most sad people slump down and make their body limp. Would you breathe heavy and slow or breathe rapid and short? Probably a little slower. Would you tilt your head down or up? Down. Just for one solid minute make yourself feel sad.

When I do live seminars, there is always at least one person who goes past sadness right into massive depression in four seconds or less. This person has practiced this emotion a lot. And there is usually someone else who is too busy giggling to really get into sadness.

They have a well-trained brain for happiness.

The reason good actors can pretend to have certain emotions in such a convincing way is that they are excellent at actually creating the desired emotion on command. For most actors, nobody ever explained to them they could take the same skills and apply it to every waking moment. You are about to recognize a skill you have had all your life and learn how to use it every day.

Now, take another moment and make yourself exceedingly happy. Stop reading. Stand up for a second and change your state. Come on. Read this paragraph then put the book down and play along. You have 60 seconds to make yourself unbelievably "happy." Stand up, jump around, make noise, think dirty thoughts, hear happy voices ... do whatever it takes to get out of sadness and into "happiness." Just smile from ear to ear and open your arms wide. Get excited. Yell, jump, laugh, smile.

DID YOU PLAY ALONG?

Are you happier than you were a second ago? Do you feel different? Is your blood pumping? Did you break a sweat? Is your brain spinning? If you didn't play along - shame on you. If you use your body AND your brain ... you can change states instantly. And, isn't happiness just a state of mind? Learn to use your body to guide yourself into any emotional state. Any good actor knows this. In order to "be" a character, you must "feel" that character's feelings.

The reason I lead people at my seminars to jump up and down and act like they just won a million dollars is so they can experience first hand the powerful effect that physical movement has on your "state of mind." Intense movement or other physical sensations creates instant "chemicals" to be shot through your bloodstream. The faster and more intense you move, the more intensely the chemicals are dispersed. That is why it is very hard to feel depressed when someone is tickling you or you are laughing hysterically.

Imagine walking through the woods enjoying the peaceful scenery. Then, 20 feet away you spot a twelve-foot-tall grizzly bear growling in your direction. How quickly does your heart start beating? How fast could you run if he takes one step towards you? How fast would your body change from "joy and peace" to "fear and anxiety?" Scientists call this the "fight or flight" response. Chemicals shoot through your bloodstream instantly to protect you. Well, if you are walking around with a pharmacy in your brain ...why wait for external circumstances to push the "dispense" button?

Just for fun ... try this. Close your eyes and see how fast you can go from happy to "sexually aroused." Remember a time you felt sexually aroused by someone. You will find that making noise or moving your body will accelerate the process of "feeling aroused." If you direct your thoughts to paint pictures or run full screen movies in your head - you will quickly feel that sexy state of mind. If you turn up the volume of those movies where you are the lead character - you will get there even quicker. And finally, if you allow yourself to "feel" the same feelings as the characters in your mental movie - it will feel real.

What must you think about in order to go from sadness to happiness in under sixty seconds? What voices or thoughts did you hear yourself say in order to make that emotional journey? And finally, what did you do with your body to quicken the process?

For most people in live seminars, they can do negative emotions with very little coaching. Is your brain wired to access those emotions faster than total elation? If so, start rewiring it now. There have been long books written on this form of state management. For that reason, I will not go into massive detail on this important topic. However, I will give you the big chunks of information and urge you to take actions to master your emotions. The difference between a champion and an "also-ran" is how effective the athlete is at controlling their internal state of mind. The mental part of sports is really about controlling levels of enthusiasm, motivation, anger, energy, internal pictures, internal dialogue and physiology. Life is no different. Each day you should interact with your spouse, your co-workers, and your children like every emotional state you feel could affect the outcome of your life.

Sadness is a "program" you unconsciously run when certain events occur in your life. You may have other, more troublesome "emotional programs." Do you ever accidentally hit the "run program" button on these: Anger, frustration, upset, misery, pity, guilt, sorrow, jealousy, fear, anxiety, depression, hate? If you ever experience any of these limiting emotional states realize this fact: These emotions are a result a very specific process that you "do." You don't just feel jealousy ... you "run" jealousy.

People who can control their emotional states have more "peak states" and fewer "bad days." Therefore, these people tend to be more productive, attract and keep better relationships, and have more energy to get things done. In short, you want to be a "state management expert."

There are three basic methods for controlling your emotional states.

1. **Physiology** - Learn to adjust your body.

2. **Internal Images** - Learn to control the pictures in your mind.

3. **Internal Dialogue** - Learn to control the words, phrases, and sounds inside your mind.

All three of these techniques can be used to influence the kinesthetic/feeling part of you. Let's face the simple and brutal truth. If you can create states of silliness, happiness, and sadness in under 60 seconds, why aren't you happy all the time? The answer is that you haven't made up your mind to "do happiness" all the time.

The mind and body are not seperate, they are one. You cannot use one without affecting the other. The way to master your mind is through your body. The way to master your body is through your mind.

PHYSIOLOGY

Your body is one huge chemical manufacturing plant. As I discussed in an earlier chapter, even a small micro movement in your finger fires off very specific neuro-pathways in your brain. Imagine what happens when you do ten jumping jacks or fifty pushups. Imagine what chemicals shoot through your body when you hear a train coming toward you while your car is sitting on the railroad tracks. Those fast, instant, fearful feelings you might have are actually the result of chemicals shooting through your bloodstream in an effort to get you to take action. You don't need an actual event to take place outside yourself in order to spark the chemical rush. All you have to do is be proactive with your body! Movement is a key to controlling your state of mind. Holding your body in certain positions or moving them in specific motions triggers pre-set feelings that might be associated with that movement. Clapping your hands, jumping rope, or jogging in place might spark instant emotions from times past. Learn to get up and use your body to induce powerful emotional states.

INTERNAL PICTURES

Sad thoughts create sad emotions. Some people visualize a time when something sad happened (a funeral, their dog died, the close of a business, loss of a game, etc.). The key to quickly gaining emotional access from a mental picture is to adjust the way the internal picture is played inside your mind.

You can adjust your own internal pictures in many ways. You can make the image bigger or smaller, darker or lighter, bordered or flush, colored or black & white, grainy or clear, closer or farther away. Remember the submodalities we discussed in chapter four? All these techniques will adjust the emotional intensity of any memory or internal picture. It's like playing with the dials on your TV set. When you adjust these "sub modalities," you affect your own level of emotion.

Many people use perspective to adjust the internal emotions. You may find that a memory seems more realistic when seeing the event through your own eyes. This is called "first person visualization." First person is the most effective way to go back and feel memories of past events. This is also useful to know in order to stop feeling emotions from past events. If you want to gain some emotional distance from the memory, you simply change your perspective to "third person." This is named for an imaginary person who could be observing you from 20 feet away. The term "second person" would be used if you were remembering talking to a friend and decided to imagine the entire conversation through her eyes. Simply switching to a third person perspective dramatically reduces the emotions you feel as you recall painful events. Once psychologists and hypnotists discovered the power of these simple changes and sub modalities, they became very effective in assisting clients in overcoming severely limiting emotional blocks such as traumatic memories, fears, and phobias. (These techniques come from the field of NLP.)

INTERNAL DIALOGUE

Most people talk to themselves via an inner voice. Using the power of language, you can learn how to talk to yourself in a way that induces specific states. Car manufacturers have discovered that both men and women actually "buckle up their seatbelts" if they program a woman's voice to remind the driver to put on their seatbelt. If car manufacturers can change the voice in your car, why can't you adjust the voice in your head? You could make the voice strong and bold, soft and sexy, yelling, begging, giggling, singing, laughing, etc. Some people can even adjust the location the voices come from, and it makes a big difference whether or not the commands come from behind your head instead of in front. The concept of tonality is especially useful in giving your unconscious commands. Commands are defined as words that end in a lower note than when they started. Say to yourself, "I'm going to win." Now, say it like a question instead of a statement. "I'm going to win?" Notice the intonation changes on the last word. Learn to control the words, phrases and sounds in your mind, and you will have a more powerful influence on your own state management.

USING THE POWER OF DECISIONS TO CONTROL ANY EMOTIONAL STATE

What happens the moment before your brain goes into an emotional state? What must you do before your mind directs you to feel such enticing states as passion, lust, happiness, laughter, joy or peace?

Your brain does one key thing ... it makes a decision.

This sounds simple, but it is powerful. You make a decision to allow yourself to "create that state." For instance, if you were to actually see the bear in the woods, your unconscious mind would make the decision for you to feel the "fight or flight" response, leveraging on your autonomic nervous system. In this case, you make an unconscious decision to create an emotional state: terror. Terror pumps adrenaline through your veins and you can run faster than ever before. A very useful state when being chased by a bear.

The problem with most people is they believe events in the outside world control their emotional states. When in reality, the outside world gives you events. You decide what that event means for you. Your brain makes a decision as to whether that event means sorrow, fear, joy, laughter, etc.

Here is a how it works...

1. Some Event Occurs. --->

2. You Assign a Meaning to that event. --->

3. You choose which emotion is appropriate for that meaning. --->

4. You decide to have the emotion (or not). --->

5. You experience the Emotional State.

Would you agree that "happiness" is an emotional state? Is it a "state of mind" that you have felt before? If so, could you put yourself into that "state of mind" instantly? According to the above chart you can have the emotional state of happiness simply by participating or observing in some event in which happiness is the appropriate emotion. Like a chain reaction, you will experience happiness each time this event occurs. In the field of NLP, this is called a trigger or an anchor.

Examples:

Your lover whispers in your ear, "I love you." --> You feel loved.

Your lover kisses you on the neck. --> You feel sexually aroused.

Your lover gives you that "don't you dare" look. --> You feel tension.

It feels like this: 1. Event ---> 5. Have the Emotion

The reason you sometimes skip steps 2, 3, and 4 is that the event had occurred so many times in the past, you have already made the decisions of 2, 3, and 4 and those decisions became unconscious habits. Steps 2, 3, 4 are hard-wired into your nervous system to be at the beckon call of each event.

Inanimate objects can hold instant triggers to past events. You already count on this mechanism to make you feel good. Sometimes triggers can be a great part of being human. Think about the various inanimate objects in your life that spark an immediate emotional reaction: Perfume smells, religious symbols, sentimental songs, team logos, high school letter jacket, photographs, etc. Often, triggers can work against us in ways that are unproductive. For many people, the mere mention of their ex-spouse's name puts them into an instant state of anxiety. For many, the sight of the Nazi war symbol fills people with anger and sadness. (There is clearly justification for such emotions. However the symbol is the trigger to have the emotions. When you allow something outside of yourself to become a set trigger - you give up having choice over your emotions.)

Furthermore, with a bit of further education and practice, you can intentionally set specific "triggers" so you can feel good automatically. It is also possible to erase a trigger even though it seems to have been programmed unconsciously. It takes conscious awareness, intense emotion, and a specific event. In the chapter on grapho-therapy, I recommended you actually think about your goals and even listen to inspiring music while you practice your handwriting changes. The intent is to have the mere viewing of the letter "t" serve as a trigger to feeling confidence. The t-bar changes work without the added emotions that music or correct visualization brings. At the same time, when you have the tools to make yourself happy - use them!

You can spend your whole life trying to control all the outside events, so they constantly start the emotional chain reaction. This is an act in futility. You can spend all your energy trying to control other people, the traffic, your boss, the economy or your spouse. And, I agree, it would be wise to surround yourself with people and things that push the "positive" emotional buttons as often as possible. Likewise, if you have buttons that create negative emotions, it would be prudent to avoid people who push those buttons, too.

However, there is an easier way. Just take control of any decision in steps #2, #3, or #4. At every point, you make a decision that eventually affects your emotional state. Let's face it. You are going to have an uphill battle if you try to control #1 (all events in the world). But, it will be much easier to decide for yourself what meaning the event has, or what emotions to feel, or even if you choose to feel any emotion.

So, here is the big secret to being happy: Make a decision to be happy in the moment.

This is so important I'll say it again. What it takes to be happy is very simple. It takes a decision to be happy in that moment. Yet we go through life, and we let everything else screw up our attitude. You get a speeding ticket, so you get pissed off at the cop. Don't you? You get stuck in traffic, you get angry, frustrated, stressed, etc.

WHAT DOES THE EVENT REALLY MEAN?

Pretend you are a woman dating a man. How do you feel when your "lover" doesn't call when he said he was going to call? You are waiting by the phone. Are you mad, worried, indifferent? Let's assume you are typical and you get mad as hell. Anger. Right?

"Yeah, okay. He should have called - the lying bastard." You might think, "He didn't call because he doesn't really love me!" In other words, since you fear he doesn't love you, you feel rejected (emotion). When you feel rejected, you might process this rejection via anger, sadness, or tears. Some event --> some emotion.

Think about it. We go through our life allowing our external circumstances to drive our emotions.

What if you found out he didn't call because he stopped to help a lost puppy find his way home in the freezing storm? Oops. New meaning. New emotion ... instantly. Notice that when you change the "meaning" of an event you feel a new emotion instantly. At the unconscious level you probably changed the movie that was playing in your head. Instead of the movie of your boyfriend in a hotel with another lover, you ran the movie of him saving a dog's life. New movie = new emotion.

So, what if you believed that the place you are right now is all the external stimuli you needed to move to step #4 and decide to be happy?

You have already proven that in less than 60 seconds you can make yourself feel happy. So do it all the time. Take control of your internal thoughts, sounds, and pictures.

The highest possible stage in moral culture is when we recognize that we ought to control our thoughts.

— Charles Darwin

EXERCISE IN TRIGGERING HAPPINESS

How many things do you do every day with the intention of making yourself happy? Stop, take a moment and write down the emotional states you would like to feel on a daily basis. Then, write down some physical movement, exercise, specific memory, or some clever phrase that will instantly remind you how that state feels. This list will become your first set of "emotional triggers." These thoughts or actions will be tools to instantly induce the states you want to feel. (Fill in all the blanks with your own processes)

Target State	Specific Technique I can use to trigger the emotion
Silliness	I visualize Jim Carrey making funny faces.
Vitality	Drink fresh carrot juice
Peace	5 deep breaths and imagine a tropical waterfall.
_____	_____
_____	_____
_____	_____
_____	_____
_____	_____

WHY AREN'T YOU HAPPY ALL THE TIME?

Most people have been letting other people and outside events control their happiness. Were you one of those people? If you were, I'll tell you the big secret.

You are not happy all the time, because you have not made up your mind to be happy all the time.

I only know this because I used to run the "unhappiness program" without even realizing it. In 1998, I should have been emotionally "on top of the world." I was on a seminar tour in India. I

had a loving girlfriend, plenty of money, good health. I was traveling in another country having adventure and helping others. All of
my needs were being met. I was even being treated like a king. I
remember in New Delhi, this one guy with a white turbine walked
up to me, bent down, kissed my feet, and said in a thick Indian
accent, "You are my guru gee, you're my guru gee." I said, "No,
dude, I'm just a handwriting expert teaching a few tools. Get up off
the floor before someone thinks you've dropped your contact lens."

But there I was - a guru in a foreign land. I had created all these
things I had always wanted since I was a kid. (I had a published
book, a feeling of fame, a loving woman, freedom, adventure, etc.) I
found myself sitting in my hotel room later that night and thinking,
"I'm experiencing everything I've ever wanted, and I'm not happy."
Then, I began to ask a very "un-empowering question." I kept asking, "What's wrong with me?" It just struck me as very irritating
how I had all these skills at my disposal, and yet I still had not mastered the concept of just being happy in the moment. Remember
that if you ask a question enough times, you will get an answer. I
found out what was wrong with me, and I will explain how I fixed
it in the following chapter.

What was occurring was my focus was on #1 - the events. I was
successfully controlling the events in my life to give me what I
thought would make me happy. But, I had not been putting enough
time or energy in controlling the specific thoughts or emotions that
occurred as a result of my unconscious thinking, physiology, or
actions.

Once I decided that it wasn't the external events that would
make me happy, I looked on the inside. I began an intense investigation of my health, my purpose, and my emotional states. After
intense investigation, I realized I had been ignoring certain aspects
of my health - which caused me to lose balance. In that situation,
the cause of my dark thoughts was as much related to my health as

it was to my control or lack of control of my internal images, thoughts, and soundtracks. Because we are spirits living in this human body, we must realize that the biochemical, structural, and energetic essence of our humanity does have an effect on the quality of our lives.

Once I made the decision to be happy all the time, I started making changes. I cleared out all things that triggered unhappy feelings from my house or in my life. I stopped spending my time with "depressing people." And, most importantly, I took back total control over my physiology. I studied and mastered the best little "happiness" drug inducing chemical plant known to man: my own body.

The next chapter reveals my health discoveries that keep me in a jovial state of mind.

This is the true joy in life, the being used for a purpose recognized by yourself as a mighty one; the being thoroughly worn out before you are thrown on the scrap heap: the being a force of nature instead of a feverish selfish little clod of ailments and grievances complaining that the world will not devote itself to making you happy.

— George Bernard Shaw

Universal Truth # 14

We are spiritual beings visiting this planet in the form called "our body." The duration & quality of our time here depends upon our own commitment to maintaining the health & well being of our physical body.

CHAPTER 12

HEALTH SECRETS OF THE SUPER HEALTHY

Health and money are a lot a like. You don't really miss them until they're gone. For most people health is simply the absence of pain. I think that definition lacks a true understanding of the incredible pleasures of experiencing vibrant health. Pain is your friend. Pain is just a blinking red light on the highway of life telling you your body needs some attention. Stop doing what you are doing. Just taking pain killers is like closing your eyes and running the red lights. You are asking for a bigger warning light down the road. You may be asking for a head-on collision.

It's hard to lead a person out of poverty if you can't get your butt out of bed. Let's face it. If this vehicle that you get a 100-year lease on stops working - your mission on this earth is entirely compromised. Most people take better care of their cars than they do their body. At least your car comes with an owner's manual. Your body gets conflicting advice.

I have discovered that it is a NECESSITY to maintain a vital, balanced, healthy body. It's difficult to be a peak performer when you're sick. It's hard to be in a peak state when I feel like I'd rather be sleeping. You can't get very far on the road to success without fuel and a working vehicle. I have every intention of living beyond 100 years old in a state of vibrancy and exuberance. I'll spend my last 10 years on this planet dancing, singing and making love. I won't have tubes in my throat or using a walker. What's your plan for your 100th birthday? You might want to start thinking about it.

In the meantime, it is easy to lose your focus and motivation when your body feels lethargic. In almost all cases of those "crappy Monday" feelings, I can trace my loss of motivation back to poor eating, drinking, or health related choices. I felt miserable. I know what it's like to be in the downward cycle. (Sugar, caffeine, no exercise, etc.) I also know how to break that cycle and get my body back on track.

When your body is not in optimal health, you are less creative, more moody, less energetic and mentally sluggish. Many times I have found myself seeing the glass as half-empty, feeling depressed or introverted. As soon as I recognized these emotions were occurring – I evaluated my health quadrant. Sure enough (every time), I had not been making enough emotional and physical "deposits" into my own health.

As soon as I recognize I am out of balance – I take action. Crank up the vegetable juices, put on the running shoes, turn on the blender full of super green algae or protein shakes, and out comes the vitamin bottles. For me, symptoms of fatigue, pessimism and depression are simply warning signs telling me my body is out of balance. It is craving proper nutrients, exercise and attention. As soon as I give my body what it needs, it rewards me with energy, vitality and sharper thinking.

WHAT IS YOUR BODY TELLING YOU IT NEEDS?

This chapter is not really designed to be a treatise on health. The topic is just too complex. But I thought it was extremely useful to mention some of the techniques I have found effective for me in increasing energy, avoiding disease, boosting my immune system, and keeping fit while guiding my body to an optimum healthy level.

The healthier you are, the easier it will be to keep a state of peak performance.

BOOST YOUR IMMUNE SYSTEM

I recently invited a friend to stay with me while she was in town. I hadn't seen her face-to-face in over 5 years. It was fun to catch up on old times and rekindle the friendship. Staying with someone 24 hours a day gives you a real nice snapshot of how much they value health and health related education. The sad truth was she had no understanding of what her body needed or what made her truly healthy. She complained that she was "always getting sick." She knew her immune system was weak, so her solution to her weakened immune system was to become a clean freak. She went as far as to not use the same spoon as someone else when eating ice cream. So, she adapted her world to deal with her "compromised immune system." She tried to change the outside world instead of changing her inside world. It never occurred to her to go investigate the source of the problem and fix it.

As I watched her food choices, it was obvious why she had some health challenges. First, she chose to eat red meat at every meal. She preferred hamburgers and French fries to anything vegetarian. She kept a bag of chocolate candies in her purse for snacking. She even bought four pints of ice cream while visiting for just two days. None of these things are horrible in small quantities. But making these food choices over a lifetime can lead to dire consequences.

Because she was thin, her poor eating habits were not obvious to the average person. She was unwilling to learn the art of giving her body optimal nutrition so it can fight it's own battles with full power. She was unaware of the value and necessity of fresh live food (vegetables) in her diet. She was unaware of the need to drink lots of water and eliminate or reduce her caffeine intake. She was unaware that too much caffeine overworks the adrenal glands. In a nutshell, she was simply ignorant about the commonly known fact that nutritional choices have direct correlation to your health. She simply thought, "I'm skinny. I must be healthy."

The art of medicine consists of amusing the patient while nature cures the disease.
— Voltaire

MACBETH: Canst thou not minister to a mind diseased, Pluck from the memory a rooted sorrow, Raze out the written troubles of the brain, And with some sweet oblivious antidote Cleanse the stuffed bosom of that perilous stuff which weighs upon the heart?

DOCTOR: Therein the patient must minister to himself.

— Shakespeare

She had never heard of alternative medicine, nutritional supplements or homeopathy. She was ignorant of how to manage her body. In fact, she was running it into the ground with the value of being "skinny" above being healthy. The sad part is she actually "tried" to do the things to keep her healthy. She avoided germs and took prescription medicine from her doctor. Many medicines such as "antibiotics" (anti-life) actually kill small micro-organisms. This is useful the first few times. However, if you take antibiotics over many years, your body builds up immunity to the drug and your body ends up creating more difficult strains of viruses to kill. In essence, the doctor's medicine compromises your immune system over time.

Most people think prescription medicine heals sickness. In most cases, prescription medicine simply stops the pain or stops the symptoms. Think about the last time you had a headache. You really just wanted the pain to stop. Right? Pain medicine is designed to stop the pain - not cure the problem. We all dislike pain so we want pills to cover the pain. But pain is just your body's way of communicating with you. Listen up.

Truthfully, only your body can heal itself. In many cases, useful therapies, medicines, holistic treatments, vitamins, and even operations simply help get the "blockages" out of the way or give your body that extra boost so it can heal itself. If you give your body what it needs... it can heal itself.

The four basic food groups and antibiotics were nice theories in the 1950's, but in the new millennium these outdated health methods are just ignorance waiting for a disease to come get you. If you give your body what it needs, it can fight off any disease, supply you with endless energy, and keep you alive and kicking for over a hundred years.

WHAT DOES IT TAKE TO LIVE FOREVER?

Dr. Alexis Carrel conducted a research experiment that lasted 34 years that ended in a startling conclusion. Dr. Carrel, a nobel peace prize winner in 1912, hypothesized that a single living cell could live forever if it was kept free of toxins, given proper nutrition and a healthy supply of fresh oxygen. He set out to prove his theory by taking the living tissue from chickens (which normally live an average of eleven years) and kept the tissue alive indefinitely simply by keeping the cells free of their own wastes and supplying them the nutriets they needed.

These test cells lived disease free in petri dishes until the experiment was cancelled by the Rockefeller Institute because they were convinced the cells could be kept alive indefinitely. Think about how this applies to your body. You are nothing but billions of living cells. You must keep yourself detoxified (flushing your body with water is the key), supply your body with lots of oxygen (exercise, movement, breathing.) and proper nutrition. If you fail at any of these three you are inviting disease to find you.

It may sound like I have no appreciation for western medicine. Not so. I deeply appreciate and respect the dedication, intent, and breakthroughs this philosophy and scientific field have brought to the world. There is no other place I'd rather have a car wreck than in North America. I would get the finest trauma care available. I have a current western doctor and consider his advice carefully for all my medical decisions.

However, when it comes to preventive treatments and the study of wellness - the system of educating western doctors has some serious flaws. Most western medical doctoral students spend a majority of their education (8-12 years) researching and studying disease. In fact, they are experts on disease. (The average doctoral student gets less than 4 hours of nutrition as part of his training.) If Dr. Carrel says nutrition and toxic free living are the basis for the fountain of youth ... don't you think you should spend some time studying how to be toxin free and nutritionally sound?

If you were modeling "success" to learn wealth, would you listen to the financial advice of someone who has studied poverty all his life? No, you would listen to people who have studied and perfected the art of wealth building. So, when you think about gaining optimum health, don't wait until a disease hits you to seek the advice of a disease specialist (a western medical doctor). Start by studying what it takes to live with optimum health now ... while you are healthy. There are many sources of wisdom and expertise in the alternative health field. Below are some of my personal success tips that have assisted me. In addition, I would strongly encourage you to investigate the many books I have recommended on health related issues. I keep an updated list of my recommended health books and my favorite health resources on the Internet.

http://www.bartbaggett.com/health

The following success tools are divided into these topics:

1. Exercise

2. Nutrition

3. Happiness tips - avoiding depression

EXERCISE, EXERCISE, EXERCISE

Exercise is one of the major keys to having long and vibrant health into old age. Only self-deceit or laziness could support a lifestyle with no physical movement. Human bodies are dynamic, They are designed to move - not sit behind a desk for long hours. Exercise is the fastest route to supply fresh oxygen to every living cell while exercising certain cell groups to make them stronger. If you are not exercising regularly, then you are just asking some form of health crisis to come knocking on your door to serve as motivation. Don't wait. Be proactive. Take action now. Exercising isn't just to prevent future pain, it has it's own current pleasures.

Being in excellent shape helps me stay balanced in times of crises, because my body is conditioned to handle more stress. If I have an emergency, I could eat poorly or skip exercise for a while and still not get sick. I have built up health reserves.

There are two basic forms of exercise: aerobic and anaerobic. Aerobic simply means with oxygen and an-aerobic means without oxygen. Aerobic exercise includes any movement that increases the oxygen flow to your muscles such as jogging, yoga, walking, aerobics, or climbing the Stairmaster. Anaerobic exercise includes those activities that create an oxygen deficit in order to get a burst of power - sprinting, weight lifting, power lifting, power yoga, etc. Both forms have their advantages. If you are low on energy - focus on aerobic. If you are low on strength- anaerobic will be very useful for you. Personally, I alternate both weekly so I am balanced in strength and stamina.

WEIGHT TRAINING (ANAEROBIC EXERCISE)

In a normal week I invest about five hours into my health quadrant via exercise. I usually spend one hour at the gym - three days a week. Then I jog, ride the stationary bike, or do some form of yoga for another 60 combined minutes during the week. I also figure I invest an hour into dressing, undressing, and getting to the gym.

When I have the extra time, I'll exercise for five days (3 weight and 2 aerobic sessions) and take two days off for rest. I use a simple yet powerful routine that I recently learned from author Bill Phillips in his book *Body for Life: Twelve Weeks to Mental and Physical*

Strength. If you are interested in weight training or need to lose weight, I recommend you visit my health recommendation's web page and order Bill's book. Bill maps out an easy-to-follow routine that works wonders at burning fat and strengthening muscle in less than one hour per day. I've been lifting weights (off and on) since I was 15 years old. Bill's program is the first that I have used that actually proved to give me fun, fast, recognizable progress in my size and strength the first 30 days. When you add up the numbers, he asked that you invest just under 40 hours over a 12-week period to have the body of your dreams. Wow. Small investment - great reward.

In addition to all the boosted energy and confidence you feel with a great body, you will also be 40 hours more intelligent. You see, a small investment in a portable walkman and a few hundred dollars into some educational audio programs will equal two college courses. While you exercise, you learn via audio tapes. Health and learning become two emotional values you get to feel on a daily basis!

I'm a believer of the phrase, "Use it or lose it." If muscles aren't exercised on a regular basis, they atrophy, sag, and weaken. They become of little use to you. And believe me, it is hard to find your inner strength, when your outer strength is gone. Simple weight training is a great way to build and maintain strength. If you've never been to a gym or feel like your body lacks muscular defini-tion, then I recommend starting a weight-training program immedi-ately. Join a gym or buy some inexpensive portable dumbbells to keep near your desk. You will be amazed at how many dumbbell curls you can do while talking on the phone. Weight training might be painful at first, but it becomes addictive in a good way. Weight training actually causes minor tears in the muscle fiber. As your body rebuilds these tears, using protein and amino acids, you are rebuilt stronger and firmer.

You'll notice after weight training for a while, the stronger your muscles feel, the stronger you feel on the inside. (Hey, you look sexier, too!)

In a recent study of the positive effects of weight training, they found 70-year-old men and women who did daily weight training out performed 30-year-old men and women. Your muscles do not have to get old and weak. They only atrophy when you don't exercise them regularly.

AEROBIC EXERCISE

I like to balance my exercise routine between aerobic and anaerobic. So on Tuesdays and Thursdays I focus on exercising my cardio-vascular system: I get my lungs pumping. Also, fast movement is excellent for the lymph system. Because your lymph system has no organ to pump out the toxins, movement is the only way this system gets flushed. Aerobic exercise is where I really strengthen my stamina and feel that burst of endorphins to my brain. Research shows that aerobic exercise is essential in healing all forms of depression.

I have many options to get that legal dopamine rush: I can get my lungs breathing heavily and increase my heart rate by jogging, fast-walking, swimming, bike riding, Kung-Fu, aerobics, etc. I'll do this for as little as twenty minutes some days. According to Bill Phillips, you don't need to do cardio exercises for an entire hour. Twenty is plenty. According to other health experts, you should warm up for fifteen minutes and exercise in your zone for forty minutes or more. I don't know who is most accurate - I just know what works for me.

I suggest finding an exercise you enjoy doing. Some people prefer bike riding, while others love jogging through the park. For me, I like to mix it up. I'll ride my bike one day, go jogging another. Make sure you stretch and warm up for at least ten to fifteen minutes before any hard workout. I stretch using yoga poses or a light jog to warm up.

On weekends, I give myself the freedom to rest if I so choose. After all, I've put my body through 3-5 days of exercise, so it could use a couple of days to regenerate for the upcoming week. What is more often the case, I usually have so much leftover energy that I like to do a fun physical activity on Saturdays like hiking, dancing, mountain biking, skiing, or playing football with the boys. There is nothing like pure physical play to make you feel young again! "Throw me the ball! I'm open!"

YOGA / TAI CHI / KUNG FU

While weight training and running are great for building strength and stamina, I'd like to recommend a couple of exercises that increase the body's flexibility and balance. After spending time with some 70 year old men who look about 35 – I'm convinced that proper nutrition and exercise are the secrets to the fountain of youth.

Yoga is a form of exercise that combines body postures with deep breathing. Although Yoga is somewhat new to the western world, it was developed several thousand years ago in India. For the past 30 years, Yoga has grown in popularity in the west. It is a great exercise for stimulating vitality, increasing flexibility, enhancing overall good health and the ability to relax. I highly recommend taking a Yoga class and exploring how it can benefit you. I find that after every Yoga class I take, my mind feels relaxed and at peace, while my body is tingling with energy. Any stress I had that day is gone. For me, Yoga is a moving meditation. And if you think Yoga is for sissies, try "Power Yoga" – the same poses, only longer and more strenuous. It will challenge you and make you sweat.

ANCIENT TIBETAN RIGHTS

No matter how busy you are, you can always find 7-10 minutes a day to stretch and bend in the middle of the floor. There are a few basic "Tibetan Yoga" moves that will strengthen, stretch, and energize your muscles. You can read about these simple, yet powerful exercises in a book originally written in 1939 called the *Ancient Secret of the Fountain of Youth* by Peter Kelder. This book has been a godsend for everyone I know who has back or neck pain of any kind. The book is based on Peter Kelder's first hand research of a remote village in Tibet where men and women routinely lived to be over 125 years old. These exercises were part of their daily ritual.

This set of stretching exercises aligns the spine, releases endorphins, balances your chakras (energy meridians of the body), and stretches your muscles. When I was younger, I used to have lots of lower back pain. After doing these simple exercises for less than one week, the back pain disappeared completely. Plus, it stays gone as long as I keep up these "ancient rights" and take care of myself. Everyone I know who has used these simple thousand-year-old techniques has seen profound results.

The basic set of moves consist of a variety of ways to stretch your spine. Here is a taste of a few of the moves. Take a yoga class or get the book for the full story.   www.bartbaggett.com/health

TIBETAN 7 MINUTE YOGA WORKOUT

#1 Spin - Stand facing forward with your hands extended outward. Spin around in a circle until you become slightly dizzy. Remember to spin from left to right (clockwise.)   This is supposed to speed up or actually spark the vortexes or 7 chakras into spinning.   Be careful not to spin too much until you get used to it. This one will make you a bit dizzy. You will also feel like a kid again. That's fun.

TIBETEN 7 MINUTE YOGA QUICK REFERENCE GUIDE

#2 Leg lifts - Lie flat on your back with your palms facing down. Tilt your head up so your chin touches your chest. Lift both legs into a vertical position. Hold. Repeat. This will strenghten your stomatch and lower back muscles. It is also supposed to further stimulate the seven chakras.

#3 Neck Bend - Crouch on your knees (both feet behind you/ bottom of toes touching the floor.) Put your arms to your sides. Tilt your head back so you can see the ceiling above and behind you. Then tilt your neck forward until your chin touches your chest. Repeat. Don't fall backwards. This stretches your neck and back muscles. If you work at a computer all day, you will notice this will be a wonderful tool to loosen your upper back and neck tension.

#4 Back Bend - This is the most challenging for someone who is really inflexible. Work up to it. The process is to move from a sitting position to a squared off back bend. Start by sitting with your hands to your side, palms down, chin to your chest, toes up, legs extended in front of you. (Sitting position not pictured.) Then, in one movement, bend everything back by pulling your pelvis toward the sky. Keep your head aligned horizontally with your torso. Don't arch your torso like a rainbow. Keep your body squared off. Repeat.

These next two moves are key movements from modern Yoga. They are essential in keeping your whole body flexible and strong. You will notice your shoulders getting stronger as you are able to hold these positions for a longer duration.

#5 Yoga Full Body Back Stretch - Lay flat on your stomach with your palms face down next to your shoulders. Push your torso up, leaving your hips flush to the ground. Point your nose to the sky. Hold for 30 seconds. Then, go directly into #6 "down dog". See the illustration. Alternate # 5 and #6 increasing the hold time as you gain more experience.

#6 Down Dog - Lay flat on your stomach with your palms face down next to your shoulders. Push your entire body up into the air so that your butt forms the point of a pyramid. Keep your heels touching the floor if you can. This position is called "down-dog" in modern day yoga. Hold for 30 seconds. Alternate with #5. This will elongate the spine and actually help align your spine.

If you do these simple exercises daily, you will notice a profound difference in your energy level, decreased or eliminated back & neck pain, and overall feeling of wellness!

TAI CHI / KUNG FU

I have always been enthralled at the acrobatic maneuvers I witnessed in those Chinese Karate movies. It wasn't until I was an adult that I began to realize the health and spiritual benefits of the martial arts. Before I studied Kung Fu, martial arts were some strange mystical fighting style for those guys who enjoyed fighting. Actually, most real eastern martial artists are spiritually balanced, peaceful, and very unlikely to actually start a fight. What's more, I discovered in Korea and China that the martial arts instructors also worked as the villages' medical doctors? Why? The concept of managing your Chi explains it all.

In eastern medicine, Acupuncture practitioners believe that sickness is caused by a blocked flow of Chi - or energy. So, the art of managing your Chi could be accomplished through martial arts as well as health practices. In fact, since I've been studying with Master Song, I have seen him prescribe Tai Chi to most of his patients over 35. Stretching and strengthening the muscles are an essential step in recovering from injury. Plus, when you add the benefit of learning to control your Chi - it is a powerful elixir!

Developed in China, Tai Chi is a "soft" martial art that focuses on building internal strength as opposed to the "hard" martial arts,

DON'T BELIEVE EVERYTHING
YOUR DOCTOR TELLS YOU....

The principles of Washington's farewell address are still sources of wisdom when cures for social ills are sought. The methods of Washington's physicians, however, are no longer studied. — Thurman Arnold

For the majority of people, smoking has a beneficial effect. -Dr Ian G. Macdonald, Los Angeles surgeon Quoted in NEWSWEEK November 18, 1963

Louis Pasteur's theory of germs is ridiculous fiction. — Pierre Pachet Professor of Psychology At Toulouse, 1872

One-half of the children born die before their eighth year. This is nature's law; why try to contradict it? — Jean-Jacques Rousseau Author of the most widely read child-rearing manual of its day. 1762 like Kung Fu, that also focuses on outer strength, competition, and combat. When you take a Tai Chi class, you will learn to move your body in ways that increase the flow of energy. The Chinese call this energy Chi or life force. For me, Tai Chi is like a very slow dance, where you gracefully move from one stance to the next. You can literally feel the tight parts of your body "releasing and opening up." Tai Chi also clears the mind of all that unnecessary chatter and brings you to a state of inner peace. I've found that Tai Chi is excellent for keeping you balanced and stress-free. Again, it is a moving meditation.

TIME & EXERCISE

Now for those of you who might be thinking you "don't have enough time to exercise," that's just your old limited belief system working against you. Ignore it. You must think of exercise as a necessity - like food and water. It is the fuel for your body. Exercise is what gives you the strength to make the rest of your life run more smoothly. In reality, we all have the same amount of time in the day. We have all the time that there is. Personally, I find that a five-day workout plan actually gives me so much energy I can reduce my sleep requirements more than 90 minutes per night. So, instead of eight hours of sleep, I can get up feeling refreshed after just 6 - 6.5 hours of sleep when I'm exercising regularly. In my experience - exercising gives you MORE TIME.

When you search your busy schedule you will discover you really can find the time to squeeze in a little exercise each day. Think of it this way. There are 168 hours in a seven-day week. As I mentioned earlier I invest just over 4 hours a week into exercise. When you look at the big picture, just four hours a week can net you twenty extra healthy years. Or, if you are motivated by pain that four hours you didn't exercise could cost you a lot of pain and suffering during the final years of your life. Now, I bet if you were really committed to feeling your best, you could find 4-5 hours out of the 168 hours you have to choose from each week. Remember, use it or lose it!

SIGNS OF DEPRESSION OR JUST POOR THINKING PROCESSES?

In the previous chapter, I alluded to a time in my life when I should have been happy but wasn't. Those dark thoughts led me to an important lesson in biochemistry. I have no idea if this section will apply directly to you or to a loved one of yours. Because I am writing a book on happiness, it makes sense to discuss one of the major causes of unhappiness — depression. According to recent studies, one in eight Americans (12.5% of the U.S. population) suffers from depression. If that statistic is true, that means there are a lot of unhappy people out there turning to their doctors for help. One of out of every twelve people you know could be struggling with the chemical side of un-happiness. Don't be quick to judge them for not simply controlling their thoughts. There might be a chemical basis for such emotions.

When the word depression first entered my reality, I thought I was struggling with some existential crises about the meaning of life. I found myself thinking, "I've created everything I want, but I'm still not happy." For me, I thought I could control everything with my mind. What I couldn't control with my mind, I could control through physiology. I was right, but I didn't understand what I was dealing with. It wasn't until I realized the significance that brain chemistry has on my "state of mind" that I made serious effort to get all the facts about how to keep my brain in optimum performance mode. Until I acknowledged my brain was out of balance, I was unable to find a way to keep it in balance.

Do you know anybody who has taken prescribed anti-depressants? The most common psycho-pharmaceutical drug in America is

Prozac. This brand name is a drug sold for treating depression or social anxiety disorder. Even if you are not at all depressed or never ever take this drug, it is useful to understand what this drug does to the brain and why it is prescribed to millions of people a year worldwide.

Research shows Prozac does affect certain seratonin levels in the brain. Seratonin is the natural "happy" chemical released by the brain. So for many people, Prozac does have a direct effect on the level of happiness they experience. According to the best selling book *Listening to Prozac*, this drug can turn shy people sociable, depressed people happy, suicidal people stable, etc. Wow. A pill can do that? (Yes, a pill can do that and a properly mixed batch of Korean health tea can, too.)

Prozac was the first FDA approved selective seratonin reuptake inhibitor introduced to the American Market. Today, there are many other brands of medicine to treat depression (Prozac, Zoloft, Wellbutrin, Paxil, Celexa, Nardil, Parnate, Elavil, Anafranil & more). There are many other "natural treatments" that don't get near the attention.

www.stop-depression.com or   www.bartbaggett.com/health

Since 1988, Prozac has been used by over 38 million people worldwide. It has been prescribed so much because it has amazingly positive effects for many people. I would be the last person to endorse psycho-pharmaceutical drugs considering my life's focus on the power of the mind and bent toward alternative natural medicine. However, after experiencing the effects of this type of drug first hand - I now have a deeper level of empathy and understanding for this condition. If you are seriously depressed, then just by "understanding" that you are not losing your mind but instead have only a chemical imbalance can provide tremendous relief to a struggling spirit. That being said, I don't recommend staying on prescription medication more than a month or two. There are natural treatments that have no side effects and won't raise your insurance premiums.

It may be an effective treatment if you are one of the people who doesn't get the short term side effects. But you should be aware of the side effects of taking Prozac. One common side effect is total loss of your SEX DRIVE. That alone would make me depressed! The following numbers are percentages of people having symptoms from the drug and the percentages have the same symptoms on a placebo: nausea (23 vs. 10 percent), headache (21 vs. 20 percent), insomnia (20 vs. 11 percent), anxiety (13 vs. 8 percent), nervousness (13 vs. 9 percent) and somnolence (13 vs. 6 percent). I don't have any statistics to tell you the long-term side effects. I do believe this though: taking a drug of this type does not help you heal the cause. It only affects the symptoms and can lead to a lifetime of dependency on the drug. As with any dis-ease (mental or physical), look for a completely natural solution before you turn to prescription medicine. Losing your sex drive is not fun!

The three important lessons I learned from taking prescription anti-depression medication for two months was this:

1. Medications have horrible side effects that your doctors don't always warn you about or might not even know about.

2. Medication can have a fast and positive effect on the symptoms of depression. It works.

3. Happiness can be induced by chemical changes in your brain chemistry.

Knowing what I know now, I take extra care of my mind and body to insure I keep my brain chemistry balanced. I don't take prescription anti-depressant drugs and never will again. I found a natural alternative to keeping my brain chemistry balanced. (Nutrition, vitamin supplements, and exercise.)

WHAT IS ECSTASY?

Have you ever heard of the designer street drug called "ecstasy" or "X"? Well, there is a good reason they call it ecstasy. It's because this drug makes you feel the emotion called "ecstasy." In America, around the turn of the century (2000), ecstasy passed up all other drugs (except alcohol) as the drug of choice for American teenagers. Back in the 1980's, ecstasy was legal and very trendy. I tried it once during college. It was truly an awesome brain high. It's just plain and simply a "get happy" drug. It kick starts your own little internal pharmacy and injects the "feel good chemicals" right into your bloodstream.

In my non-scientific opinion, I think ecstasy is like 20 Prozacs hitting your bloodstream at the same time. It essentially sucks the seratonin from the reserves in your brain and shoots dopamine out into your bloodstream. Essentially, dopamine is the brain's happy drug. Prozac simply adjusts the "vacuums" and inhibits the self-created chemical from dissipating as quickly. Ecstasy actually sucks your brain dry of all your storehouse of the chemical and treats you to an overdose of your own happy juice. So, you experience higher levels of your own happy drug. It's no wonder kids love it. It is happiness in a pill.

Is happiness really just an emotional reaction to a chemical reaction in your brain? Are you creating dopamine & seratonin when you get up and dance, make love, or laugh? Are you actually creating drugs in your bloodstream naturally? Yes. Your brain is actually "shooting" the chemicals into your bloodstream. Most of the chemicals are already made and waiting for the right "cue" to come out and play. You don't need drugs to experience happy feelings. So, learn to start pushing your own happy buttons.

So the secret to happiness is to take ecstasy. Who said that? No ... I'm kidding. Happiness does have a chemical component to this emotion. If you are chemically out of balance, achieving the state called happiness will be an uphill battle. Take efforts to give your brain chemistry what it needs. If you want to take some herbal supplements like St. John's Wort or Ginseng to start the chemicals flowing, do so. After much research, I found some side-effect-free all-natural pills that keep my brain in balance. They are called Moonbeams. They are inexpensive and effective. Many people take them daily just because it adds to their happy juice! Even if you don't feel down, you might want to give them a shot and see if you can feel any happier! (www.bartbaggett.com/health)

The secret is already right there in your brain. You don't need a drug or even an herbal tea to start the chemicals flowing. You can start the chemicals flowing by a decision to direct your thoughts. You direct your thoughts through controlling your physiology, your mental pictures and your internal dialogue. You have lots of options to rid the symptoms of depression and choose happiness.

Boost Your Energy
Uplift Your Depressed State

The state of low energy or depression can be a real momentum breaker on your way to the top. Whether you feel down because of physical or emotional reasons ... taking physical action can provide instant state shifts. Furthermore, consistent maintenance via nutrition and exercise can send the blues away for good. Whenever you notice that your body is low on energy or you feel depressed, try some of these techniques.

Deep Breathing – Breathing sounds simple, but don't underestimate the power of this under utilized energy pump. The "ha breathing technique" is an exercise that gets the oxygen pumping up your body and to your brain. It's quite fast and effective. This is great to do before a workout or while just sitting at your desk to give yourself that extra pep. Years ago, I taught hypnosis seminars to assist people to stop smoking in one session. Hypnosis works because it allows your own mind to function roadblock free. Most smokers believed the act of smoking gave them energy. Actually, the deep breaths (albeit filled with smoke) actually provided an oxygen rush which they normally didn't get. Apparently, I was the first person to give them permission to just breathe deeply without a burning cancer stick in their mouth. Give yourself the gift of pure oxygen. Here is how.

First, take a deep breath, inhaling through the nose for about 5 seconds. As you do, raise your hands to shoulder level as if guiding the breath up your body. Then, as you exhale, make a long "ha" sound that lasts the length of your exhalation, about 10 seconds. While doing this, push your hands from your shoulders down to your waist. Repeat this three more times. Expanding your lungs and moving the breath up and down your body will increase the blood flow in your body, and you will notice that you feel more energized.

If you are at work and are a bit self-conscious about making loud "ha" sounds while sitting at your desk ... relax. The mere act of taking a very deep breath, holding it in for a few counts and expelling it for a longer count will triple your oxygen intake. Remember to expel every last breath of air so you get all new fresh air on the next intake. Don't be surprised if this exercise gives you a fun head rush at first.

Get Your Body Moving – Sometimes when I feel unmotivated, I take a walk, jog, or go hiking. Now this may sound like the opposite of what you feel like doing when your body is lethargic. But you'll be amazed how this simple act of "movement" changes your state. I've found that sometimes all my body needs to increase energy is to get up and move. So I suggest doing anything that gets your body moving: walk, jog, dance, do jumping jacks. Moving your legs and working your lungs increase the oxygen to your brain and release happy brain chemicals called endorphins. After just fifteen minutes of walking you will feel your energy increasing. There have been many days when I was under a deadline to work hard and keep going, but all I felt like doing was taking a nap. The decision to jump on the mini-trampoline for ten minutes or do fifty pushups has literally bought me two hours of effective work time. If you have the luxury of being able to take a walk in nature - you will really feel rejuvenated. (Remember, humans use oxygen. Trees and plants emit oxygen.)

Play Some Fast, Upbeat Music – Music is a very quick and powerful state changer. There is something magical about upbeat rhythms that excites the brain and lifts the body's energy.

Do you remember the theme song from the movie *Rocky*. Whenever the boxer Rocky Balboa was training hard, the sound-track played very upbeat, energizing music to match the audience's feelings with Rocky's drive to be a champion. Every time I hear the *Rocky Theme* song, I feel like boxing, jumping up and down, and waving my arms like he does when he reaches the top of those steps. Moving your body is the fastest way to change your state. Music accelerates this process. The scientific study of brain waves and brain synchronization gives us scientific reasons why we experience different states while listening to different musical beats. Baroque music actually has the beat as our Alpha brain patter. You are relaxed and learn faster in an Alpha brain state. (This is the target brain wave pattern in hypnosis and meditation.) The Beta brain wave is a much faster, short sound wave. This beat is often found in disco, rap, Hip-Hop, Big Band, and modern Dance/Industrial music. You can't help but get pumped up when you listen to music with this beat. So, pick your tunes carefully. I shake my head in pity when I see an office environment with a "no music" rule. How do they expect their employees to keep up their tempo?

Since sadness and fatigue have a very high correlation with slow moving brain wave patterns, I highly recommend that whenever you're feeling down or unmotivated, play some dance music, swing music or fast rock n' roll. Then, get up and dance and shake your groove thing.

Take Vitamins / Minerals – The conversation about vitamins and mineral supplementation could take up 12 books and not even scratch the surface. I will say this. In today's fast food world with a farming community of chemicals and depleting top soil minerals worldwide - it is highly unlikely you are getting all the essential and trace minerals you need just from your food alone. Now, you may be fanatical about getting your pure organic foods in every possible combination. But, in most cases, you are low on key vitamins and minerals which could dramatically change your health. I have seen men simply add copper to their diet and their gray hair turns back to black. I have seen a simple liquid potassium supplement double people's energy and cause spontaneous healing of aches and pains. I have seen the consumption of shark cartilage free arthritis sufferers from winter pain. My mom takes flax seed oil to give her smooth skin and strong nails. My dad eats raw garlic to keep the colds away - it works. There are hundreds of unconventional and effective natural remedies that work by giving the body what it needs to heal itself. You have to decide to discover what works best for you.

I have found that in addition to a basic multi-vitamin, I function better on extra doses of vitamin C and complex B. These help in my energy creation and immunity. I also notice a profound difference in my "life energy" when I consume fresh real Blue Green Algae, Ginseng, Spirulina or Chlorella. If you buy the powder form, you can just mix it into a fruit smoothie in the morning.

About ten years ago, my friend Dana Margolis suggested a vitamin mixture to help me have more energy. She told me to just visit the local health food store and ask for 500MG of Vitamin C, 250 MG of Vitamin B-6, and 500 MG of L-Phenylalanine. She said this combination would make me feel better. Funny thing happened, it

Do not take life too seriously.
You will never get out of it alive.
— Elbert Hubbard

I don't do anything that's bad for me. I don't like to be
made nervous or angry. Any time you get upset it tears
down your nervous system.
— Mae West

To hate and to fear is to be psychologically ill.
It is, in fact, the consuming illness of our time.
— H. A. Overstreet

Positive attitudes—optimism, high self-esteem, an outgoing
nature, joyousness, and the ability to cope with stress—
may be the most important bases for
continued good health.
— Helen Hayes

The health of the people is really the foundation upon
which all their happiness and their powers
as a state depend.
— Benjamin Disraeli

lifted my spirits immediately. She didn't tell me until two years later that this combination of these three inexpensive over-the-counter nutritional supplements was her secret formula for getting her "depressed" client off of prescription medication and onto something natural. I didn't think I had symptoms of depression, but I felt so much better - they clearly gave my body something it was missing. Your natural state of being is happy, pain free, and energetic. If you aren't experiencing that right now - your body is talking to you.

Any nutritional supplements can have unexpected effects, so please test them for yourself. I don't use L-Phenylalanine anymore because it seems to eventually make me tired from its tendency to over spark my adrenal glands. St. John's Wort had the same effect on me (eventual fatigue), but this is not common for most people. St. John's Wort (an all natural supplement) dominates over 50% of the anti-depressant market in Germany. Give the natural brain elixirs a shot. You might feel even happier!

TUNE YOUR BODY

The physical body is an interesting machine. It moves us to where we want to go, it keeps us alive, it motivates us to eat, to sleep, keeps our blood flowing and organs doing their job. Also like a machine, the body gets a few kinks in it, and thus doesn't run as well as it could. You feel this in the tightness of your muscles or perhaps a pain in your lower back. What do you do when your car stops working properly? You take it into the shop, right? Give it a tune up, and it's ready to go again. Well, sometimes your body needs a tune up, as well. Below are some resources for keeping your body attuned for success.

Chiropractor: These doctors specialize on releasing any blockages in the body. Some chiropractors adjust the spine directly by popping the vertebrae back into alignment. While others do a softer method by adjusting the legs and applying acupressure to key meridian points. I prefer the softer method myself, and I have this done at least once every couple of months.

Massage: Your skin is your largest organ. It actually produces vitamins and helps you maintain health in a variety of ways. Even something as simple as getting some sunshine fills your body with Vitamin D and makes you feel more alive. So, treating yourself to a massage every once in a while is both healthy and a great way to live with prosperity consciousness.

Your body holds both physical and emotional tension. A good massage can make you feel more emotionally relieved than a good cry. Those knots of tension in your muscles are meant to stay there. You'll find this to be a great stress reliever. The Swedish massage is very gentle and relaxing. The Sports massage works on those more stubborn tension knots. It can be painful, but the stress relief you will feel will be worth the pain and money. Very therapeutic.

Acupuncture: This is one of the oldest health practices on the planet and still has extraordinary results. This health practice is based on the premise our body is electrical and the natural state of our electrical energy is to run freely along meridian lines. When the energy is blocked ... health problems occur. Acupuncture works to clear the energy path and allow the body to start healing.

(I can't say I fully understand or grasp the scientific concept. In fact, I'm still not sure how TV or electricity works. I'm pretty amazed I can turn on the TV and see pictures beaming through space of an event on the other side of the planet. I've learned to accept what works.) You should seek out a trained acupuncturist.

Acupuncture is an Asian technique that uses round-pointed needles to release energy blockages in the body. The needles, which don't go very far into the skin, are placed at specific points of the body along the meridians. These imaginary energy lines called meridians are connected to certain organs or parts of the brain.

The needles don't actually hurt. It may look strange - but it's effective. Treatments are between $50-$90 per session and covered by many insurance policies.

Acupressure: Very similar to acupuncture, only the trained practioner presses the meridian points with their fingers instead of needles. This is a great alternative for people who can't handle the needles. I have personally seen miraculous results from acupressure. You can do some of these techniques with your own hands by pressing specific spots on your body to affect other body regions. I have eliminated back pain, headaches, and even runny noses by pressing the right spot and holding it. My dad has literally worked bruises into his skin pressing an acupressure point too long. However, the bruises were worth it because the pressure relieved muscle spasms in his legs and lower back that medicine could not relieve. Many times acupressure was the only treatment that worked enough to allow him to leave the bed when he had disk problems in his back. I encourage you to read more about it.

BART'S QUICK ACUPRESSURE TIPS:

Runny Nose: Pressing down on the tips of your fingers will stop a runny nose. (Top finger on your nail, bottom finger/thumb underneath.) Hold for thirty seconds. Repeat until nostril clears.

Back Pain: Press on the sore spot in calf or buttock to release lower back pain. (Use baseball for leverage. Ouch this hurts, but works.)

Endorphine Rush: Find sore spot on the hand between the thumb and pointing finger for a general endorphin starter. Good for any pain anywhere on the body.

Headache: Press finger into the lower back soft spot at the base of the skull to rid a headache. (Difficult to self-administer this one. Find a friend.)

Meditation: Meditation is both a physical and a spiritual foundation for people worldwide. I find it is the one thing that consistently helps me keep my mind and body balanced. Meditation is simply the practice of being alone with yourself in a quiet and peaceful way. Most meditation teaches the art of quieting your mind and attempting to actually stop thinking - turn off the inner chatter. Deepak Chopra describes meditation as focusing your mind on the spaces between the actual thoughts. Some people see prayer as another form of meditation. I think my own power-naps are a form of meditation, but some people disagree.

You'll be amazed at how meditating on a regular basis will help you to be calmer during stressful situations. Crises just won't upset you as much, because you are able to keep your body tension-free through deep relaxation.

There is no right or wrong way to meditate. Study all the paths or make up your own. If you are new to meditation, start with this technique:

Find a quiet, comfortable space where you won't be distracted. Turn off the phone and make sure you are alone so you won't be bothered. I suggest turning the lights down and lighting a candle. This can create a very calming atmosphere. If you choose to listen to music – select instrumental music that has a very slow rhythm. Start with silence until you find music that simply blends into the nothingness. I suggest you sit on the floor with your back against a wall or in the lotus position (legs crossed). Avoid lying down as you might fall asleep. Put your hands in your lap palms facing up.

Once you've created the proper setting, just close your eyes for a while. Take several deep breaths and do your best to focus your mind on nothingness. Turn the volume to zero on all your internal dialogue. Put any mental movies away in storage for later. Focus on a blank screen.

Quieting your mind may take getting used to at first, but eventually you'll get the hang of it. If your mind is still full of chatter, keep repeating the word "relax" in your mind slower and slower and slower. If it helps, count backwards from 100 very slowly. This usually puts me into a meditative state very quickly.

If you want to use meditation to solve a specific life problem or ask your higher self to give you answers, instead of focusing on nothing, simply repeat the question over and over until your unconscious floods you with possible answers. Remember that meditation is not a time to judge yourself. *Just be.* Allow what comes in and let your mind keep bringing up images, sounds, and thoughts. Let your mind flow in a state of peace.

If you believe that thoughts create your reality - then the act of meditation is the most direct activity you can do to direct your thoughts to create your future. I recommend meditating every day for at least half an hour.

FOOD IS THE FUEL FOR LIFE

I cannot over emphasize the importance of gaining mastery over your food choices. There is no more direct route to your mental and physical state of being than your diet. Over 200 years ago Benjamin Franklin said, "Most men dig their own graves with their teeth." Ben was a vegetarian in an age where there was no research to support such a drastic dietary choice. He outlived the average colonial male by 40 years.

There is no hard and fast rule about do's and don'ts that work for everybody. But, if you are not consciously choosing foods and drinks for their overall health value - you must invest some time into your food knowledge bank.

One basic rule of thumb you can go by is the "cleanse vs. clog" theory. Ask yourself if the food you are about to put into your mouth is going to clog your intestinal tract or cleanse it. Remember detoxifying your system is key to being disease free. Live food and water cleanses. Dead animals, dairy and processed foods clog your system. Since your body is over 70% water, you might consider making 70% of your diet water rich live vegetable foods. Do it for a week - you will feel energized!

Food clogging our system is one of the number one reasons our bodies feel weak and tired.

Rather than write a whole book on nutrition (there are plenty I can recommend), I'm just going to mention a few of my eating habits that work for me. If they help you, use them. If they don't appeal to you, find your own.

First, I rarely eat heavy red meats like steak, hamburgers, beef fajitas and pork. Red meat is one of the worst body cloggers. It can stay in your colon for days, weeks even. It's also very high in cholesterol and can make you constipated. Ever felt like taking a nap after a huge meal eating lots of red meat? Well, that's because it takes most of your body's energy to digest that animal flesh. Too much heavy digestion can really slow down your momentum for the rest of the day. Now I admit I love a great hamburger every now and then, so I'm not asking you to stop eating the meats you love. I'm suggesting that you limit your heavy meals and increase your intake of light vegetarian meals. For instance, try eating vegetarian every other day, or at least every other meal. You'll notice a huge increase in your energy level, because you're giving your body time to digest the meat from the previous meal. Some vegetarian alternatives are salads, grilled vegetables, tofu, veggie burgers, pastas and rice dishes. When you do decide to eat a meal with meat, choose chicken or fish over beef or pork. Chicken and fish are leaner and easier to digest. If you eat in restaurants frequently, ask the server if they have a vegetarian option. Most chain restaurants offer a few vegetarian entrees. You will be surprised at how full you feel and the great flavor.

Some health experts suggest you eat only fruit or vegetables for breakfast. For me, this doesn't work. I function better having some protein in my breakfast. My brain is sharper when I have a small serving of eggs, tofu, or even some turkey in the mornings. Or, I like to have a fruit smoothie with some protein powder. Test your food choices and judge for yourself.

THE SECRET OF MAINTAINING YOUR BLOOD SUGAR LEVEL

Now let's talk sugar. That's right, all those desserts, cakes, muffins and cookies … they're enemies to the successful person. Forget about the fat issue. That's obvious. Sugar content controls blood sugar level. I only truly understood the power of blood sugar while dating a diabetic woman in 1994. I didn't understand that even "healthy foods" like fruits and pastas quickly turn to sugar and send your blood sugar levels skyrocketing. Diabetes is one of the #1 diseases in elderly people. In my opinion, it is caused by all the work they forced their pancreas to do while they were young.

Sugar is the enemy of the sugar sensitive person. White sugar is notorious for bringing your energy spiraling down after a brief high. There is an abundance of great information at the website: www.weightlossdoctor.com about the effect of sugar on your system. The information will astound you at how sugar affects your body, weight, and energy level. Most of my chiropractor friends that are trained in Applied Kinesiology say sugar is a pure poison that short circuits the electro-magnetic nature of our body. I sure like the sweet taste. Darn.

So the next time you are tempted to eat a donut for breakfast, remember that that sugary food choice will bring your energy down after the initial high. Not a great way to start the day. Skip the cookie that you might have eaten with your lunch. Eat a slice of cheese, yogurt, or turkey (protein) instead. Again, I love a good dessert on occasion. But I eat sugar foods sparingly and not on days when I can't afford a huge spike and crash in my blood sugar level. Protein gives you slow burning energy. Sugar gives you spikes of energy.

Here's an idea that may help you keep track of your sugar intake. Make yourself some dessert coupons allowing yourself to eat one heavy sugar based dessert each week. Whenever you're tempted to eat a candy bar, you can pull out your coupon and ask yourself, "Do I want to spend my one dessert a week on this or save it for something better?" Some people find keeping track in this manner helps them make better eating choices. I have found that repressing our desires for fun foods can be counter productive. Flat avoiding foods we like often causes resentment and a negative association with the healthy lifestyle. Keep it all in moderation.

Caffeine has similar effects on your energy level. Coffee increases your acidity level, overworks your adrenal glands and dehydrates you. Tea and Coke also contain high amounts of caffeine and sugar, too. I recommend bottled water with lemon with every meal. (I don't see how you can get your 8 glasses of water a day if you drink Cokes and Coffee, too. You would spend your whole day in the bathroom!) Too much caffeine borrows tomorrow's energy for today. Eventually, it will cost you. When I want to drink coffee, I bargain with myself. I agree to drink two large glasses of purified water for every single cup of coffee I have. You don't have to eliminate anything completely. Just recognize what is harming and what is healing your body. Life is about choices.

CLEANSE YOUR BODY OF TOXINS

If a cell can live forever if it is kept free of toxins, how do you cleanse the toxins. Many diseases like lung cancer, colon cancer, and kidney failure are a clear result of a toxic amount of impurities creating a "toxic" environment in the body. If you wonder why it is so important to keep your body toxin free, think about this ...

remember the TV images of the Alaskan coastline covered in oil when the Exxon Valdez spilled millions of gallons of oil in the shipping accident years ago? I can't erase the images of oil covered geese getting stuck in the oil and dead fish covering the beaches. When you fill your body with toxins and don't clean it up, your cells become like those struggling geese. They can't function normally.

Cleansing your body on a regular basis is just as important as eating healthy. The easiest way is to drinks LOTS of water each day (at least eight glasses). Eating a dependable source of fiber in your diet will also cleanse your colon. If you're not regular, then you're clogged. And if you're clogged, you are creating a toxic wasteland at the base of your colon. If you think you aren't full of toxins, I dare you to go get a professional colonic. Even the healthiest eaters get toxins and need cleansing. A colonic will let you view with your own eyes what's been eating you. When you get unclogged, you will be surprised at how light and energetic you will feel. When I detoxify myself and eat a pure vegetarian diet, I sleep better, need less sleep, have more energy, and think clearer. (When I do that, I must take amino acids and iron supplements. Test everything on your own body.)

Here are my suggestions for keeping the inside of your body clean and working properly:

Fiber - Eat high fiber foods like bran cereal, apples, pears, prunes and vegetables like carrots and broccoli. I've discovered a whole grain cereal called Kashi that you can find at the grocery store. You boil it like pasta and eat it hot. It has a chewy texture, and tastes great when you add honey or syrup. Kashi works fast to clean out the body and gives you a boost of energy as well. Try it.

Colon Cleanser – If the idea of a professional colonic frightens you, use the slower route. You can fast for a few days on juice, water, or nothing. Or, there are colon-cleansing supplements at your local health food store that work wonders at keeping your digestive tract on track. In fact, these supplements do much more than just unclog you. Many provide healthy bacteria that your intestines need to function at optimal levels. I always keep a bottle of Live Acidopholous in my refrigerator to assist me in digestion when I eat too much or ingest too much coffee. (Caffeine kills good stomach bacteria thus increasing stomach acid. Live bacteria in the form of acidopholous helps digest and re-balance intestinal flora. (It doesn't taste as bad as your might think.) I recommend doing a colon-cleansing program once every quarter for general body maintenance and taking intestinal flora enhancers if you eat a high acidity diet. (meat, caffeine, sugar).

Drink Water – Drink lots of water. You have heard this for years and yet you probably still don't drink enough. Think about Dr. Carrel's cell living forever. It takes water to flush out the toxins. It takes liquid in your body to distribute the nutrition to each cell. Keep fresh water flowing through your body. Water flushes out all the toxins and helps keep your kidneys clean. Read any diet book, and they'll tell you that water helps you stay slim. It can also help you slow aging. Here's something to make you think. The human body of a twenty-year old is over 80% water, while an elderly person is about 60% water. Do you think there's a correlation between the body dehydrating and growing wrinkles? Perhaps if we drank more water, we'd age less.

DO PREVENTATIVE MEDICINE

There are many benefits of preventative medicine. Most people only go to the doctor when they're sick. They wait for their body to breakdown before seeking any kind of treatment. I recommend going to the doctor when you feel healthy. It will save you in medicine costs and down time. (I even recommend calling into work for a "well-day." Heck, why should I be punished for not ever getting sick. I take lots of well-days and I work for myself!)

What is preventative medicine? Preventative medicine is the science of avoiding diseases before they even get started. By keeping the body healthy - you don't create a toxic place for germs and viruses to breed disease. You might visit an alternative practitioner every couple of months and check the overall conditions of your health. You might go to a chiropractor for a spinal adjustment or some Applied Kinesiology, a Chinese Herbalist for a balancing formula or acupuncture. Or you might go to a nutritionist for a general health analysis and recommendation of vitamins to keep you healthy. The idea behind preventative medicine is that you take measures to keep yourself in optimum shape.

I've gone through many flu seasons, when everyone was getting sick around me, and I remained perfectly healthy. The reason is when your immune system is strong you've got more defenses against people's germs. Germs don't cause sickness. Germs that infect a body with lots of toxins and no defenses cause sickness. Visiting a preventative doctor periodically and incorporating alternative health practices into your daily life is a 21st century Success Secret of the Rich and Happy!

WORK ON THE CAUSE, NOT THE SYMPTOM

I am constantly amazed at people's response to their own lives. For some reason the concept of being totally responsible for their own circumstances eludes most people's brains. Give yourself a quick test. If you noticed water on the floor of your kitchen, what would you do?

a) Gripe, complain, and live with the puddle of water in your living room.

b) Clean up the water.

c) Clean up the water and then discover the cause of the water and fix it.

Now, most people reading this would choose answer (c). Now be honest with yourself. If you had a source of irritation in your life, would you take the same approach?

Imagine that you woke up one day and you are broke - poor - living paycheck to paycheck. What do you do?

a) Gripe, complain, blame the system, your parents, your boss, and live with it?

b) Go to work tomorrow just like you did today (but keep your thoughts to yourself)?

c) Take 100% responsibility for your current situation. Evaluate what you did to get yourself in that situation and fix it.

Now, be honest, would you have picked (c) in this scenario. Most people do not. If you are reading this book, I suspect you did pick (c) at some point in the recent past. You found yourself less than "happy," or less than "rich." Good job.

I keep two doctors in my life: a western medical doctor (Dr. Koval) and an eastern medical doctor (Dr. Edward Song.) Both are very qualified, but they approach the world by asking different questions.

I'll relay a rather personal story. A bit embarrassing, but I think you will learn something from my experience. I was showering a few months ago when I noticed a small nodule in my left chest. Since I have been on a structured weight lifting program, I was noticing my chest was getting bigger and stronger. But a lump in the left pectoral that hurt when touched was not part of the training program. I thought it was nothing and it would go away in a few days.

That weekend I was in New York visiting a friend of mine. He showed me a three-inch scar underneath his nipple from surgery he had just two months earlier. He said it was from a non-cancerous lump in his chest that he didn't have checked out until it was so big his shirts looked funny. That was all the motivation I needed to get my butt into gear. First, I called my western doctor. I had to know if this was a freak of nature or if I was turning into a woman. I had heard of lumps in a woman's breast, but never a man's. And, I did not want to sit in the waiting room for a mammogram. No thank you. So, I made an appointment. As soon as I returned home to Dallas I was in Dr. Koval's office getting my chest examined.

After the examination, Dr. Koval began asking himself two questions: "Is the lump cancerous?" and "How can we get it removed the fastest?" It turns out such nodules were quite common in men, and he recommended I get a biopsy immediately to find out if it was cancerous. The statistics say that if you spot cancer early, it can often be treated successfully. So, from a western perspective this was the right recommendation. They would most likely have the lump surgically "cut out." Ouch. Now, this is sounding pretty painful and expensive. I keep health insurance, but knives and surgery are not my idea of fun.

So, I said "Thank You" to Dr. Koval and drove straight over to Dr. Song's office. (Dr. song is my eastern philosophy Oriental Medical Doctor. Yes, they have 8 year colleges for OMD degrees.) I was never the kind of kid who settled for an answer I didn't like. Dr. Song and I sat and shared some green tea before we began discussing my medical problem. It's nice to actually visit with your doctor for more than three minutes. (Dr. Koval visits with me, too. But no green tea.) After the tea, Dr. Song inspected the swollen area and began asking me some questions.

"Have you been eating anything different?"

"How long has it been there?"

"Have you been taking any medications?"

Clearly, Dr. Song was asking a very different set of questions than my western doctor. Dr Song was asking himself, "What is the cause?"

Well, upon thinking about Dr. Song's question, I remembered I had been taking a popular hair loss drug called Propecia (aka Proscar). I began taking it two months ago when I noticed my hair thinning a little bit on top.

"Ahhh," Dr. Song said. "You must stop taking that right now! You have been taking female hormones - that is what causing your problem. I will make a batch of custom herb tea that will make lump go away." (He has a rather thick Korean accent - but it is worth listening to him extra close for the pearls of wisdom.)

Then, it clicked. My friend in New York had started taking the same hair loss drug one year ago. Hmmm. That could be the cause.

Notice Dr. Song began looking for the cause - not trying to simply "remove the symptom." Dr. Song wanted to give my body what it needed to heal itself.

Let me set the record straight about my thinning hair. Losing one's hair is a common thing for men, especially after they turn 30. But, my hair has always been my best feature - and I was determined to hang onto it. My father lost his hair and has been happily bald since he was 23. Since my mom still had a full head of hair, I thought my chances were 50/50. So, when it began happening to me, I was noticeably perturbed. I was not giving in to nature without a fight.

So, I asked Dr. Song what he was going to do about me losing my hair. (As if it was his fault that I couldn't take the hair loss medicine anymore. Ha.) Anyway, after a long lecture about testosterone, genetics, and green tea, I realized I couldn't just take a pill to stop the aging process.

To make a long story short, here is what happened over the next two weeks. I paid Dr. Song for a custom brewed set of Korean tea -

bad tasting liquid sealed in little brown packages. I took it three times a day and threw away the Propecia. The lump slowly shrank and then disappeared. (All without surgery.)

The point of this story is quite simple. You are at cause of everything that happens in your life. (You may never find out what the cause is ... but believing you are at cause gives you great power.) You also have many options. You have to look.

When I spoke to my western doctor (Dr. Koval) the next week, to inform him of the good news, I asked him a very direct question, "Have any of your other patients that have taken Propecia also had breast lumps?" He said, "Yes. It is not uncommon." I asked why he failed to mention this critical piece of information to me. He said, "They all had lumps in both breasts, not just one. I didn't think it was related. In any case, the safest route was a biopsy." Yet, knowing this pattern ... he still didn't try to find the cause.

I wasn't upset because Dr. Koval wanted to fix the symptom - that was his job. Medicines have so many side effects, it is impossible for any one man to keep them all straight. Dr. Koval is one of the most well read physicians I know on herbs and alternative natural health. He always supports my unconventional eastern cures. But, he has years of training to ask a different set of questions. The same questions he was taught in western medical school. He means well. His intentions were good and his methods were proven - from his own belief systems and own experiences and literature supplied by drug companies. I would probably be okay using either method.

The reason I have two doctors is because I want the best of both worlds. I want to choose which belief system, which methodology, and which process is going to work best for me. In this case, it seemed obvious to me that the drug caused the lump. Stop taking the drug - lump stops growing. Take special herbs - heals the wound. I took total control and total responsibility.

Find the cause and fix it.

HOW THIS LESSON CAN APPLY TO YOU & YOUR MONEY

This lesson can apply to any problem in your life. If you are constantly broke - fix the cause. Some people start looking for a new credit card or a loan. They refinance their house. They start looking for a higher paying job. Or, they might work really hard to elect a new politician to change the system. These are all ways of fixing the symptom and not dealing with the cause of the money problem.

We will go into more depth on the cause and effects of not having enough money. But here is a basic quick fix.

First, you are most likely spending more than you make. In America, this is practically a modern day ritual. Cut up the credit cards, stop spending as much money, save 10% of every dollar you earn, and stop the bleeding.

Now, make a plan to build financial security.

What is the cause of you being the age you are and earning the level of income you are earning? What decisions did you make last year, five years ago, etc? What path did you choose? What are your beliefs about how much money you can earn? How important is being rich to you? What choices can you make this year to build more wealth?

The truth is all you have to do to take inventory of your mindset is to look around you. Take inventory of you life. The reality you are living in right now is a direct result of your thoughts and beliefs about the world. If you're alone, poor, stressed out, or unhealthy …

your thinking is at the root cause. Begin changing your mind now, and your body and world will start changing. It may take six months for the changes to be obvious, or you may notice changes immediately - but start now.

By the way, after I got my body and hormones back in balance ... my hair loss stopped. I believe because I made such a firm decision to keep my hair ... my head obeyed. I also decided to become detached whether or not it happened. Let me explain that last statement. I made a decision of the outcome I wanted: To keep my hair. But, because I also accepted the possibility of losing my hair, I stopped worrying about it. I stopped putting focus on what I didn't want to happen. Remember your mind is a creating machine. It tends to manifest into reality your most dominant thoughts. So, if you focus on what you do not want to happen ... that is often what you get.

You might want to check my photos ten years from now. Let's see how well my hair obeys my brain. Hey, according to my 62-year-old father, women dig bald men. What? Me worry?

If anything in this chapter has sparked some curiosity or you want to learn more about how to take total control over your body, please visit a special page I have designed just for you. I have included links to other websites and referenced many books that contain expanded information on most topics I discussed in this chapter. Getting control of your health will change your life entirely.

Other resources:

www.bartbaggett.com/health

www.stop-depression.com

www.weightlossdoctor.com

Universal Truth # 15

The quality and meaning of your
communication is the response you get
(regardless of your intent.)

CHAPTER 13

THE SECRET POWER OF RAPPORT

I was in the back seat of a New York taxicab with a very wealthy and successful man named David Palgon. We were doing a joint venture selling my Grapho-Deck Flash Cards via full-page newspaper ads. He was a veteran marketing genius and a man I respected deeply. Every time I get a chance to visit with someone whom I deem successful, I ask them the same question, "If you had to identify one thing, one element of your life or your personality, that has been the key to your success in life, what would that be?"

David thought for a minute and said, "My black book. That's been the most important thing to me. It's because of the wide circle of people I know that I am constantly presented with fantastic deals and excellent advice. When I was just twenty, I only knew a handful of people. Now, I can call up the CEO of major corporations. Because they take my calls, I get things done. My friends are my most valuable resource."

Because I was looking for a personality trait, his comments added another dimension to my research. David was saying very clearly that his success was not achieved alone. He was wise enough to attract, choose, and maintain relationships that lasted a lifetime. He realized the value that other people brought into his life. I don't know if David consciously or unconsciously developed the skills necessary to make people like him. I do know that you don't maintain close relationships with hundreds of people if you are unable to make people like you.

For many people, just living by a strict moral code of integrity is enough to create a sense of trust with your circle of friends. If you make it a habit to treat everyone you meet with fairness, kindness, and generosity, these people will be around to support you for the next thirty years. Even if deals go sour, your behavior in the deals will be remembered.

Before you can call up a friend from five or ten years ago and ask him to help you achieve a goal... you must have done something to create that friend years earlier. Everyone reading this book has a few good friends. But, ask yourself honestly... how big is your black book? How many people can you get on the phone and have instant sincere trust and rapport?

It is my belief that the larger number of people that you can put into your black book, the larger your emotional and financial bank account will become. Investing in relationships is a sound investment.

Some people seem to naturally make friends easier than others. Good sales people have mastered the art of developing quick rapport with total strangers. Sales people are traditionally one of the highest paid positions in any organization. This statistic alone should tell you the value of understanding and relating to people.

In the early 1970's my father, Curtis Baggett, worked as a financial planner for a company called IDS. At just 35 years old, he consistently sold more insurance, mutual funds and financial services than any other salesperson in the company. He has often relayed the real reason he became an entrepreneur. He said, "Most of the time I worked for IDS, I earned more money than the vice president earned. For some reason, he felt threatened by a young salesperson out-earning him. He didn't want me to earn more. Jealousy, I guess. So, he kept reassigning me to the worst territories so my income would drop. But, like clockwork, I would build that sales team to #1 in the nation. Eventually I got tired of working against my own company and started my own."

The reason my young father was earning more money than the 55-year-old vice president was simple. Curtis was much more effective at creating rapport, establishing trust, and influencing a larger number of people. Today my dad still has contact with many of his customers he met back in 1972. He has leveraged these relationships to do new and different deals for over three decades. If you learn one skill - learn the art of establishing rapport and maintaining long-term relationships.

There are dozens of effective books on the art of establishing rapport, influence, and selling. Personally, I think every teenager should be forced to read Dale Carnegie's *How to Win Friends and Influence People*. This book written in the 1950's teaches us the fundamental people skills. Although some of the advice is rather elementary, I am surprised at the number of people who don't really know when to shut up and listen, ask questions, say please, and send thank you cards. If you want to immerse yourself in the modern art of influence, there are much better live seminars and more effective techniques that incorporate more modern 21st century psychological tools. I'll share a few of these tools with you here.

As I was learning and mastering these advanced "rapport" tools over the past 15 years, my friends and family noticed I was making some major shifts in how I got along with people. My father especially was impressed with my new ability to create rapport with anyone. However, when I explained the specific techniques, he said, "That's nothing new. I've been doing this for 20 years!" True, Dad has always been a natural at creating rapport, and the techniques have been around for ages. But what is new is we are now able to teach rapport in a step-by-step analytical way. The reason we know these techniques is because researchers studied the most charming, the most influential, and the most effective communicators on the planet - and modeled their behavior. Dad was correct in that many of the techniques were not new to him. However, until now, he couldn't effectively teach the skills to a new person because he was just doing it naturally. Some of the definitions didn't even exist until the late 1970's when Richard Bandler and John Grinder pioneered the field of NLP (Neuro-Linguistic Programming.) Terms like "matching, mirroring, pacing, and leading" are commonplace in communication workshops, dating books, and sales training world-wide today. As much as they have been absorbed into the training and self-help community, I am still shocked at the profound value these "rapport skills" have on the vast number of participants in my live seminars. Even if you are a social butterfly, take a few minutes to really memorize and practice this set of rapport tools. You will be shocked at both the simplicity and effectiveness of doing a few things differently. You will notice people, even the most difficult people, will begin to treat you as if you were their best friend.

THE SECRET OF RAPPORT

Think about a time when you just instantly clicked with another person. Think about someone whom you feel like you've known for years. Go back to that time and imagine being completely in sync with them. It might have been a family member, a friend, or some-one you just met. Go back to that time and think about what it was about that person that made you feel so attuned. Chances are you felt you were alike because you lived in the same towns, liked the same movies, held the same beliefs, or even had similar patterns of speech. Whatever the reasons that came to you for the sense of warmth you felt is based on the concept of rapport.

Most people can't put their finger on why they like someone or why they do not. Most people just have a "good feeling" about someone or an "awkward or creepy feeling." This is why most peo-ple feel so helpless in the dating scene. They are just rolling the dice with hopes that someone happens to be a match.

The good news is researchers have discovered specific process-es that occur when people are in rapport and different processes that occur when people have no rapport. You can now take conscious control of what many people call "chemistry." The applications of this in a romantic setting are obvious. Instead of waiting around for the one person in a million that turns your motor - you can push the emotional buttons, and ignite a relationship with yourself and that person. My first book, *The Secrets to Making Love Happen*, and the audio course, *The Secrets To Creating Chemistry*, are very thorough resources to apply these techniques to romance if that is your outcome. In addition, you can use these same skills in you interpersonal relationships, with your family, with co-workers, and with total strangers. What I'm offering you here is the ability to truly connect with people on their level so you can understand each other fully. People will thank you for making them feel so understood.

IT FEELS LIKE WE HAVE SO MUCH IN COMMON

You already know the secret of gaining rapport with people. You do it all the time. When you first meet someone at a party, what do you do? You both ask a series of questions until you find something in common. Right? As soon as you find something in common, you feel a sense of connection. If you discover that you grew up in the same town or went to the same college, you experience some commonality. You look for clothes in common, people you both know, and even movies you like. The more things in common you find, the more comfortable you begin to feel with this person. And you'll notice the more "chemistry" develops.

There is a basic rule for all rapport. The more similarity - the more rapport. The more difference you have - the harder it is to maintain rapport.

Rapport simply means the ability to enter someone else's world, make them feel you understand them so that you both feel a strong common bond. It is the ability to go from your map of the world into their map of the world. Rapport is the essence of successful communication.

The downfall to simple conversational skills is that all the rapport is based on "content" of the conversation. That may be useful at a party, but not in a negotiating session with an adversary. How do you make people like you when the "content" is an issue? The answer lies in the other ways that we communicate.

If you have ever been in a romantic relationship, you don't need to be told in words when your spouse is having a bad day. You can read it on their face. Imagine saying, "Hi Honey, is something wrong?" Your spouse growls back, "No. I'm fine." She falls down into the couch with her arms crossed and a frown distorting her face. You don't simply say, "Great! What's on TV?" You unconsciously sense that your spouse is in a bad mood. Even though the "content" of her sentence said she was fine, you know differently.

The reason you know your spouse's emotional state is because we are masterful communicators even without choosing the right words. Even my cat makes it abundantly clear when he wants to go outside or needs some more water. He can't talk - but he communicates.

We communicate with both our bodies (physiology & body language) and our voice (word inflections, word choices, and tone of voice). Studies reveal that the most effective tool is the use of our physical bodies in communicating what we really mean. That means the crossed arms and the pouty face speaks more truth than the words "I'm fine." Furthermore, the way someone says, "I'm fine," speaks more truth than the word choices alone. You must listen to the intonation, inflection, volume, pitch and even rhythm. All these things you already know intuitively. You just might not have ever separated the various aspects of communication into such finite detail. When you begin to recognize the different parts of communication, you can then adjust your own style to be more effective.

When you are "in rapport," you are experiencing similar emotions as the other person. Positive emotions are what make people want to trust you, like you, love you, and even listen to you. Because emotions are chemical processes that occur in our physical bodies, it makes sense that we can then influence other's emotions through the medium of our physical senses.

The simple art of "mirroring" or "matching" another person might seem silly or simplistic. Actually, this is one the most powerful tools for creating instant and long lasting rapport you will ever learn. Ever since I learned the art of mirroring and matching at age 19, my ability to get along with people has improved ten fold. I still use these skills in every telephone call I make, every radio show I appear on, and in every person-to-person meeting I have. Naturally, since these skills works so well in business, I use them to make my relationships smoother as well. Once you feel the results for yourself, you will keep these tools within arms reach whenever you are interacting with other people for the rest of your life. They are that powerful.

THE ART OF MIRRORING

Can you remember those hilarious black and white comedy slapstick movies filmed in the 1940's starring the Marx Brothers? Remember Groucho, Harpo and Chico? I vividly remember a scene where one of the brothers pretends to be looking into a full-length mirror and the other brother is facing him (from inside the mirror). Obviously, there is no glass in the mirror and the other brother mimics every move he makes. He moves his arms fast, slow, dances, whistles, spins around, etc. This "mirror" image is why they call gaining rapport through matching someone's physical movements "mirroring." Technically, the word "matching" is the same thing, but you would move the same arm as your partner, instead of the opposite arm. The technical differences between the two terms are really unimportant. In my mind, they are interchangeable words. In a nutshell, you move just like the person you are talking to moves. You sit like them, stand like them, hold the same postures, breathe the same.

When people first try this concept, they feel self-conscious. They confuse mirroring with mimicking. In my mind, mimicking is what younger siblings do to their older siblings in order to irritate them. Mimicking is copying to the point of being obnoxious. On the contrary, mirroring is the subtle art of matching the body position of the person you are talking to. If she leans back, you lean back. If she puts here left hand on her hip, you put your hand on your hip. If she laughs, you laugh. If she talks really fast, so do you.

When researchers have studied couples in love or two business people experiencing a deep state of rapport - mirroring occurs naturally. There is evidence that when two people are in deep levels of rapport, the rhythm of their breathing are strikingly similar. It is common to see their body postures exactly alike. They even speak with the same volume and cadence. The next time you are at a restaurant, notice the way people are sitting across from each other. When in deep rapport, you will notice both people are leaning forward together or leaning back together. You might even notice that their hands are resting in the exact same position. They don't even realize they are matching and mirroring one another, because most of rapport is on an unconscious level. So when you match and mirror people, they won't notice you doing it. What they will notice is that they suddenly like you more and feel very comfortable with you.

Try this simple experiment. Choose someone as a test subject (preferably someone you don't know) and move your body in the same direction, manner, and movements as they do. During live seminars, we have partners stand facing each other face-to-face in order to match and mirror each other's body movements. For instance, if you tilt your head, your partner should tilt his head. If he/she lifts his foot, your partner should mirror that. And so on. Your job is to simply follow the other person's lead. After doing this for a few minutes, you will find yourself feeling connected to the other person. In a seminar, the results are often comical and silly. Even though both partners know what the purpose is something interesting invariably happens. The two partners like each other much more than they did before the exercise. Even when exchanging no words, people feel a sense of connection with each other.

I challenge you to mirror someone's body positions today. The most common concern about using this rapport tool is that the other person will catch you and think you are mimicking them. This will not happen. In fact, most people are so self-absorbed, they won't even notice your movements at a conscious level. You will be surprised at the number of times people will simply say things like, "I know we just met, but it seems like I've known you for years."

You don't have to just use your body to mirror someone. I was forced to master the art of matching someone's voice when I started appearing on radio shows by telephone. Out of the 1300 radio interviews I have been featured on, I would guess over 1,100 of those have been by telephone. Because of this fact, I was essentially handicapped from using my body language to create rapport with my audience or the host. It didn't matter what I was wearing or what I looked like. I was forced to learn how to adapt my voice alone to meet the various criteria of all three types of people. I often spoke fast, slow, loud, soft, etc. I was often the host's favorite guest, because I sounded just like him. Because I grew up in Texas, my natural speaking voice contained a slight southern accent. I learned very quickly that New Yorker's don't care much for a slow talking Texan. Therefore, I would turn my accent on and off depending on which part of the country the radio show was airing in. People occasionally ask me why I don't have an accent. I simply tell them it was costing me friends and money, so I "got rid of it."

THE SECRET WORLD OF REPRESENTATIONAL SYSTEMS

What researchers have found is that there are three major representational systems that we use to communicate. NLP refers to these channels as the Visual, Auditory, and Kinesthetic channels. Visual refers to anything you can see or visualize in your mind. Auditory includes all things that you can hear or any sounds that you create, including voices inside your mind. And of course, the Kinesthetic channel is the part of you that feels things using your body or emotions. Actually, there are two other channels (smell and taste.) However, I'm not going to discuss these two other systems in detail, because they don't apply to this conversation about influence and rapport as much as the other three.

The Five Representational Systems

1.	Visual	See
2.	Auditory	Hear
3.	Kinesthetic	Feel
4.	Gustatory	Taste
5.	Olfactory	Smell

Many people communicate primarily using just one representational system. All of us have experience using all three. If you think about these channels as different ways to receive information, they are easy to memorize. Imagine the visual channel as a movie screen or TV set on with the volume turned down. Imagine the auditory channel as the telephone or stereo speakers. Finally, imagine the kinesthetic channel as a Braille book, a feeling in the heart, or a big hug from a friend. You use all three of these channels to give and receive information. The one you are most comfortable with is your primary channel. Master communicators use all three channels in balance.

Effective communication is the ability to create rapport by matching as many of these "channels" as possible. If you think about one of your best friends, it is likely, you both utilize the same primary channel to tell stories and share information. Personally, I speak very fast and tend to move my hands a lot when I speak. This style is indicative of someone who functions primarily from a visual channel. That's true. I tend to see images in my head before I start to communicate. Because I am so visual, I even talk on the phone using visual word choices. I often say, "I can see what you are saying. I'm picturing it this way. It's not clear." These words are clues to the people who I am talking to that I really like using my visual channel. If they want instant rapport with me, they can do two simple things. First, they can speed up the pace of their speech to match my fast talking style. Second, they can choose words that have a visual reference. It doesn't matter what the content of the conversation will be. If they speak using these two techniques, I will unconsciously like this person more. And I will understand their communication much quicker.

I've been aware of these techniques for over a decade and they still work on me. This is how we are programmed. Just because I am aware of my programming doesn't change the fact I build rapport faster and more naturally with people who communicate in my primary channel. I invite you to match me.

As a professional speaker and writer, I am extremely aware that my audience may not prefer the visual channel as much as I do. Therefore, you will see me intentionally write using words that inflect a more auditory meaning or a more kinesthetic meaning. These words allow my reader to "feel more in tune" with me. The words are like serving the same dinner on a paper plate or fine china. The food could be exactly the same, but depending on your cultural upbringing, you would be completely at home with the right plate or feel totally alienated by the wrong plate. I know people who would rather starve than eat off a paper plate. So, if you try to convince someone of your opinion, and your facts are being served on a paper plate - they will never even taste your opinion. Simply by switching channels, the same opinion gets delivered on fine china. When you switch to their primary channel, they feel you are "one of them" and immediately open their mind to your opinion.

Take a moment and test your current awareness of representational systems. Complete the following pop quiz:

REPRESENTATIONAL SYSTEM QUIZ

Which of the three categories do the following phrases fit? (Visual, Auditory, Kinesthetic)

See it clearly

Shake down

Solid idea

Tune him out

Brilliant example

Rings a bell

Tone it down

Pretty as a picture

Years ago, I once shared the stage with a guy who loved to talk through his K-channel. (Kinesthetic.) He would speak very slowly and even take long contemplative breaths between sentences. He would feel the need to hug me all the time and couldn't get a concept until he could stop and "feel it." Needless to say, this man drove me bonkers. In order to communicate effectively, I was forced to slow down my speech, breathe slower, and use words from the kinesthetic word chart. You see, because of the difference in our natural communication style, we didn't have automatic rapport. Because I was able to adjust my style, we could have rapport. Now, working this guy was never effortless, but it was possible. If you master the ability to adjust your communication style, you can have rapport with anybody.

Take a look at the following chart and make a note of which column of words you tend use more frequently. If you are totally balanced, that's great. However, if you always use visual words (like I used to) and never use kinesthetic words (like I used to), then you will be unable to effectively establish rapport with someone who communicates primarily through his kinesthetic channel. This used to be a big problem for me. Now, after over 10 years of awareness, I have instant unconscious flexibility in my speaking and writing patterns.

REPRESENTATIONAL SYSTEMS KEY WORDS

Visual	Auditory	Kinesthetic	Unspecified (generic)
See	Hear	Feel	Sense
Look	Listen	Touch	Experience
View	Sound(s)	Budge up against	Understand
Appear	Make music	Get a handle	Think
Show	Harmonize	Solid	Learn
Crystal clear	Mellifluous	Suffer	Conceive
Flash	Dissonance	Hard	Be conscious
Imagine	Attune	Make contact	Know
Focused	Overtones	Throw out	Perceive
Twinkle	Chant	Turn around	Insensitive
Clear	Question	Grasp	Distinct
Foggy	Be all ears	Get hold of	Motivate
Dawn	Rings a bell	Slip through	Consider
Hazy	Silence	Catch on	Change
Sparkling	Be heard	Unfeeling	Process
Reveal	Resonate	Concrete	Decide
Envision	Deaf	Scrape	Contemplate
Illuminate	Tune in/out	Link	Reward
Shine	Clatter	Cram	Express
Dim	Tell	Tackle	Feedback
Dark	Noise	Warm	Logical
Glow Shout	Sharp	Organize	
Scan	Talk	Soft	
Pretty	Say	Fall	
Zoom in	Babble	Shape	
Reveal	Shrill	Tension	

HOW TO PUT IT ALL TOGETHER

If the essence of rapport is sameness, then the overriding principle is to become the same as the person you are talking to. There is an animal in the reptile family called a chameleon. This little creature's strength is not speed, strength, or intelligence. The chameleon has the ability to change its skin color to blend into its own surroundings. You must be a chameleon.

One of greatest benefits of being able to create warm and fuzzy states in others is they begin to listen to you. Before you can effectively influence anyone, you must first gain rapport. As soon as you have this emotional connection, you can begin leading them to your way of thinking. The most interesting experiment you can do for yourself is lead someone using your posture. Find someone to mirror that is totally unaware of the fact you are going to mirror them. Once you have mirrored their posture, leg positions, arm positions, and even head position - start changing. In other words, you move your leg and see if his will follow. You will be surprised at how easy it is to get people to follow your lead. Likewise, once you establish rapport on this level, you can lead them to your opinion, idea, or toward your product or service. Rapport is the beginning point of all effective persuasion. I once mirrored a CEO while he was sitting behind his big mahogany desk. After gaining rapport, I crossed my legs in my chair. Less than thirty seconds later, I heard a "thump" under his desk. He had unconsciously tried to cross his legs under the desk. He was following my lead and he didn't even realize it.

You can pace or lead people in a variety of contexts. If they are tapping their finger on the desk, you can move your finger in the same rhythm. If they are blinking their eyes rapidly, you can blink your eyes at the same pace. You can even tap your toe to the same rhythm as they tap their finger. If someone is sitting with their mouth tense, you can tense yours. Then, after you gain the connection, you can lead people into other states.

If you are a telephone sales person soliciting people at their work, you usually have to pace them into talking to you. If a busy real estate agent answers the phone out of breath sounding terribly busy, you must enter her world. I would say something like this in a clear, fast, rapid, speaking voice, "Beth, you sound so busy! Can you squeeze one minute to answer a quick question?" If she says, "Yes. But only a minute." I then must match her fast-pace voice for about fifteen seconds before I stop speaking, take a deep breath, and hope she follows my lead. In order for Beth to feel I respect her and connect with her in her manic busy state of mind, I have to meet her on her turf. Then, after I have matched her world, I can lead her into my world. Even if I were able to establish rapport with Beth in under one minute, I would then tell her my sixty seconds was up and ask her for a few more minutes. Otherwise, I would offer to call her at another time. If I offer to hang up after one minute, she feels respected and she already knows I can talk fast. If she liked me in that first sixty seconds, it is likely she will want to hear what I have to say. It may be tough to gain rapport over the telephone in under sixty seconds, but it is great practice. Truthfully, people make judgments about you everyday in less time than that. Using just your voice inflections, speed, and volume are all you need to master telephone relationships. I am still amazed at the number of cold-calls I get at my office that do not even attempt to gain rapport with me. I'm wondering if these people just aren't trained well or just hate their job? No rapport, no sale. No rapport, no influence. No rapport, no relationship.

After people test these simple rapport tools, they are amazed. However, there is always one person in the audience who has a problem with using them. They say something like this, "I don't feel comfortable manipulating people with these techniques. If people don't like me for who I am, then I don't think it was meant to be." I sit. I listen. And I resist my urge to say something sarcastic. That kind of thinking reminds me of a single guy I know named Alex who thinks all women are weird and difficult. Alex refuses to read any self-improvement books or practice the techniques of rapport building. He rarely dates and the few dates he has usually end in the phrase "Let's just be friends." Naturally, anyone who isn't willing to analyze his own behavior is going to continue living an uphill battle in relationships. Alex holds onto the pipe dream that there is one woman out there who will just effortlessly "click" with him and love him "just the way he is." He doesn't believe he needs to change anything about himself. I am in no position to say whether his dream woman exists or not. Because Alex is 43 and has never had a relationship last more than six months, it seems to me his strategy for life-long romance is not working. It would behoove him to start changing himself because "who he is" is repelling all the women he dates. Likewise, if your ability to instantly connect and create long lasting rapport with people is drastically underdeveloped, you owe it to your future friends to learn the skills. When you make people feel comfortable, they will thank you for it. They will appreciate having someone who understands them. People are not born "charming." People learn charming. If you were brought up in a family of introverted engineers, your social skills might not be as effective as a child who was brought up by a politician.

Here is my advice to anyone reading this who has a problem with utilizing the rapport skills outlined in this chapter. If what you are doing isn't working - try something different. People will appreciate you matching them. You will enter their world and they will love you for it.

Universal Truth #16

Ask and you Shall receive.
(But, please ask correctly and specifically.)

CHAPTER 14

TOXIC VOCABULARY

I remember my dad teaching me the power of language at a very young age. Not only did my dad understand that specific words affect our mental pictures, but he understood words are a powerful programming factor in lifelong success.

One particularly interesting event occurred when I was eight. As a kid, I was always climbing trees, poles, and literally hanging around upside down from the rafters of our lake house. So, it came to no surprise for my dad to find me at the top of a 30-foot tree swinging back and forth. My little eight-year-old brain didn't realize the tree could break or I could get hurt. I just thought it was fun to be up so high. My older cousin, Tammy, was also in the same tree. She was hanging on the first big limb, about ten feet below me. Tammy's mother also noticed us at the exact same time my dad did. About that time a huge gust of wind came over the tree. I could hear the leaves start to rattle and the tree begin to sway. I remember my dad's voice over the wind yell, "Bart, Hold on tightly." So I did. The next thing I know, I heard Tammy screaming at the top of her lungs, laying flat on the ground.   She had fallen out of the tree.

I scampered down the tree to safety. My dad later told me why she fell and I did not. Apparently, Tammy's mother was not as an astute student of language as my father. When Tammy's mother felt the gust of wind, she yelled out, "Tammy, don't fall!" And Tammy did... fall.

My dad then explained to me that the mind has a very difficult time processing a negative image. In fact, people who rely on internal pictures cannot see a negative at all. In order for Tammy to process the command of not falling, her nine-year-old brain had to first imagine falling, then try to tell the brain not to do what it just imagined. Whereas, my eight-year-old brain instantly had an internal image of me hanging on tightly. This is why people who try to stop smoking struggle with the act of stopping smoking. They are running pictures all day of themselves smoking. Smokers are rarely taught to see themselves breathing fresh air and feeling great. The language itself becomes one barrier to success.

This concept is especially useful when you are attempting to break a habit or set a goal. You can't visualize not doing something. The only way to properly visualize not doing something is to actually find a word for what you want to do and visualize that. For example, when I was thirteen years old, I played for my junior high school football team. I tried so hard to be good, but I just couldn't get it together at that age. I remember hearing the words run through my head as I was running out for a pass, "Don't drop it!" Naturally, I dropped the ball. My coaches were not skilled enough to teach us proper "self-talk." They just thought some kids could catch and others couldn't. I'll never make it pro, but I'm now a pretty good Sunday afternoon football player, because all my internal dialogue is positive and encourages me to win. I wish my dad had coached me playing football instead of just climbing trees. I might have had a longer football career.

Here is a very easy demonstration to teach your kids and your friends the power of a toxic vocabulary. Ask them to hold a pen or pencil. Hand it to them. Now, follow my instructions carefully.

Say to them, "Okay, try to drop the pencil."

Observe what they do.

Most people release their hands and watch the pencil hit the floor. You respond, "You weren't paying attention. I said TRY to drop the pencil. Now please do it again."

Most people then pick up the pencil and pretend to be in excruciating pain while their hand tries but fails to drop the pencil. The point is made.

If you tell your brain you will "give it a try," you are actually telling your brain to fail. I have a "no try" rule in my house and with everyone I interact with. Either people will do it or they won't. Either they will be at the party or they won't. I'm brutal when people attempt to lie to me by using the word try. Do they think I don't know they are really telegraphing to the world they have no intention of doing it but they want me to give them brownie points for pretended effort? You will never hear the words "I'll try" come out of my mouth unless I'm teaching this concept in a seminar.

If you "try" and do something, your unconscious mind has permission not to succeed. If I truly can't make a decision I will tell the truth. "Sorry John. I'm not sure if I will be at your party or not. I've got an outstanding commitment. If that falls through, I will be here. Otherwise, I will not. Thanks for the invite." People respect honesty. So remove the word "try" from your vocabulary.

My dad also told me that psychologists claim it takes seventeen positive statements to offset one negative statement. I have no idea if it is true, but the logic holds true. It might take up to seventeen compliments to offset the emotional damage of one harsh criticism. These are concepts that are especially useful when raising children. Ask yourself how many compliments you give yourself daily versus how many criticisms. Heck, I know you are talking to yourself all day long. We all have internal voices that give us direction. So, are you giving yourself the 17:1 ratio or are you shortchanging yourself with toxic self-talk like, "I suck. I'm fat. Nobody will like me. I'll try this diet. I'm not good enough. I'm so stupid. I'm broke, etc. etc." If our parents can set a lifetime of programming with one wrong statement, imagine the kind of programming you are doing on a daily basis with your own internal dialogue.

Here is a list of Toxic Vocabulary words. Notice when you or other people use them.

But	*Try*
If	*Might*
Would have	*Should have*
Could have	*Can't*
Don't	

<u>But</u> - negates any words that are stated before it.

<u>If</u> - presupposes that you may not.

<u>Would have</u> - past tense that draws attention to things that didn't actually happen.

<u>Should have</u> - past tense that draws attention to things that didn't actually happen (and implies guilt.)

<u>Could have</u> - past tense that draws attention to things that didn't actually happen but the person tries to take credit as if it did happen.

<u>Try</u> - presupposes failure.

<u>Might</u> - It does nothing definite. It leaves options for your listener.

<u>Can't / Don't</u> - These words force the listener to focus on exactly the opposite of what you want. This is a classic mistake that parents and coaches make without knowing the damage of this linguistic error.

EXAMPLES:

Toxic phrase: "Don't drop the ball!" Likely result: Drops the ball

Better language: "Catch the ball!"

Toxic phrase: "You shouldn't watch so much television." Likely result: Watches more television.

Better language: "I read too much television makes people stupid. You might find yourself turning that TV off and picking up one of those books more often!"

EXERCISE:

Take a moment to write down all the phrases you use on a daily basis or any Toxic self-talk that you have noticed yourself using. Write these phrases down so you will begin to catch yourself as they occur and change them.

Toxic Phrase   Re-written

PART FOUR:

THE SECRETS TO BUILDING WEALTH

Universal Truth #17

We are living in a world of abundance.
If you are living in any state less than abundance,
you are denying the very nature of your being.

CHAPTER 15

FUNDAMENTAL CASH FLOW
SECRETS OF THE AGES

I am about to tell you a few things you might not want to hear. I say that because many people are continually looking for a magic pill or a trick technique to getting something. In the sport of soccer, you might remember Pele's trademark scissor-kick where he falls to

his back, upside down, swinging his legs over his head and torpedoes the soccer ball into the corner of the net. We all love those winning plays. But, if you talk to any professional coach or athlete, they will tell you those plays are only possible when and if the player has mastered the "fundamentals." As children, we practice mimicking our heroes only to wonder why we are never as effective as they are. I used to watch Chinese Martial Arts movies and run around the house karate chopping the curtains. Without the fundamentals, you simply can't achieve mastery. As an adult, I took three years of Kung Fu from Master Edward Song. Many times during the first year I was tempted to quit because learning the fundamentals was often arduous, tedious, and boring. I later found out that Master Song still practices every single move - every basic move- once a week. He realizes the power of mastering the fundamentals. He told me the reason more people don't complete their training to become a "black belt" is most people do not have the discipline to master the fundamentals. This holds true for professional athletes, salespeople and musicians.

Universal Truth # 18

Pay yourself first.

This chapter is designed to reveal the fundamentals of getting rich. Before I discuss these basic 2000-year-old truths, ask yourself this question, "Am I willing to master the fundamentals - no matter how boring, tedious, or risky they might seem?" If you aren't willing to follow the proven route, what's the use in even reading the map? Are you willing to get past a silly childhood belief that said, "I'm not good at math," in order to grasp an essential element of money? Warning... there may be a spreadsheet in this chapter! Are you willing to read this entire chapter twice? Are you willing to analyze every chart and really study every graph? Okay, if you are committed... read on.

When I was a teenager, Dad gave me a book called *The Richest Man in Babylon*. This easy to read story of an ancient metalworker contains as many applicable money truths as any of today's best sellers. The main character, Arkad, found himself working in the proverbial "rat race." He worked long hours bending metal to make shields and weapons. It was a respectable middle class job in the thriving city of Babylon. Like many of you reading this book, he barely made ends meet and wondered how to ever get ahead. The story goes onto reveal how he formed a relationship with the wealthiest man in Babylon and learned his secrets. The reason this little book made such an impact on me is that I was too young to appreciate it. In other words, I read the words, but I didn't get the meaning. I didn't follow the advice and it cost me.

The first ancient principal shared by the rich wise man was this: "Pay yourself first."

Pay yourself first applies to many areas of your financial life. For example, if you learn the simple habit of saving at least 10% of every dollar you make, you will quickly be sitting on a small nest egg of cash. This may sound difficult, but every one I know who has committed to paying themselves first had this surprising reaction, "I didn't really miss the money at all." This is a tip you can use

Universal Truth # 19

Do not work for your money. Make your money work for you.

no matter how much money you are earning. Most people spend wasteful money on sodas, cigarettes, or even $3 cups of coffee at Starbucks. They don't stop to think what that $1 or $2 a day could grow into in 20 years. Many people feel buying weekly lottery tickets is their retirement plan. It's a great plan only if you want to retire flat broke. Research indicates that the one single behavior that poor people frequently do and rich people rarely do is play the lottery. There is an undeniable statistical inverse correlation between your net worth and playing the lottery. In my opinion, lottery is a tax on people who are very bad at math. (1 in 40 million are not odds I want to take.)

I recently read about a school bus driver who saved just $3 a day and retired with over 3 million dollars in assets, because he was willing to live below his means. Can you say no to lottery tickets and dessert? See the spreadsheet on the next page labeled Spreadsheet 15-1 busdriver.

LIVE BELOW YOUR MEANS

Most people are not willing to live below their means. In fact, when Americans get a raise at work they immediately think of ways to spend the extra money. A few months later, they're living expenses have risen again to exactly meet their earning power. Sound familiar? It is a cycle that traps people in the maze we call "the rat race." You can't get out because you've spent all your exit tokens on crap you didn't need. You overspent. So now you are paying for it with your freedom.

The insightful book *The Millionaire Next Door* screams this principle even in its title. The reason the millionaire is next door is because he is living in the same neighborhood as you. The difference is he is making a few critically different decisions. While you were accumulating more debt, he was building wealth. He was buying assets, you were signing up for liabilities. The book also goes on to explain that even though all of the millionaires in the study could afford a bigger house, a newer car, or more expensive jewelry, they didn't choose to spend their money there. It was these same fundamental habits that got them to the place of a balance sheet over a million dollars. They save a portion of every dollar earned and live below their means. Eventually, they are worth so much money they do buy luxuries. Those luxuries are still below their new means.

Actually, when I say "save," I actually mean "invest." They do spend a portion of income on living expenses, entertainment, or miscellaneous goods. A small portion of every paycheck is earmarked for a pool of money that earns more money. Depositing your "nest egg" money into the savings account at the bank earning just 4% interest is about as stupid as letting your brother-in-law invest it in that restaurant bar scheme! However, it is smarter than leaving it under your mattress. But, with just a bit higher risk and a bit of financial education, you can earn ten times the amount of profit using the power of compound interest.

The secret to how the school bus driver turned that $3 per day into $3 million is in the second piece of wisdom.

The bus driver spent those boring hours while the kids were at school studying investments, stocks, and financial strategies. He wasn't any smarter than the other bus drivers. He was more disciplined and more educated than the other guys. The main difference was he was willing to learn how to make his small savings grow and grow and grow. While the other bus drivers played cards and watched TV, he became rich (slowly). He mastered the fundamentals, and his kids attended the finest colleges.

The Power Of Compound Interest
Bus Driver

Year	Gross Salary	10%	Year End Bank Balance w/ 4% Compound Interest	4% Interest Earned	Year End Bank Balance w/ 20% Compound Interest	20% Interest Earned
1969	$13,000	$1,300	$1,352	$107.64	$1,606.80	$267.80
1970	$13,390	$1,339	$2,798.64	$167.11	$3,583.16	$329.39
1971	$13,792	$1,379	$4,344.92	$230.62	$6,004.45	$349.99
1972	$14,205	$1,421	$5,996.09	$298.37	$8,961.13	$362.63
1973	$14,632	$1,463	$7,757.62	$370.59	$12,561.83	$373.94
1974	$15,071	$1,507	$9,635.26	$447.50	$16,936.92	$385.24
1975	$15,523	$1,552	$11,635.03	$529.35	$22,242.90	$396.82
1976	$15,988	$1,599	$13,763.22	$616.40	$28,667.65	$408.72
1977	$16,468	$1,647	$16,026.42	$708.91	$36,436.62	$420.99
1978	$16,962	$1,696	$18,431.53	$807.14	$45,820.45	$433.62
1979	$17,471	$1,747	$20,985.77	$911.41	$57,143.95	$446.62
1980	$17,995	$1,800	$23,696.68	$1,022.01	$70,796.93	$460.02
1981	$18,535	$1,853	$26,572.18	$1,139.25	$87,247.23	$473.82
1982	$19,091	$1,909	$29,620.52	$1,263.48	$107,056.31	$488.04
1983	$19,664	$1,966	$32,850.37	$1,395.03	$130,898.00	$502.68
1984	$20,254	$2,025	$36,270.75	$1,534.27	$159,580.94	$517.76
1985	$20,861	$2,086	$39,891.15	$1,681.59	$194,075.57	$533.29
1986	$21,487	$2,149	$43,721.44	$1,837.38	$235,546.49	$549.29
1987	$22,132	$2,213	$47,771.99	$2,002.06	$285,391.25	$565.77
1988	$22,796	$2,280	$52,053.61	$2,176.06	$345,287.04	$582.74
1989	$23,479	$2,348	$56,577.62	$2,359.84	$417,246.50	$600.23
1990	$24,184	$2,418	$61,355.84	$2,553.87	$503,684.92	$618.23
1991	$24,909	$2,491	$66,400.65	$2,758.65	$607,500.70	$636.78
1992	$25,657	$2,566	$71,724.96	$2,974.70	$732,172.00	$655.88
1993	$26,426	$2,643	$77,342.30	$3,202.57	$881,872.70	$675.56
1994	$27,219	$2,722	$83,266.78	$3,442.81	$1,061,611.52	$695.83
1995	$28,034	$2,804	$89,513.16	$3,696.03	$1,277,399.03	$716.70
1996	$28,877	$2,888	$96,096.87	$3,962.85	$1,536,448.01	$738.20
1997	$29,743	$2,974	$103,034.02	$4,243.90	$1,847,413.85	$760.35
1998	$30,635	$3,064	$110,341.46	$4,539.88	$2,220,683.15	$783.16
1999	$31,554	$3,155	$118,036.77			

Total no interest earned $65,003   Total using compound interest $2,220,683.15

Spreadsheet 15-1 Busdriver

"Compound Interest is the greatest mathmatical discovery of all time!"

— *Albert Einstein*

He was reflecting on the Rule of 72 which assists financial planners to deter-mie how many months it will take for your money to double depeding based on your interest rate.

THE POWER OF COMPOUND INTEREST

If the bus driver would have only mastered the fundamental habit of saving 10% of his income, he might have had around $118,036 of cash for his retirement. (This is if he had kept his cash in a savings account at his local bank and earned the traditional 4% compounded interest.) By the way, if he had kept that cash under his mattress for twenty years, he would only have $65,003 for his retirement. Just the act of earning a meager 4% a year in a no risk savings back almost doubled his savings.

What the bus driver did was he mastered another principle: compound interest. If the bus driver had invested his 10% monthly savings into the typical mutual fund during 1969-1999. He would have retired with over 2.2 million dollars! Now, because the bus driver actually played the stock market and his money performed better than the average mutual fund, he earned over $3 million dollars. Do you see the secret power of compound interest?

The concept of compound interest can be illustrated many ways. I find I learn best when people let me see visual examples. If you learn better when you see, hear, feel and touch... you are not alone. A spreadsheet is about the least entertaining teaching prop ever invented. Play along with this story and you will get it.

Imagine you have two twin kids, Jack and Jill, who grow up

wanting to be pig ranchers. (Work with me here. Imagine they are adopted if the thought of pig ranching is beneath you.) On their 20th birthday, you make them a very simple offer. You will invest to get them started in the pig ranching business. You tell them very clearly that this is a simple contest. The kid with the most pigs bred and living on their ranch on their 40th birthday inherits your entire 10 million dollar estate.

THE RULES ARE AS FOLLOWS:

You will give them both a ranch of equal size, the same amount of money, and four pigs each to start with. Each year, you will give them four more pigs to add to their stock. They can't buy more pigs from outside. They must breed them. So, the contest begins.

The first few years go along smoothly. Each kid happily gets four new pigs every year and the pigs do what pigs do. They eat, play in the mud, and mate, creating lots of little piglets. Each kid is up to about 35 animals when Jack decides he wants a new car. So, he sells five of his pigs and drives a shiny new car into town and impresses all his girlfriends. Jill smiles and continues to drive her two-year-old car that she purchased for less than two pigs in a trade with a neighbor. She hated to spend her savings on a car, but it was an emergency. Jack continues to rob the kitty at least once a year for "special occasions." (Rumor has it Jack became quite a bacon aficionado!)

So, another year goes by when both their ranches are hit by a terrible storm. They each loses ten pigs. Wow. Jack thought it would have been wise to have some of their fortune invested in ducks, but Dad made the rules.

The kids seem only a few pigs apart during the first five years. But, in the sixth year a stroke of good luck occurrs. A new chemical is added to the pigs' feed that allows pigs to breed almost twice as fast. Jill jokes it is pig Viagra, but she likes the result. More pigs. A year later the drug is recalled and pig production goes back to normal.

As the years go by, Jill's stock of pigs get so large, she has to expand the ranch a few acres. Truthfully, she wonders if it was worth all the trouble. Since she became a vegetarian for health reasons people think she is really weird being a pig rancher! By the fifteenth year, it becomes clear Jill is going to win. She has over ten times the number of pigs. Jack scratches his big sagging-over-the-belt belly in confusion. He asks, "How could a few pigs taken here and there make that much difference?" As his skinny sister stares at her overweight twin brother, she explains the power of compound interest.

After a blank look came over his face when she used math, she tries the brutal approach. Look at your belly. Do you think one slice of bacon did that? No. It was one slice of bacon, every day, for 15 years. You were making your belly fat simultaneously making your wallet thin, one slice at a time. You have heard of the goose that lays the golden egg, haven't you? Well, you ate the pigs that bred 10 million dollars. On Jack's 45th birthday, Jill gladly pays his medical bill for the triple bypass surgery on Jack's heart. She is a good sister. Jack isn't a stupid fellow. He just doesn't understand the power of compound interest, and he lets a few bad habits ruin his physical and financial health.

The other application of paying yourself first has to do with taxation. In most western countries, an individual is taxed between 25%-60% of their income depending on how much money they make. Without discussing the fairness of this policy or not, one can clearly see that giving your money away to the government is like giving away two pigs a year...with no benefits! Therefore, it is highly recommended you educate yourself on how to legally pay less taxes.

Right now, I'll reveal to you the number one method rich people use to avoid taxes: corporations. The corporation is an amazing invention that gives you back control of your cash flow. Let me explain. Most poor and middle income earners are working too hard for wages to ever imagine having time to run a successful corporation or even a small business. There is no law that says you have to be successful. In fact, many small businesses and corporations go four or five years without ever turning a profit.

You may be asking, "Are you recommending we start a business that loses money? That would leave me with even less money than I started with!" Nope. Your math is bad. What I am suggesting is that you KEEP YOUR MONEY out of the hands of the government as long as legally possible. You see corporations have a different set of tax laws than individuals. Did you know that corporations pay about the same percentage of tax as you do... but they pay it only on NET INCOME. Net income is the money left over after you've paid out all your business expenses.

In other words, if a corporation earns $100,000 from one client and spends $100,000 on rent, labor, and expenses, the government gets to tax the difference between those two figures:

$100,000 income

<$100,000> expenses

$0 Net Profit

33% tax on $0 = $0 taxes owed.

Pay tax on your net income, not your gross income.

This is such an important concept to start applying immediately. You must learn to earn more money on your savings and have more money to live on. You can accomplish both these things by paying yourself first and paying the government last. This is more difficult to pull of working as someone else's employee than working for your own company/ being self-employed. You must get creative and find a legal way. There are many paths to the same goal. For many Americans, the first step to financial freedom is turning in your employee badge and starting a career of self-employment.

Now, I want to make one thing clear. I do believe it is appropriate to pay some taxes to the government. There are many great government funded institutions that benefit society as a whole, like having police officers on the street, a strong military, paying teachers to educate our children and paying construction workers to build better roads. All these come out of our tax contributions. However, if you are not careful, you can become so heavily taxed that you will feel like you can never get ahead. This is because the government, with all its good intentions, will suck more than its fair share of money right out of your wallet. Think about it. When you get a paycheck, the government pulls out a considerable chunk for income taxes, social security and welfare. So, you worked all those long hours and only got a portion of what you earned. Then you take that leftover money and go buy stuff: car, food, clothes, toys, computer, etc. And you will notice that nearly every time you pay retail for something, you pay an additional sales tax. Guess who gets that? Da government. Then if you live in certain states in the U.S.A., you might pay an additional state income tax. Who gets more of your money? Da government. Then if you're buying a home, you pay a property tax to fund the schools. That's an additional tax you pay after your paycheck has been deducted for income tax, state tax and sales tax. The government, designed to work in your best interest, even taxes you when you die. In order for your heirs to receive the house, car and stuff you left them, they often have to pay a probate tax. And it's pretty hefty. So my point is this. If you only work for a living without putting your money into any tax exempt investments, you will find that most of your hard-earned money goes to the government. If you do that all your life, you will feel financially stuck, because it is nearly impossible to build wealth, when you give it all to the government. So when I tell you to look for ways to avoid paying lots of taxes, what I'm saying is pay as little taxes as legally possible and no more. Put the rest of your money in places that are legally acceptable to the government. That's how the rich people keep most of the money they earn. You can keep most of your money too, if you are open and willing to learn new ways of managing your money.

YOU MUST LEARN BETTER TAX STRATEGIES

If it angers you that rich people don't pay more in taxes, don't write your congressman – join the rich. The laws allow you to behave like the rich. Rather than fight them, join them.

You see, as an employee, you pay the government its money first. In America, the employer is required by law to deduct the expected amount of taxes out of your paycheck and send it to the government for safekeeping. Those lawmakers in Washington know the average person would spend every penny and have none left to pay their taxes when April 15th rolled around. They are right about most people, but not about you. You have discipline and you know the law.

Your mission is to keep your money and let it grow using smart investing as long as you possibly can. Then, if you actually owe taxes, you pay them out of your bank account at the end of the fiscal year. Why should you let the government use your money interest free for a full year? (Imagine Jack loaning out his best pig nine months out of the year. She can't have piglets, if she ain't here.) You can't earn interest on money that you don't have.

What if there was a legal way to pay the same 33% tax on less money than you actually earned?

This concept is called tax deductions. If you own a small home based business, you automatically qualify for up to 30 deductions you didn't have before. (You can deduct part of your phone, your car, childcare, even part of your rent.) If you are reading this and you do not own some type of part-time business, go find one. Remember, you don't have to ever make a dime or turn a profit. If you can't think of anything to do, just sign up as an independent distributor for some multi-level marketing company and begin taking deductions today. (See some low start-up cost, home-based businesses at Bartbaggett.com/business.)

The more legal deductions you have, the more of your money you get to keep. And I highly recommend getting a good tax attorney and especially a tax accountant to figure your taxes at the end of the year. A tax accountant knows all the new tax deductions (and they change yearly). He knows what the government will let you get away with and what will raise a "red flag" and make the IRS suspicious. Rich people have tax experts on hand to ask advice and keep them paying the least amount in taxes while acting within the tax codes. If you are ready to act like the rich people, then it's time you surround yourself with some tax experts. They are worth the investment. If they are good, they will save you more money each year in taxes than they will cost to hire them.

How Edward Took Back His Tax Money

Here is one example of how one resourceful friend began to take back his money from Uncle Sam. Edward is a very successful Internet consultant for X-Corporation. He routinely earns $60,000 per year working in the Internet Division. He noticed that even though he was making $60,000 per year, 33% of it was going to taxes. That's $19,800 of his hard earned money. This frustrated him because such a huge chunk was getting deducted before he ever got his paycheck. After paying for the costs of living and sales tax on everything, he found that he had only a little left over to invest and

Edward As an Employee

	Paychek	Taxes -33% Deducted	Take Home Pay
Jan	5,000	1,650	3,350
Feb	5,000	1,650	3,350
Mar	5,000	1,650	3,350
April	5,000	1,650	3,350
May	5,000	1,650	3,350
June	5,000	1,650	3,350
July	5,000	1,650	3,350
August	5,000	1,650	3,350
Sept	5,000	1,650	3,350
Oct	5,000	1,650	3,350
Nov	5,000	1,650	3,350
Dec	5,000	1,650	3,350
annual	$60,000	19,800	40,200

19,800 Tax Due

20% interest of $1650 = $28 per month profit

Edward As a Corporation

	Paychek	Taxes -0% Deducted	Take Home Pay	Edwards Small Business Deductions	Adjusted Net Corporate Taxable Income	20% Interest Interest Earned On Tax Savings
Jan	5,000	0	5,000	2,000	3,000	28
Feb	5,000	0	5,000	2,000	3,000	28
Mar	5,000	0	5,000	2,000	3,000	28
April	5,000	0	5,000	2,000	3,000	28
May	5,000	0	5,000	2,000	3,000	28
June	5,000	0	5,000	2,000	3,000	28
July	5,000	0	5,000	2,000	3,000	28
August	5,000	0	5,000	2,000	3,000	28
Sept	5,000	0	5,000	2,000	3,000	28
Oct	5,000	0	5,000	2,000	3,000	28
Nov	5,000	0	5,000	2,000	3,000	28
Dec	5,000	0	5,000	2,000	3,000	28
annual	$60,000	0	$60,000		$36,000 Taxable	330 Interest

x 33%

$11,880 New Tax Due

Snapshot:

	Gross Income	Taxes	Interest	Net Income
As an Employee:	$60,000	(19,800)	0	$40,200
As a Corporation:	$60,000	($11,880)	330	$48,450

$8,250 Net Gain from Incorporating

*$8,250 x 20 years compounded = $1.8 million

347

build wealth. Then one day he met a friend, Judy, who was also an Internet consultant making $75,000 per year. Only Judy was self-employed and ran her client fees through a corporation she had formed. She showed Edward on paper how her clients paid checks directly to her company. This was her "gross" income. Judy then deducted all the business expenses she could legally deduct: partial rent of her home office, laptop computer, cell phone, company car, postage, business lunches, etc. Then after she had subtracted her expenses, what was left over was her "net" income. For an entire year, Judy received the sum total of $60,000. She deducted $24,000 worth of expenses. That left her a net income of $36,000. At the end of the year she paid 33% ($11, 880) to the IRS. Interesting. Edward had earned the exact same $60,000, but he paid $19,800 to the IRS. In other words, he paid $8,250 more than Judy to the government. Now, imagine how quickly he could have grown his wealth, had Edward had an additional $8,250 0 to invest. Well, as the story goes, Edward quit his job and for less than $500 incorporated himself. And now he's watching his money grow, because he gets to keep more and more of it each year.

The bottom line is this: If Edward had stayed at his job, he would have had little after-tax money left over to build for a solid retirement. Now, if he keeps earning at least $60,000 through his corporation for 20 years, that $8,250 tax savings would become over $1.8 million compounded at 20% per year.

If you are an employee, the government tax system is stealing your retirement.

So what are you going to do about it? Naturally, Edward found his own way to work within the tax laws. Edward didn't even have to quit the career he loved. He just changed the way he made money for the same services. I don't know how you are going to start paying yourself first. Remember to keep asking the question and you will find the answer.

OWNERSHIP VS. OCCUPATION

Let me ask you a question. Do you really care if the car you are driving is in someone else's name? What if the house you are living in is officially owned by XYZ Corporation? Does that bother you? If you really think you own something free and clear, think again. Don't pay your property tax and see who really controls your property. (The government does). Ownership is really just paper permission to occupy the premises. If a war breaks out you will quickly see who can roll their tanks through your yard. Begin focusing on "controlling" the things you want, not necessarily "owning" them. Did you know you could own 100% of a corporation stock and that still doesn't mean you own your house? Even if you lose a lawsuit, the creditor can't just take the house. The creditor would have to take control of your stock, take control of the company, then try to get your house. Corporations can provide valuable protection from lecherous lawyers, creditors, and pissed off ex-spouses. You never want to expect those negative things will actually happen, but it is wise to set up your financial house so one natural disaster doesn't wipe out the whole pig ranch.

So far I've talked about four key principles that RICH live by and the poor do not:

1. Pay Yourself First.

2. Live below your means.

Invest 10% of every dollar into your future.

Use tax deduction strategies & corporations to keep more of your earned income.

3. Have your money work for you. Don't work for your money.

If you eat the golden goose, it never lays eggs. Your money is your 24/7 non-stop staff of employees. If they are working for you,

you can relax. Learn the techniques of putting your money to work for you. (Mutual funds, real estate, stocks, bonds, joint ventures, etc.)

4. <u>The Power of Compound Interest</u> - small deposits can make your rich over time.

You can't benefit from compound interest if all your extra money is being paid to a credit card company at an interest rate of 19.9%. You are going backwards — You are being bitten, by paying compound interest to someone else. That is why your debt never seems to get paid off. This power works for and against you. Pay off your debt.

Now, remember the ancient story of *The Richest Man in Babylon* I discussed earlier. That little book places the main characters in one of the richest places and times in history. But by listening to the characters, you would think the world was full of poverty, debt, shortages, and hard work. You and I are living in the most free, most abundant, most technologically advanced, and richest time in all of history combined. Sustained wealth has never been completely dependent of who was president, what the interest rates were, or if we are in a recession or not. The principles work regardless of what is going in your world.

Arkad, the character in the book, successfully saved 10% of his income for the first year. Then, he had a big party, bought the finest clothes and drank the best wines. It was a killer party. He killed the goose. So, after a long talking to by his rich mentor - he learned his lesson. He worked another year of hard labor and he was presented with the problem of where to invest his money. He knew at just 4% he will eventually be secure... but not rich. Like many people learning a new skill, he made a bad decision. Arkad sent his gold on a trip to buy diamonds from the Far East. He trusted his friend, the chariot maker, to pick the finest diamonds in the land. He expected to triple his money. Instead, his friend brought back the finest glass replica diamonds in the Far East. They both lost their life savings. Arkad learned another costly lesson: choose your advisors wisely. Don't trust a chariot maker to buy diamonds. You would hire a diamond cutter to build a chariot.

For some reason, most people give more credence to their own circle of friend's advice than a qualified expert. They feel that sincerity and intention somehow replaces experience and actual knowledge. Go find the best advisor you can afford and follow his advise. I knew a guy who took the advice of his three divorced buddies regarding his troubled relationship with his wife. Also, he flat refused to pick up a best selling relationship book or schedule an appointment with a therapist that has counseled 400 people. That befuddles me. When it comes to tough decisions, get advise from experts and then weigh them carefully.

I know of what I speak. When I was fourteen, I started saving money for my first car. My stepfather, Tex, kept a written journal of all my savings he was holding for me. It was fun to watch my money grow. He made me a great offer. For every dollar I saved, he would match it dollar-for-dollar. That makes a big impression on a fourteen year old that money grows if saved. When I turned sixteen, my real dad, Curtis, bought me a car. I didn't need the money Tex was saving for me, so I let my savings keep growing. Years later, when I finally decided to cash out from my step dad, I got some bad news. My step Dad had lost all of my money (and his money) in the stock market. I was crushed. As I sat there feeling betrayed, I remembered the story of Arkad and his diamond scheme.

Tex was honest, educated, and had good intentions. But he wasn't a professional stock trader. My real dad told me all along to put it in a mutual fund. (My real dad was a financial planner - he was a professional. I listened to the wrong dad on that investment.) Truthfully, Tex earned thousands on good investments over the year. Professional stock traders have flops, too. Spreading your money out over 30 different stocks lowers your risk. I'm sure you've heard the phrase "Don't put all your eggs in one basket." A mutual fund does that for you. Diversify and invest a little of your money in a variety of stocks.

Before you jump to conclusions about my dear stepfather, Tex, the story doesn't end there. A few years later, Tex surprised me with an envelope full of cash. He felt responsible for my savings, so he has paid me back every penny out of his own pocket. Yes, he doubled my initial amount. To this day, I deeply appreciate the integrity and responsibility he took. And, he didn't have to pay me back. I made the investment decisions. I took responsibility that I lost the money. I learned three lessons in one: integrity, compassion, and financial risk.

Key Principle: Choose your advisors carefully.

Before I wrap up this brief and incomplete discussion on investments, there is one more key concept I must cover: Assets. What is an asset?

When studying for my business degree at Pepperdine University, my accounting teachers told me very clearly what was an asset and what was a liability. However, I'm beginning to change my mind. According to my new financial hero, Robert Kiyosaki, they have it all wrong.

In his book *Rich Dad Poor Dad*, Kiyosaki says this, "You must know the difference between an asset and a liability, and buy assets. If you want to be rich, this is all you need to know. It is Rule #1. It is the only rule. This may sound absurdly simple, but most people have no idea how profound this rule is. Most people struggle financially because they do not know the difference between an asset and a liability. Rich people buy assets. The poor and middle class acquire liabilities, but they think they are assets."

I remember thoroughly hating accounting class. I remember now the reason I hated it was I was always confused as to which column the numbers went under. It was tough for me to learn the rules for the credit and debit column. I'm not the only one who found it challenging. I realize now why it wasn't so clear.

Can you tell me if a house payment is an income or expense?

Can you tell me if a car is an asset or a liability?

Can you tell me if a $30,000 payment goes in the credit or debit column?

The answer to all of the above questions is ... both answers are correct depending on who's paperwork you are looking at. To the landlord, the house payment is income. To the renter, the same payment is an expense. A car is an asset on your balance sheet, but it costs you money every month. Hmmm. A $30,000 payment goes into the credit column if you are getting it, debit column if you are writing the check. So, how do you keep up?

Leaning on Robert Kiyosaki's rich dad's wisdom, I've adopted entirely new definitions of assets and liabilities. His rich dad said, "An asset is something that puts money in my pocket. A liability is something that takes money out of my pocket."

Remember, rich people buy assets. Poor and middle class people buy liabilities, and they think they are assets. A perfect example is the car in your own driveway. You might think that is an asset. But, using Kiyosaki's definition, it is a liability. Unless your car actually puts money in your pocket, it is a liability. Oh, your house is definitely an asset. My banker tells me it is my best asset. Here is a fact you may not like. Your house is your banker's asset. It is your liability. Why? Your mortgage payments put money into his pockets, out of your pockets. It will only become an asset the day you sell it for a profit. That is only if you sell it for a profit. If you sell your house for a loss, then it is definitely a liability … money out of your pocket. Whew. Hard truth to hear. Even some of the experts have this one misinformed.

It makes sense. Think about the first ancient principle of wealth we discussed. Do not work for your money. Make your money work for you. Your assets have to work for you, not against you. Money is just the form of energy that buys assets or buys liabilities. Money under your mattress is neutral. Money in a mutual fund is an asset. Money in your gas tank is a liability.

According to Kiyosaki, some common assets of the rich are: stocks, bonds, notes, rental property, businesses, and intellectual property. Take a moment and redraw your financial balance sheet to reflect the new definitions. You might find you are not as far out of the rat race as you once thought.

A Sample Wealthy Person's Real Balance Sheet

Assets	Liabilities
stocks	my automobile
cash in savings	my home (until the day I sell it.)
	my kids
rental houses	my clothes
IRA retirement fund	food

Most people think because you own a house or a car you have a valuable asset. It is usually the bank's asset. According to the new definition of an asset, if something doesn't earn money for you - it is not really an asset.

THE SECRET TO EXITING THE RAT RACE

The secret is when your passive income exceeds your expenses! That's it. Your assets give you passive residual income. Want to be your own boss?

When I ask people what they want in life, one of the most common phrases I hear is: "I want to own my own business." You have probably thought about this, or said it, one time or another in your life. After reading this section, you might question the merits of this goal. When people say they want their own business, they are really telling me a list of what they want and what they don't want. They have a false belief being their own boss will immediately deliver all the wants and eliminate all the don't wants.

TYPICAL REASON FOR WANTING TO OWN YOUR OWN BUSINESS:

WANT	DON'T WANT
More money	Financial struggle
More free time	A schedule
Pay less in taxes	Government getting paid first
More variety	Boredom
Sense of ownership	Work for someone else
Sense of purpose	A meaningless job
Feel significant	Feel insignificant
Creative outlet	No creativity
Certainty	Uncertainty

For many people, owning their own business is a giant leap in lifestyle compared to the option of working for someone else as paid labor. However, if you want to be rich, self-employment is not your outcome. It should not be your ultimate goal. If anything, self-employment is just the next step along the path to financial abundance. Let me explain.

Remember the financial wisdom that states "Do not work for your money, make your money work for you?" If you simply exchange one boss for another - you are still an employee. In fact, when you start your own business, you are the worker, the boss, the accountant, the sales team, the marketing department, and the trash detail. You have traded one job for six jobs. In exchange, you do get the emotional benefits of freedom, significance, variety, creativity and ownership. Also, you take back control of your tax situation. There are many other benefits, too. However, the reason over 80% of small businesses fail within the first five years in the United States is because rarely does one person have the skill or energy to fill all six roles. You might make excellent widgets, but have poor skills selling them. Or you might sell lots of widgets, but you can't manage the cash flow.

Small business management aside, what is the real purpose of working? I think there are two purposes: 1.) Become rich as fast as possible. 2.) Spend your day doing something that you love to do. Have passion for your career and it won't seem like work.

In my humble experience, once you have reached the first goal (financial independence), finding work that fills you with passion and fulfillment is easy. The challenge for most people is finding a great paying job that meets their inner most emotional desires. Listen carefully, even if you find that great job... you are still not guaranteed wealth. You might be able to create a high cash flow and a way to spend your day working a job that you love. But, you are still a few steps away from financial freedom.

Here is the definition of financial freedom: You are financially independent the moment that the profit generated by your assets (passive income) exceeds your expenses on a consistent and predictable basis. Notice that nowhere in that definition is the word job, work, career, etc. The basic model of financial abundance is not dependent on employees and employers. These two methods are really the starting point.

Work is basically exchanging your time for some amount of money. As long as you work for money, you will be somebody's employee. (If you are your own boss, you are your own employee.) The way to gain riches is to have your money go to work for you.

If you are a bit confused, this diagram should solidify the point I am hammering home. As you read this today, ask yourself which of the following categories you fit best into?

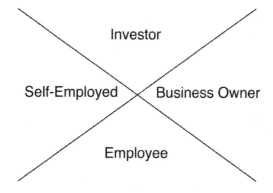

a. Employee

b. Self-Employed

c. Business Owner

d. Investor

Most self-employed people assume they are business owners. They are not. If you cannot leave the country for at least one year and come back to a business that is worth more than when you left it... you are not a business owner - you are an employee.

You must begin to think like an "investor" or a "business owner" in order to become financially free. Don't get me wrong. You can keep working as long as you find it fulfilling, but don't confuse your work with your financial purpose: acquiring assets that earn you money.

Residual Income > Expenses = Financial Freedom

Most people think that if they save enough money to quit their job they are free. Not true. If your assets are not paying you enough profit monthly to cover your expenses, without dipping into your cash savings, you are just on vacation between jobs. If you pour all your savings into your own business, you become self-employed with the potential for massive profit or bankruptcy. If you take the same money and buy assets, you can earn an immediate positive cash flow and move yourself into the two quadrants that the rich live in.

Have you ever noticed that the wealthiest people have the least amount of titles on their business card? I used to wonder why. Now I realize that because super wealthy people are not employees, they have no title. They are in the business of buying and selling assets. Those assets could be businesses, houses, stocks, etc. Because they no longer have the employee mentality, they don't have a flashy title on their business card. Less is more.

I am not dissuading you from self-employment. As an entrepreneur, I like this life. However, I have learned self-employment is not the easiest or shortest route to wealth. Look at all the options.

Most people believe that owning their own business is the shortest route to wealth. It might be for you if you become an educated business person. If you are determined to run your own business, please read Michael Gerber's book *The E-Myth*. In his book, Mr. Gerber outlines a very clear model for running your business by successfully replacing yourself at every job position. He illustrates clearly that as long as the business depends on you, it cannot replicate itself and be self-sufficient. Gerber explains how to grow a business from the self-employed quadrant into the business owner quadrant.

I was washing my car one day at one of those self-service car washes that requires you to put in four quarters to spray wash your car. I never thought about who owned those little self-operating businesses until I saw a man dumping hundreds of quarters out of the machine into a large bucket. As I visited with him, he explained that he purchased this little car wash for less than $20,000. He spent about one day a week collecting the money. All the other duties, such as refilling the soap, cleaning the stalls, and repairing the machines, were handled by his one employee. He said he gets the money himself if he is in town. He thinks his employees are honest, but buckets of cash would be an easy temptation for anyone. As I discovered, this little car wash in my neighborhood grosses this guy about $1500 per week in income. So he invests a few hours a week in an asset that earns him a huge residual income. Here is a guy who gets the value of being a "business owner". This asset pays him cash. If he could only find a trustworthy person to collect the money, he would be a pure business owner and not even have to spend an hour working as an employee. All in all, he made a great business decision. There are businesses you could buy in your own neighborhood. How many car washes did you pass by this week? Start looking for assets!

Remember, these quadrants are not a ladder. You don't have to experience one to make the transition into the other. Most people graduate from one to the next because of cash flow restraints. You can take a short cut if you make up your mind to do so. But you have to make a decision that is your outcome.

DANIEL RETIRES AT AGE 28

I know one person who took the shortcut to financial freedom starting the day after graduating college. Daniel Tibeto was a close friend of mine while we attended Pepperdine University. He knew something when he was 19 that I didn't learn until I was 29... the secret of wealth is buying assets. I spent my twenties moving slowly from quadrant to quadrant. Daniel spent his early twenties buying assets. He spent his late twenties in semi-retirement with his lovely wife and their new baby. Hmmm. I wonder why I didn't learn this earlier. Daniel was very clear on his intent. His only purpose from the day he graduated college was financial freedom. He knew that the only way to get financial freedom was own assets that paid him a monthly residual income. So, he basically skipped the whole job thing. He skipped the whole self-employment thing. He focused on one thing only: buying assets.

For two to three straight years, he lived in a crappy apartment in Santa Monica, California existing on nothing more than peanut butter sandwiches and tuna fish! He drove the same 1970 yellow Karman-Gia car he owned since high school. He got up early every day and went to bed late. He and his partner were searching for real estate deals in the Los Angeles area. They knew if they found the right deal, they would have cash flow for life. After two years of missed deals, failed closings, and struggle... they signed their first deal. It was a real estate development deal that turned ugly. After a year of struggle, both Daniel and his partner lost several hundred thousand dollars and had to get real jobs to pay off the debt. It was a big risk that didn't pay off. However, Daniel relays that bad deal taught him to be more educated, more prudent, more calculating, and be a better investor. Daniel didn't give up. He took a part-time job as a real estate appraiser to learn about the things he didn't know the first time. After another few years, he started risking his own money again.

He found a good deal on a pair of houses in Santa Monica. It wasn't a huge deal, but it created enough cash flow to look for bigger deals. Then, disaster struck. A major earthquake totaled his one piece of property. He turned disaster into opportunity by using the insurance money and a loan to convert this old piece of property into a sixteen-unit apartment complex. This one deal still earns Daniel and his wife over $10,000 a month in residual positive cash flow. You might say he got lucky because of the earthquake. Nope. Luck finds those who are prepared and ready. Or another way to put it: preparation meets opportunity. If the earthquake hadn't hit, it might have taken another three years to earn the cash or qualify for the credit to do a bigger deal. In any case, Danny would still have been retired by now if he chose not to work. The stroke of luck just speeded up the path. Daniel was clear on his outcome - buy assets and retire young. He could have just quit after the first loss. It set him back a few years. All-in-all, he still took the fast track to residual income. He was willing to live below his means, sacrifice his ego, learn from his mistakes, and work toward one goal: positive cash flow. Now, it is time for you to create your own plan.

Key Points:

1. Avoid getting stuck as an employee who earns about as much as your expenses.

2. Owning a business is different from being self-employed. If you can't leave the country for a year or more and come back to see the business is worth more than when you left - you are self-employed.

3. Wealth is created by owning assets. Only by living in the "business owner" and "investor" quadrants can you build and sustain wealth.

4. Be detached and honest about which quadrant you are living in. Don't get so emotionally attached to owning your own business

that you let it drain your cash reserves. Your "nest egg" is for buying assets. If your own business is not creating positive cash flow - it is a liability.

By the way, the definition of rat race and the concept of cash flow have never been illustrated better than in Robert Kiyosaki's worth-every-penny board game called *Cash Flow*. I highly highly recommend getting this game. When you play the game with your family or your friends, you will be forever affected. The principle is simple: get out of the rat race. Build investments that create passive income to support your living without having to work for it. The goal sounds simple, but the execution is something 90% of the world never does in real life. The way you get out of the rat race is to buy enough "assets" so that the cash flow from these "assets" surpasses all your living expenses. When that occurs, you no longer need a job. You are a full time investor. You are financially free.

If you don't understand money, how are you going to be comfortable being rich? Make money your partner in life.

Other Resources:

You can find out more about *Cash Flow* and other recommended financial resources at our webpage.

www.bartbaggett.com/cashflow

www.bartbaggett.com/finance

Universal Truth # 18

God wants you to be rich.

CHAPTER 16

THE SPIRITUALITY OF PROSPERITY
ABUNDANCE MENTALITY & PROSPERITY THINKING

I'm going to ask you to mentally stretch a bit during this chapter. I'm a very practical guy. If I can see it, touch it, or even feel it, then I can be convinced of its existence. However, the spiritual aspect of money does not have such an immediate feedback mechanism as to prove it is accurate or true. I suppose what I am about to describe is like describing God. Evidence is all around, but it takes a bit of faith to really grasp the whole thing.

When I use the term Spirituality, I don't mean religious. The concept I am introducing will apply to any religion or anyone who has no religion. In fact, physics actually plays an important role in the theory of Prosperity. It's hard to argue with physics.

Did you know that according to the laws of physics matter never actually disappears? Things are just energy in various forms of movement or non-movement. Energy can change forms. The most common example is the molecular structure H_2O. One part hydrogen and 2 parts oxygen is called ice when it finds itself in an environment below 32 degrees Fahrenheit. If you put the piece of ice on a warm stove it becomes liquid (water). Then, if you heat it up, it changes forms again into gas. This makes sense even to me as a guy who never took a physics course. But, when the scientists go on to explain that everything on the planet eventually changes form and recycles itself, it boggles my mind. If you think about the amazing planet we are on ... it makes sense. There is no huge trash dump where things we need anymore just go and pile up. Our planet is a living ecosystem that produces and consumes and changes forms over thousands of years. Our trash, our homes, our exhaust, and even our bodies eventually are recycled into the earth. So, if you get out of your own small body for a minute and look at the world as a whole: you realize you are just part of one big system. You can fight it, but in the end you are part of the one-ness with the planet.

This one-ness is the key to abundance thinking. If you have the firm belief that there are unlimited resources to take care of you, then you think, act, and speak in a very different way than if you believe in scarcity. As human beings we have an ego that creates separation from each other and the planet. Since our ego drives us to meet our basic needs (food, water, reproduction, etc.) it makes sense the ego separates us from other humans in an effort to guarantee we get our needs met first. The ego isn't very spiritual. So, to move beyond our basic ego needs and into prosperity consciousness, we must imagine the universe as a part of ourselves.

When you realize that money is just a form of energy exchanging hands, it loses it mystery. Money is just a form of energy that some government printed on paper. These days, money isn't even printed on paper. Right now, where you sit, there are billions of dollars being sent through your body in the form of radio waves, TV signals, and satellite information. Even worldwide banks transfer billions of dollars nightly around the world in the form of simple electrical pulses. You are already in the flow of more wealth than you could possibly spend. The trick is to tune your body to the right channel so you can take your turn directing the money. Really, that's what you do, direct. You don't ever really possess money or things anyway. If you look at the planet from outer space, do you really think the house, the car, or money in your pocket is yours? No. You are just occupying them during your short stay on this planet. Clothes will be purchased, food bought, and money spent by someone. Commerce is just a big swap-meet of people exchanging energy for things. From this perspective, it makes sense that you have as much "right" to direct the flow of money as anyone else walking this big rock. Right?

When you lose your attachment to owning, possessing, or controlling things - you open your mind up to the free-flow of money spiraling into your life in unexpected ways. All you really want to do is direct the flow of money into places of your own choosing. When you see yourself as simply a person who redirects a portion of the billions of dollars a day that flies around this planet, the job of being wealthy seems so much easier. You are just a traffic cop on the highway of wealth.

Now, in order to begin to "see " the billions of dollars that are flying around your head as we speak, you must adjust your financial vision receptors. People stuck in poverty consciousness are blind to the fact we live on a planet of total abundance. They only see scarcity.

DO YOU HAVE FINANCIAL GLAUCOMA?

Imagine an overflowing river of fresh mountain water flowing beneath your feet. You can dip in and sip water anytime you want. That river has been flowing since birth and you expect it to be flowing long after you die. If that is your reality, do you need to fight over the water with your brothers and sisters? People burdened with financial glaucoma can't see the flowing river of money all around them. In fact, poverty consciousness forces people to see only drops of water where there are buckets. Scarcity thinking feels a draught coming when there are rainstorms over the mountain. Scarcity thinking changes a happy loving river community with unlimited water resources into a miserable, thirsty, water-hoarding town of bickering siblings who fight and sue each other over buckets of water. When people feel scarcity of a needed resource (love,

"The source of all wealth is giving."

— Buddha

money, shelter, etc.) their ego takes over and creates struggle or conflict.

Look at your model of the world and ask yourself honestly this question, "Is money like an abundant river that can be shared by all with plenty left over for people downstream?" Or, "Is money like a trickling stream that should be damned up, fought over, and stored for the future? "

If you see the flow of money like a trickling stream, you've got to change your thinking.

Author Stuart Wilde says that our ego separates us from the flow. Most of us would always give the last sip of water or the last bite of food to our close family members. We feel connected, so we take care of our own. In fact, just at a family picnic with baskets of food - we are generous and loving. "No, you take the last chicken wing. Oh! I insist, you drink the last Root Beer, I'll take the Dr. Pepper." There is an unwritten rule that our family shares all our resources, and there will always be enough if we stick together. Hmm. What if you could imagine yourself as part of the entire universal family? What if you imagined that everyone on the planet and everything was pulling for you to get your piece of the pie? Would that change your attitude?

THE UNIVERSAL LAW OF GIVING

If you knew absolutely beyond a shadow of a doubt that you will never go hungry ... would you be more generous with your own food? If you knew you had millions in the bank, would you be more generous with your money?

Most of us have been taught since we were age two that you get back what you give, but many can't see past today to reap the rewards of their sowing. Most religions teach that there is a universal cycle that gives us back what we put forth. The eastern belief systems call it Karma. You get what you give. Yet when it comes to money, we feel the pressure of today is more pertinent than the Universal Law that says we will get back tomorrow what we give today.

Have Abundance in Love, too

The same concept of abundance can be applied to other areas of your life besides finance. The term "jealousy" is in direct conflict with abundance thinking. Jealousy is based on a fear of loss of love. You can only fear a loss of love if you think the love in question is limited and finite. If you feel love is in abundance and always flowing, you wouldn't feel threatened by your spouse loving another, too. I'm not suggesting it is always easy to be fearless and jealousy-free. But, because we attract the most dominant thoughts into our lives, fearing loss ... brings loss. Giving love brings love. Sharing wealth brings wealth.

People who naturally live in this state of "abundance thinking" see the world as a place of unlimited resources. Therefore, the behavior, thoughts, and fears that rule a scarcity thinker's mind don't enter the thinker's reality. Effectively, they think differently. And, as you already know by now, thoughts do create our reality.

Belief Systems

Think back to the chapter in which I discussed belief systems. Prosperity thinking is rooted in a few core beliefs. If you don't already believe these statements to be true, start asking your higher self to start providing you evidence so you can believe them. Your beliefs create your reality.

1. There is enough money for everyone to be wealthy.

2. There will always be more coming my way tomorrow.

3. I will always have my needs met. (Faith)

4. In every profitable business transaction, there is a way to make it win-win for everyone concerned.

5. All the money that I give comes back to me ten-fold.

MODELING ABUNDANCE THINKING

Many people who follow Jesus Christ's teachings talk of something called "Christ Consciousness." They are constantly asking themselves how Jesus Christ would respond to their situation. When they find themselves in a situation that requires a decision, they ask themselves what Christ would do. If they think they know the answer, they act as Christ would act. This is just another form of modeling. Buddhists do the same thing with their image of Buddha. Muslims do the same thing with their image of Mohammed. If you are attempting to stick true to a belief system, it is useful to have one individual whom you can model. When I encounter situations in which I become angry or feel oppressed, I ask myself how Gandhi would react. I act as I feel Gandhi would have and I usually feel at peace. When modeling the rich and happy, you might pick one person whom you admire and ask yourself how she or he would act. This will guide you to the right actions to take with the intent of maintaining prosperity thinking.

THE SECRETS OF SPIRITUAL CASH FLOW

If the money is just billions of energy particles flying through the air, what does it take for you to reach out and direct your share into your pocket? To get your turn directing the energy flow, you must get yourself into the flow. There is a simple metaphor to illustrate this point. Imagine you are on a shoulder of a major interstate watching cars speeding by at 70 miles per hour. You want to get onto the road, and you are thinking about the best strategy. Clearly, it wouldn't be wise to just throw your body in front of a moving truck. The best way to get yourself onto the highway of wealth is to crank your car up and start rolling. If you are moving too fast, you can't enter. If you are moving too slow, you will get hit from behind. The easiest way to join the flow is to match the speed of the other cars and slide right in as one of the team. You must get your thinking moving into the "flow" of money.

The opposite of flow is struggle. Struggle not only stops the cash-flow, but is emotionally draining. Struggle causes a lot of pain because it involves a lot of negative emotion. Struggle is also a lot of hard work. Stuart Wilde says in his book *Life Was Never Meant to Be a Struggle*, "Struggle is effort laced with emotion. As humans, we are required to exert effort in order to get things done. So if you're cycling up a hill delivering loaves of bread, you will expend calories pedaling. Effort is natural, but when one's energy expenditure gets wrapped up in loads of negative emotions, that's when you flip to the unnatural—from effort to struggle. At that point you should pull back and ask yourself loads of simple questions, questions that highlight silliness."

One of the reasons I enjoy reading Stuart Wilde's books so much is his love of humor, silliness, and tomfoolery as a mechanism to live in joy and abundance. I resonate with irreverent humor. I think seriousness is a mental disease. The end result is a living death. Get over yourself. If you can't laugh at yourself, you will have to start enjoying people laughing at you, because they will be!

If you find yourself struggling, here are some questions you might ask yourself to instantly change your focus.

What little adjustment can I make to get things moving?

Are my plans realistic?

Am I too attached to the outcome?

Would I be happier if I were a blind horny-toad instead of a human?

Am I missing some key component that could make this easier?

If I'm missing a piece of the jigsaw, what does that piece look like?

How silly would I look in a pink top hat and a tutu singing *The Sound of Music*?

Okay, I sprinkled two of those questions with silly statements to lighten you up. Asking empowering questions is a fantastic way to end the negative emotion called struggle.

DO YOU BELIEVE IN MAGIC?

The universe is a magical and mysteriously connected place. I am constantly amazed at the unexpected connections that occur around the planet. Did you know a volcano blast in Hawaii can affect fish breeding in Japan? Did you know a two-degree change in the South Pole can flood beaches worldwide by a rising tide? Have you ever been on a plane sitting next to exactly the person you needed to meet? Have you ever picked up the phone and the person you were about to call was already on the line calling you? Have you ever looked down and found money right under your feet? When these things happen, you are in the flow. Some call this synchronicity.

The best selling book *The Celestine Prophecy* illustrates a belief that "There are no coincidences." As I stated in an earlier chapter, the belief that holds "everything happens for a reason" is an empowering belief that shifts you from victim-mode to cause-mode. When you put yourself at cause you regain control. Prosperity consciousness takes this concept beyond personal control. Prosperity consciousness actually insinuates that you give up direct control and put faith in the "universe" to mysteriously deliver to your doorstep what you need. If you truly believe abundance pervades the universe, then it makes sense that some of that gold will show up on

Universal Truth #19

Everything Happens for a Reason

your doorstep sooner or later. Your job is to cure yourself of the financial glaucoma and see the opportunities as they present themselves.

Get into the flow of money. Sometimes being in the flow feels like some kind of magic. Talk to any stage magician about what magic really is. Stage magic is a combination of timing, information, and skill. The universe does magical thinks all the time - only the people watching are surprised by the miracles. The universe expected the outcome. Expect miracles. Be prepared.

I call living in "the flow" the ability to live your life in a synergy of events that seem to almost happen randomly with fantastic results. This past year has been amazingly effortless for me. I have literally worked half as hard as any year in the past and have had better results. Even in areas such as my love life have been abundant and effortless. I met an amazing woman who literally showed up on my doorstep. A friend of mine parked at my house on a date with her. Months later, she showed up again to ask me out on a date. I made no conscious effort but created a wonderful romance. Effortless.

Recently, I have been asking how I can find a nice flat in New York City as a second residence. Without ever calling one real estate agent, I have had two random people mention in passing they had accommodations in New York City that would be perfect for me. So, again I created a residence effortlessly. What's more, both situations are far below retail rental rates. I asked. I expected miracles. I looked for miracles. I created effortless prosperity. Thoughts and intent are powerful things.

Even parts of this book have been effortless. After working months with an editor that missed deadlines and produced mediocre work, my long-time friend Brian Moreland surprised me with an offer I couldn't refuse. He came to me asking if he could contribute to this book project as the editor. Wow. Lucky me.

I haven't even sent one press release out about this book (which I am writing at this moment) and I have writers from two of America's most influential magazines calling me wanting to do a book review. How does this happen? I feel like I'm in the flow so it doesn't surprise me anymore. And, I'm gracious and appreciative. I have the feeling I am one lucky guy. I think we are all lucky. I just decided to live in my natural state of abundance and good-luck. The above random events can logically be traced to their source. One writer read the article about me in *Biography* Magazine. Then, she looked on the Internet for my telephone number, etc. Yes, that's the logic process for this random event. However, there is something more. People can sense when you are in this "zone" and they want to be a near you. When you are in "the flow" people and things are magnetically attracted to you. You "attract" instead of "repel."

If you have ever been single, you know the truth about dating that states, "Women can smell desperation a mile away." When you don't need a date, you get lots of offers. If you seem desperate and lonely, people avoid you like the plague. Money is attracted to more money. It is basically like the financial rapport. Like attracts like. Be like money, money will find you.

HOW TO TURN THINKING INTO MANIFESTATION

Manifesting abundance doesn't necessarily happen overnight. I have mentioned how powerful our mind really is. Because your mind is really a creating machine, one might think it just manifests anything in an instance. We are actually lucky there is a small delay between what we think about and its manifestation into reality. This delay is useful because most of us have such poor thinking skills our lives would be filled with monsters, terror, and our other darkest fears. Your mind can only give you what you focus on. Therefore, the laws of manifestation delay your gratification by asking that you invest some *thought-time* into what you really want.

In the coming chapters, I present a very effective process for speeding up the manifestation process using a simple closed eye meditation exercise. Manifesting what you want takes a combination of proper thought and well executed action.

I remember meeting a man on my most recent trip to India who was fasting for world peace. He fasted for one full year on nothing but boiled water - quite incredible. However, about ten days after he ended his fast, India and Pakistan tested nuclear bombs in this man's own backyard. I began to wonder if meditation alone is enough to change the planet. You must eventually take ACTION. Getting "in the flow" takes precise thinking and good decisions. Then when you are firmly "in the flow," you will notice the opportunities come to you. And then you take action to make your dreams a reality.

Thoughts ---> Opportunities ---> Actions ---> Results

So let me elaborate on a few principles to change your thinking in order to increase your abundance mentality.

After you become aware of these key principles, I'm going to give you action items to start implementing them. Then at the end of this book, I'll teach you a mental time-line exercise where you will close your eyes and begin to reprogram yourself at the unconscious level. Let's face it … the difference between successful people and unsuccessful people is the quality of their thoughts. Likewise the difference between happy people and unhappy people is the quality of their thoughts.

WEALTH ATTRACTS WEALTH

Let me ask you this: If I was a Financial Planner and I asked you to invest your life savings with me, and I drove up in a broken-down car with 10-year-old shoes on, would you invest your money in my deal? Probably not. If I drove up in a brand new Mercedes and wore a Rolex watch, would you be more likely to invest money with me? Yes, you would be more open because I am visibly in the flow. Wealth attracts wealth.

You don't have to be flamboyant with your spending. In fact, I don't recommend doing this with any intention of other people noticing. This is for your brain to notice only. Definitely don't buy more than you can afford, but realize every time you pinch and save, and make a decision based on your belief that there's not enough money in the world, you send a signal to the world that says, "No, there's not enough money. I might not earn anymore. Money is scarce."

It's similar to the concept of dieting. When I've done research with overweight people, I found that a lot of the severely over-weight people actually only eat one meal a day. Now that's interest-ing. You would think, "If someone is obese, they probably eat three, four, and five meals a day," but that's usually not the case. Most obese people only eat one meal per day. They are starving them-selves into obesity.

What happens is this: When someone only eats one meal per day, a message is sent to the brain that says, "I'm only getting fed once a day. I'm going to hold onto every bit of fuel (fat) that I pos-sibly can. I don't know when the next meal is coming." Therefore the body goes into hibernation phase - holding onto all the fat. It is only after months of dietary changes that the body finally realizes it will be "safe" to let go of the fat because all the nutrients it needs to survive are coming in daily. Then, the person's metabolism changes, they exercise with ease, and the natural body begins to appear as the fat dissolves. The natural state of your body is to be fit, healthy and energetic.

Likewise, your natural state of being is to be wealthy, abundant, and in the flow. Don't fool yourself into holding onto pennies when $100 bills are passing by you right now.

THE MORE MONEY YOU SPEND, THE MORE MONEY YOU RECEIVE

So your financial awareness and your unconsciousness about money work the same way. If you hold onto every little penny, you become rigid. You become obsessed with poverty; and the foremost thought is what you get. If you're always thinking, "There's not enough money," that will be what's true, and you will get that reality. So instead, simply get into the flow. Realize that the more you spend, the more you receive. You will have to spend money to make money. There is a flow. When you get into that flow, money comes to you naturally.

I can remember many days when I spent all my money on bills. I found myself thinking, "How am I going to pay the next bill? I have no event happening or no promotion going on." But I was in the flow. I knew that it would come in. Sure enough, the next day someone would call and spend money buying my books and tapes. This would be somebody who seemed to have just mysteriously shown up. I didn't advertise to them. I didn't cold-call that person. The universe just handed me some money, and I said, "Thank you." When you are in the flow, miracles happen daily.

ADOPT THE BELIEF SYSTEM THAT MONEY ALWAYS SHOWS UP AT THE RIGHT TIME

Some call it faith. Others call it "expectations." You have to have the belief system that money always comes to you. When you do, you will be in the "flow" ... the cash flow. When you think about it, most people can find evidence in their own life that money

Universal Truth #20

Donating a percentage of your income to Charity will return to you ten-fold in magical and rewarding ways.

shows up when you really need it. Some people just create a "crisis" in order to attract cash. Change your belief to "Money always shows up when I want it."

THE 10% RULE

Now I'll share another tip that the rich do to stay in the flow. They give at least 10% of all they earn to charity. That's right. 10% of every penny they earn goes back to the universe to help others. Imagine the great karma you bring yourself when you give your money away to selflessly help others. Ever heard the saying, "What goes around, comes around?" Well, in the case of money, there is a spiritual law that says whatever you give comes back to you ten fold. That means if you donate $100 to charity, your goodwill will come back to you in the form of $1000. I've tested this theory over and over and it works. When I first heard about donating 10% of my income, I thought no way can I give that much money away each month. All I kept thinking were all the things that 10% could buy me. What if I had a tight month and I needed that extra money to pay bills? The fear got to me.

Well, I decided to go on faith and give away the 10% even in my slow business months. What I discovered was there is an incredible joy to helping others. Suddenly I could hand a few bucks to a street person and feel richer. I could donate money to a children's hospital, knowing that my money was going to make some kids very happy. After a while, I didn't even miss the extra money. You will be surprised at how easily you can live off 90% of your income. Not only did I easily get along without that 10%, but I also noticed that my income was increasing each month. Hmmm. I gave away money to help the universe, and my income increased. Interesting. Now that I've been donating 10% for a few years, I am a firm believer in sharing wealth with the universe. And I truly believe this is one of the key ways of staying in the flow.

My friend Brian is also big into donating 10% and has proven over and over that any money he gives returns to him ten fold. One night Brian was walking through downtown Dallas and a homeless couple approached him. Because Brian is used to giving 10% he didn't try to avoid them or ignore them. The couple looked in dire need of some help. They asked Brian if he could spare $9 so they could stay in a shelter for the night. Brian looked into his wallet and saw he had one ten-dollar bill left. He gave them the ten dollars and a ride to the shelter. The next day Brian's dad gave him a lottery card just for the heck of it, and Brian won $100, exactly ten times what he had given the homeless couple the night before.

The universe works in mysterious ways and seems to favor those who are charitable. Donating 10% is the most direct route to train your brain in believing "I have plenty of money." This act alone will change your belief system.

PREPARE FOR ABUNDANCE BY CLEARING SPACE

I have this comedy routine that I do occasionally that pokes fun at poor people living in the back woods of some of our Southern States. I figure if the comedian Jeff Foxworthy can make fun of the hillbillies so can I. After all, I did grow up in Texas. Invariably, I make reference to the stereotype that poor people tend to keep broken down cars in the front yard and let the weeds grow up around the wheels.

I also noticed from first hand experience that really really poor people never throw anything away. They even save hubcaps for a 1965 Dart ... just in case. My dad grew up in the backwoods of East Texas poor as dirt. I think it was his serious "lack" of things that created the clutter he still lives in today. I would have a hard time remembering the last time he actually parked a car inside the garage. In every house we have ever lived, the garage has been overstuffed with so much junk the garage door barely closes. We weren't even poor - but the same belief system he learned when he lived in a one bedroom wooden house raising five siblings still runs him. "There isn't enough. I must hold onto everything. It costs too much to replace it." Now, Dad has actually gotten much better in the last few years as he and his financial situation have matured. Clutter is a sign of an impoverished mind.

I have had the privilege of visiting many ultra rich estates and houses. For most ... less is more. Their lawns are big and well manicured. They have room to park the cars in the garage. Even the house is furnished in a surprisingly sparse and elegant manner. And, of course, there are no broken down cars in the yard or washers or dryers on the front porch. If you are firmly living in abundance, you TRASH what you don't use frequently and repair or replace things that break down. If you have the core belief that more stuff will always be coming your way— you throw the crap away and make space for the new stuff!

The opposite of clutter is open space. In the Chinese art of Feng Shui, "space clearing" is the term practitioners use to clear clutter and restore the natural energy flow to a room. Feng Shui sounds like a martial art but it is really the ancient art of changing your environment to improve your life. Developed in China several thousand years ago, it is a proven science that helps you fine tune the energies of your home or workplace to resonate with your unique energies. You do this by arranging your furniture, art and plants to create a balanced and harmonious space to conduct your life.

This sounded a bit hokey to me the first time I heard of it. However, after spending time analyzing the recommendations of my feng shui consultant —they made sense. I'm not sure how painting my wall red or putting a water fountain by my door brings me success. But I know my "thoughtful intent" has some effect on my being successful. From a totally practical angle, the act of "clearing clutter" is both emotionally and physically refreshing. I notice this even at my desk. When I put all the loose papers in labeled folders and start the day with a clear desk, new opportunities find me in a state of readiness. If your garage is filled with junk, where are you going to park your new car? Clearing space prepares your mind for the flow of new forms of energy. (Things, money, jobs, people, etc.)

I bet if you were to go into your garage or rummage through you closets, you'd find clothes you never wear anymore, books you no longer read, items like old TV sets that are broken, but you've been hanging onto them anyway. All this stuff is just cluttering up your life and blocking the flow of prosperity. Part of living with abundance mentality is being able to let go of material things. Space Clearing is simply getting rid of stuff that takes up space in your life, so that new stuff can fill that empty space.

For instance, let's say you've been wanting a new television set. Your old TV is on the blink but it isn't totally broken. You're tired of it, but don't think you have enough money to go buy a brand new one. Here is how you turn this situation into an opportunity to operate in the "flow." You take that TV to the back of your car and drive around until you find someone to give it to. Yes. Just give it away! This sends a huge signal that there is an abundance of the TV energy in your life. Now, every time you look at that blank hole on your entertainment center, you will start asking how you can get a new TV. You might find one just appears to you with no money out of pocket. You might stop by a garage sale and find one for sale or a friend of yours may suddenly decide to give you theirs.

I give stuff away all the time. It seems magical, as soon as I give away an old item, a new one shows up almost immediately. That's the way the universe works when you live in abundance. Heck, this year alone, I've been given three sofas! I keep giving them away and people keep giving me newer and better ones! I don't even need a new sofa. (Isn't that the point? Prosperity flows TO those who don't need it.) Create a vacuum by your actions and you will attract things to you.

I recommend you spend a day and clear out all your clutter. Go through your home and office clearing out all the stuff that is either broken or you haven't used in over a year. Throw away all the junk and give any descent stuff to charity (The Salvation Army will send a truck to your doorstep to pick it up.) You're helping out other people and you're clearing space for new items to come to you. You might even like the feeling of being clutter-free so much, that you don't fill all the space. That open space sure is attractive.

I recently dumped pieces of furniture and all sorts of items I didn't really like. I had so much space that Dad actually put some of his junk at my house while I was out of town! Ha. Open space attracts. Make sure your clutter loving family doesn't have a house key next time you leave town.

ACTION ITEMS

Here are some action items that are typical of "abundance thinking." Now, don't confuse the actions with the intent. Many religions preach you should pray daily. However the act of praying doesn't mean you know God. The act is just an expression of who you are being. These acts are just reflections of your intentions.

° Write yourself a check for $1 million dollars and keep it with you to cash at a future date. It is rumored that actor/comedian Jim Carrey wrote himself a check for $10 million dollars and kept in his wallet for years! This was a physical act of believing in his future ability to earn millions in the movies. That was a leap of faith when he was making peanuts doing stand-up routines in L.A.! He has cashed that check many times over! Last I heard Jim's getting $20 million per movie. Now that's manifesting!

° Always keep a fresh $100 bill in your purse or your pocket. This reminds you that you always have enough money. Even if you

Great men are they who see that spiritual is stronger than any material force, that thoughts rule the world.

—Emerson

never spend that $100, this trick makes you feel wealthy. It also shows other people you are wealthy when you grab your cash to pay for things. I sometimes carry $400-$500 in my pocket just because it's fun! Truthfully, I feel more "rich" with $1000 cash in my pocket than looking at $2000 bank balance on a statement. So, do what makes you feel wealthy.

° **Enjoy spending money.** Being stingy on the out-flow blocks the in-flow. In order to make money, you have to learn to spend money happily. If you spend money happily, people will give you money happily.

° **Clear out all clutter in your life.** Get rid of junk, appliances, automobiles, furniture, clothes, and even relationships that aren't resonating with the new "abundant" you. You must create a space for new things to arrive easily. Upgrade your life.

° **Give a percentage of your income to charity.** This tells your brain there is plenty to go around while helping others.

° **Spend time around wealthy people.** Don't spend your Friday nights complaining about poverty with strugglers. Find people who are living abundantly and spend time with them. If you don't know anyone who isn't struggling paycheck to paycheck, go to the local Four Seasons Hotel and sit on the couch sipping a mineral water for two hours. Just getting used to the "feel" of wealthy places and the language of rich people makes you feel more comfortable living the rich life. Besides, you might meet some influential people in the lobby of a five star hotel!

Other Resources:

www.fengshuiwealth.com

www.barbaggett.com/spirituality

Universal Truth #21

Wisdom is not knowing
all the answers.
True wisdom is asking
the right questions.

CHAPTER 17

QUESTIONS WEALTHY PEOPLE ASK

The difference between successful people and unsuccessful people is the quality of their thoughts. Likewise the difference between happy people and unhappy people is the quality of their thoughts. Here is one shortcut to directing your mind to high quality thoughts to speed up the natural process of manifesting your desires.

What Is a Quality Thought?

Now, what is a quality thought? You can analyze people's thoughts, beliefs, history, and even their experiences. There are lots of other things, which I could go into it, but it all begins with a thought. If you've ever read Napoleon Hill's classic book called *Think And Grow Rich,* you already have realized that thoughts are things and thoughts manifest themselves into reality. If you're a veteran reader of self-improvement books, then you may have been frustrated by doing lots of positive thinking and NOT seeing any manifestation of wealth and happiness in your life. This is going to change now. The techniques in this book are different. They work. Affirmations are not enough!

The classic self-help books say repetitious affirmations train your brain. Affirmations work for some people but not for others. Affirmations are not the answer. For example, let's pretend that you are 100 pounds overweight. You want to be thin and sexy. You look in the mirror and say, "I'm skinny, sexy, and slender." That little inner voice really is saying, "What? Are you on drugs? You're fat. Really fat, and now you are a fat liar!" You shrug it off and say, "I am skinny. I am confident." The voice says, "Nope. You're still fat.

Nice try." Etc. Etc. This is why affirmations don't work consistently - they bump into reality and your brain filters them out.

Positive thinking has to be performed with the proper syntax. You might want to review the chapters on Toxic Vocabulary and Rapport to better understand how you must effectively program your own brain. The word choice and images you use during self-talk and goal planning are significant to you getting your outcome.

Turning any affirmation or desired outcome into a question is magical. This may seem like a silly assignment but it might be the most powerful habit you will ever adopt.

Instead of saying affirmations, you ask empowering questions that your brain is forced to answer.

EXAMPLES:

How quickly can I pay off this debt?

How can I increase my income now?

What is the fastest way I can earn $5,000?

Who will I meet that will be the key to doubling my income?

Where can I find a new job that pays me what I'm worth?

Most people don't know how they are going to increase their income. Heck, if everyone knew how, most would be doing it already. But, most people don't know how. Because they don't know how, they don't take the first step. That's the big mistake. You know you will figure out how as long as you keep asking the right questions and are willing to take those first steps.

Life will show you the road signs, but if you are asking the wrong questions you won't see the signs. You will be looking in the wrong direction. The best way to start your unconscious mind attracting the people and resources you need is to simply ASK. Asking questions and having a belief you will find the answer will draw the energy and resources of the universe to you. Just be open to finding answers in unexpected places.

HOW YOUR BRAIN LOOKS FOR OPPORTUNITIES

Did you know that part of your brain is already designed to search for opportunities? It's true. The lower portion of your brain, inside the Medulla, contains an area known as the Reticular Activating System (RAS). It keeps the higher brain centers alert and ready for input. The reticular activating system also filters out constant stimuli such as things you see everyday in your environment. Take for instance your living room. When you are sitting in your living room watching TV, you probably notice the program on TV, but not the other details of the living room. Your brain tunes everything but the TV out when you are focused. It would become annoying if our RAS didn't tell our brains that we don't have to consciously notice every detail in our living room. The RAS allows you to tune out everything that is unnecessary to pay attention to and to focus on what's important to you in the moment. One way to direct your RAS to focus on something specific is through asking questions.

I'll demonstrate. "What color are your eyes?" You thought about your eye color, didn't you? The color blue, green or brown probably came right to your attention. When I asked you that question, your reticular activating system had to go search for an answer. Now since you know the color of your eyes, the answer probably popped into your head immediately. When you ask questions that you don't know the answer to, it will take your mind a little longer to come up with an answer. Sometimes your brain needs to do a little research, have you talk to people or process the question a while. It could take moments, days or weeks to find the answer depending on how curious you are and how much conscious effort you put into finding the answer. But you don't even have to consciously seek for the answer. The RAS part of your brain will work 24 hours a day, unconsciously, until it finds an answer to your question.

Have you ever tried to remember the name of somebody? You kept asking your mind, "What is her name?" But you couldn't come up with an immediate answer, so you let it go and forgot about it. Then days later the woman's name suddenly pops into your awareness. Well, that's how your brain works. Even though your conscious mind had let the question go unanswered, your unconscious mind kept searching your memories for an answer until it was satisfied.

So how does knowing this information about the RAS make you richer? Well, when you ask your unconscious mind specific questions like "What is the fastest way I can earn $5,000?" you are giving your RAS a specific opportunity to look for. The back of your brain will work constantly until it locates the fastest way you can earn $5,000. Once it does, your RAS will bring the opportunity to your attention and you will experience an Aha! The key to attracting more opportunities is to become aware of what questions you ask everyday and begin to ask only empowering questions.

HOW TO ASK AN EMPOWERING QUESTION

For example, some people would say, "I'm definitely going to make $100,000 next year." Perhaps you should wake up every morning and say to yourself, "How is it that I'm going to make $100,000 next year? What am I going to produce that will create the value to earn me $100,000? How easy could it be to become a millionaire by next month? How much fun can I have while earning lots of money?" These questions actually pull your unconscious mind into a specific, creative direction. The great thing about empowering questions is they leapfrog your current belief systems.

392

QUALITY QUESTIONS CAN DISLODGE EVEN THE MOST STUBBORN LIMITING BELIEFS!

If you grew up in a poor family or had "poverty consciousness" for whatever reason, you probably have some beliefs that indicate there is a "lack of money" in the world. If you grew up around people who stole things, wore used clothes, and hand-me-down shoes, then you might have adopted the beliefs that expensive things are hard to get if you are honest. These limiting beliefs, although not conscious, do drive your behavior. Asking a different set of questions can dislodge these old beliefs.

When an opportunity falls into your lap, subconsciously you might have said, "This is too easy. Too good to be true. Money doesn't grow on trees. How could an opportunity come along that easily? What is the catch?" These poorly chosen questions crippled your chances of success. The last question sabotaged a good thing. If you ask any question enough times, your mind will find an answer. So, your brain finds some catch and you miss an opportunity to cash in on some good luck.

You must learn to "scratch" out the limiting beliefs and reprogram a "wealth" consciousness. Even if you have a bucket full of real-life experiences, parents with crappy attitudes, and a $60,000 credit card debt ... you can leapfrog past your limiting beliefs using empowering questions.

HOW BRIAN'S PROPER QUESTIONS TURNED HIS BALANCE SHEET AROUND

I'll tell you a story about my friend, Brian. A few years ago he made some poor business decisions and went through a divorce. Suddenly he found himself $50,000 in debt. Many people would have filed for bankruptcy, but Brian decided to take responsibility and keep his credit in tact. He went to work on a plan to pay back the credit cards and the people who loaned him the money.

In order to take on such a huge feat, Brian first adopted the belief system that he could pay back that money. On his current income, that took a leap of faith. He set a date three years into the future to be debt free. He charted out his debts and visualized each one going down to zero. He paid small payments to each at first, and then started paying more and more as he gained momentum. All along the way, Brian kept asking himself a series of key questions:

"How can I pay off this debt within three years?"

"What needs to happen for me to pay off this debt quickly and easily?"

"I wonder where I can earn extra money to pay this debt off even faster."

"How good will I feel when I am debt-free?"

What Brian was doing was challenging his unconscious mind to find solutions to his desired outcome. He also set a specific deadline (3 years) and a specific amount to pay off ($50,000). Sure enough, Brian kept attracting the right opportunities and finally paid off those credit cards and loans within three years.

Other people would have asked non-empowering questions and still be in debt. Some people would have asked, "Why did this happen to me?" "Why won't my ex-wife pay her share?" "What did I do to deserve this? Etc."

When you ask yourself the right questions everyday, the universe will reveal answers. If you ask the same question enough times, your unconscious mind will work overtime to find an answer for you. (If not for the simple reason that it gets tired of you asking the same darn question everyday.) It will FIND the answer so you will move onto another question. Your persistence will pay off.

Just make sure you ask the right questions. Be specific.

Many people sit around and ask very bad questions, such as "Why does this happen to me? What did I do to deserve this? Why is my relationship always bad? Why is there never enough money?" Well, guess what? If you ask those questions everyday, you will get the answer, but it's the answer you don't want.

So instead, I would suggest to you to ask questions that empower your mind to give you what you want? Ask the right questions that guide your mind in finding a solution to your current challenges.

Here are some starters for topic of financial abundance:

How specifically can I make a million dollars?

How specifically can I experience more freedom while earning more money?

How specifically can I get a better job working with people around me that I like?

What needs to happen for me to double my income in the next three months?

What steps do I need to take to start my own business now?

How easy would it be for me to get a $10,000 raise in income this year?

What are my best options for earning extra money?

SUCCESS TIP - TAPE IT TO THE MIRROR

Make a list of questions that direct your mind to find solutions. Write each question on one 5x7 index card in your own handwriting with a bold black marker. Pick one question each week and tape that one question onto your bathroom mirror. (Choose the mirror that you use each morning to brush your teeth and primp.) Every morning you get up, you read that question to yourself three or more times. Don't be surprised if the answer comes to you in the middle of the night or while you are doing something completely different weeks later! This is a habit that creates magic!

SUCCESS TIP - MEDITATE ON THE QUESTION

Use the same index cards to start a daily 15-minute meditation. Just find a quiet place to sit for a short time period without being disturbed. Put the handwritten index question card in front of you and ask yourself the question repeatedly until your eyes close. Using your internal voice, keep asking yourself the question over and over until the answers start flooding in. Don't judge the answers, just keep them flowing. You might want to keep some blank paper nearby to write all the answers that come in. Write them all down and sort them later when you will be in a more left-brained logical state of mind.

SUCCESS TIP - WHAT'S GOOD AND NEW?

Master NLP instructor Rex Sikes taught me a very fun and valuable exercise to program optimism and start off the day right! It's called the What's Good and New? game. I suggest playing it with your significant other, your family, or your roommate. You can do it alone, but after the first two weeks, it gets harder. When it gets tougher, that's when you start to learn and create new habits. If you do this simple 60 second game for one month, you might do it for life!

Each morning, before you start the day, you must articulate in words something that is good and new. It can be one thing that is both good and new. Or you can choose one thing that is good and one thing that is new. This forces you to take daily inventory of your world. We forget to be appreciative or even notice the good things in our world.

Ask your partner to keep you accountable. Don't cheat. Don't let them start their day until they speak loud and clear what they find good and new.

There is only one rule, you can't name the same item twice ... ever. Therefore, if you say, "You Honey. You're good and the milk is new." you are not allowed to pick "you or milk" ever again. This is easy for the first dozen items. But as you run out of the obvious things, your brain starts to do a mental search each day. This "mental search" actually grows new neuro-pathways while creating a habit of finding what is good and new in your world. In essence, this game is programming optimism and appreciation.

Universal Truth #22

Everyone is given same amount of time in
the day. There is no more to give.
Time gets spent whether you
spend it wisely or not.
How you spend your time is the
difference between a life of
prosperity or a life of struggle.

CHAPTER 18

THE SECRET VALUE OF TIME

One common trait most wealthy people have is that they have a clear understanding of the value of their own time. In fact, one of the reasons most self-made millionaires work so hard is to have the ability to have free time when they choose. The word free time is actually a paradox. When, in fact, all time is free. Time just exists. None of use has any more or any less time than anyone else. At the same time, time costs us money. According to economic theory, time costs you money in the form of "opportunity cost." I first learned the term opportunity cost while getting my business degree at Pepperdine University. Essentially, every decision we make can be viewed as an opportunity. Even something as simple as sitting in your car at a fork in the road. If you drive north, you forfeit all the experiences than the south road could have given you. If you turn south, it costs you the lessons the north route could have given you. In fact, just reading this page right now is costing you something else. It is costing you the opportunity to watch TV, go jogging, spending time with your family, work, etc.

RICH PEOPLE KNOW THE VALUE OF THEIR TIME. THEREFORE, THEY SPEND IT WISELY.

Earlier I alluded to the wisdom of Benjamin Franklin. Franklin penned his ideas and thoughts in the pages of *Poor Richard's Almanac* for over 25 years of his life. Of course, his pen name was Poor Richard. He was at heart an author and a publisher. (Maybe that's why I like him so much.) In Esmond Wright's *Benjamin Franklin*, he relays the story of Ben stopping his horse in front of a market with a crowd of people. As the market had yet to open, the crowd was conversing about the bad times occurring in their country. A wide set, white haired man named Father Abraham was at the center of the crowd. A man asked, "What think you of the times? Won't these heavy taxes quite ruin the country? How shall we ever pay them? What would you advise us to do?" As Benjamin Franklin watched from afar, Father Abraham stood up and said, "If you'd have my advice, I'll give it to you in short, for a word to the wise is enough, and many words won't fill a bushel."

The crowd gathered around for his words of advice. Father Richard spoke, "If time be of all things the most precious, wasting time must be, as Poor Richard says, the greatest prodigality, since, as he elsewhere tells us, lost time is never found again; and what we call time-enough, always proves little enough. Let us then up and be doing, and doing to the purpose; so by diligence shall we do more with less perplexity. Sloth makes all things difficult, but industry all easy, as Poor Richard says; and He that riseth late, must trot all day, and shall scarce overtake his business at night. While laziness travels so slowly, that poverty soon overtakes him, Drive thy business, let not that drive thee; and Early to bed early to rise, makes a man healthy, wealthy, and wise." Old Ben smiled as his words were preached by the Father. He was proud that perhaps he had made a difference. But, to his dismay, as soon as the shops opened the crowd rushed in to spend every coin in their pockets. They bought extravagantly, notwithstanding his cautions and their own fear of the taxes. Naturally, they continued to complain about the taxes, the economy, and their financial condition as they spent. He had stopped from purchasing a new overcoat. He decided he could live with the used one on his back for another month. He was a man who took his own advice. Ben got back on his horse and rode away.

"They that won't be counseled, can't be helped"

- Poor Richard

In a remarkable modern study by Dr. Thomas M. Stanley, it was revealed that millionaires in the late 20th century live by the same principles that Benjamin Franklin taught 200 years before. Dr Stanley interviewed thousands of millionaires since 1973 to determine their lifestyles, spending habits, belief systems, etc. One interesting revelation relating to time was this: The typical millionaire wakes up at 6:40 am. Only about one if five rises before 5:40 am. I had heard through the grapevine that self-made millionaires woke up at 4 am. I read that Donald Trump, the New York real estate tycoon, always gets up before sunrise. I tried that a few times. It doesn't work for me or my body. When I go to bed at 2:00 am, I sure can't get up at 4:00 am. Through his research, Dr. Stanley found this fact: "There is no statistically significant correlation between the time one wakes up in the morning and one's wealth."

So, you don't have to give up on your sleep to become wealthy, but you clearly can't sleep 12 hours a night either. The point here is you must have a clear value on your time. Here is an exercise to get clarity on what it costs you to get an extra hour of sleep or watch your favorite sitcom. Do this exercise and heed the results. Every minute of your day has a value to it. What is yours? Here is how you find out.

THE VALUE OF YOUR TIME DURING THE PAST YEAR

What was your twelve-month gross income from all sources?

Example: $50,000 gross income

Divide that dollar amount by 8760 hours in a year.

Example: $50,000 divided by 8760 = $5.71 per hour

The resulting number is the average amount you must earn every hour of every day to gross $50,000 each year. Since this is a gross income figure, not a net income figure, it can be deceiving. You might be thinking, "Sure Bart, that is if I worked 24 hours per day. Nobody works 24 hours per day." You are right, most people don't work 24 hours per day. But, self-made millionaires don't work the typical labor union's 8.5 hours per day either. Here is a hard fact to realize. It's not the hours that you work that matter. It's the amount of money you put in your asset column. The reason this number is soooooooo important is because most people burn a lot of their time doing non-income earning activities. The chances of you getting rich only working just 8.5 hours per day for someone else's company are very slim. I'm not saying you have to be an entrepreneur. What I am saying is that you must put an additional 1-3 hours of your day into learning, investing, networking, or otherwise turning your time into wealth.

The statistics reveal that the typical "millionaire" household in Dr. Stanley's study earned about $436,000 last year. This household has a net worth of $4.3 million. Over 32% of the Americans in his study are business owners or entrepreneurs. Nearly 16% are senior level executives. 10% are attorneys. 9% are physicians. The other 1/3 consist of a mixed group of teachers, accountants, sales professionals, professors, housewives, retirees, middle managers, etc. The lesson here is simple. You don't have to earn $436,000 this year to be rich. However, you do have to start investing your time as if you were already earning that kind of money. Remember ... "Act as if." Act as if you were already rich. Fake it till you make it. The secret to modeling successful people is find out what they do and live that way.

LET'S TAKE A LOOK AT WHAT ONE HOUR OF THE TYPICAL AMERICAN MILLIONAIRE'S TIME IS REALLY

WORTH:

What was your 12 month gross income from all sources?

Example: $436,000 gross income

Divide that dollar amount by 8760 hours in a year.

Example: $436,000 divided by 8760 = $49.77 per hour - 24 hours per day.

You might begin to realize your time is more valuable than people around you realize. You might also realize that if you plan to sleep 8 hours per night - you must find a way to earn $398.16 while you sleep. In other words, you must find a way for your money to make money for you while you sleep. If you don't choose that route, then, you must find a vocation where you can earn $149.31 per hour, 8 hours per day, seven days a week, every day of the year. That seems like a lot of work. Mr. Stanley says that those who bill hourly for their time in their profession charge about $300 per hour. That sounds reasonable. Even the best consultants have a difficult time billing 4-6 hours of actual billable hours in a workday.

I chose to find a way to let my business or money earn money for me when I'm not there.

BEWARE OF TIME VAMPIRES

Marketing Expert Dan Kennedy discusses "time vampires" in one of his books. After understanding how much my time is worth (or SHOULD be worth), I stopped taking phone calls from time vampires.

Time vampires can include:

Unnecessary trips to the grocery store

Visits from in-laws

People who want you to solve their self-created "drama" all the time

Television

Trips to the dry-cleaners

Any phone call that you don't initiate (Get caller ID and use it to screen your calls.)

Touching any piece of mail more than once

Sleeping late

Paying your bills by hand (Get automatic bill pay through your computer.)

Etc. Etc.

Once you realize that in order to become a millionaire, you have to respect your time like a millionaire, taking that phone call from your sister in law about her dog's rash seems less important. When I realized this, I stopped answering my office line. If you call my office, you will very rarely hear my voice pickup the phone. Before I could afford to hire an assistant, I simply let the calls go to voicemail. It might have cost me a book sale or two by not answering those calls. But the number of non-income-producing conversations was clearly less valuable than my new "hourly" rate for time vampires. And that extra hour of sleep begins to become quite costly. Doesn't it?

Here is your exercise. Decide how much money you want to gross next year. Then, figure out your 24 hour-per-day hourly rate. Then allow only the people and events into your life that are worthy of that figure.

The New Value of Your Time for the Next Year

What is your twelve-month gross income target?

Example: $50,000 gross income

Divide that dollar amount by 8760 hours in a year.

Example: $50,000 divided by 8760 = $17.12 per hour

TAKE BACK YOUR TIME

Once you decide what your time is really worth, you must start to manage it properly. Getting control of your time is an essential element to managing your busy life. Because the topic time management is so well covered in other books, I will not review it here. Suffice to say by the preceding examples is that if you are wasting time, you are wasting money. I actually use a custom made "planner" that not only incorporates my appointments, but it also incorporates my daily success habits. I actually schedule those life changing habits such as exercise, taking my vitamins, drinking 2 liters of water, appreciating my spouse, meditation, etc. I value my time so much I make sure I schedule all the important things in life to build up my reserves. If you don't manage your time, you will spend it all on urgent items and forsake what is really important – like buying your loved one some flowers on the way home from work.

Universal Truth #23

What you focus on you manifest.
A quiet and focused mind is one of the
most powerful forces in the universe.

CHAPTER 19

DESIGNING YOUR FUTURE USING TIME-LINE & MEDITATION

THE POWER OF MEDITATION

If you haven't yet decided to set aside a few minutes per day or per week to sit by yourself with no distractions and meditate...consider making this quiet time a daily or weekly habit. Most self-improvement techniques focus on "doing" or "behaving" differently. Much of what I've talked about in this book has to do with reshaping the ego/personality part of your life and interacting with the world in a new way. This is an essential component. An equally important component is to use the power of your inner spiritual self to tap into higher powers that move the world in ways we cannot see. Many practitioners of various forms of meditation actually feel, see, attract, and move energy through their body and out into the world. This may sound a bit hocus-pocus to the typical western mind, but there is lots of scientific evidence that even the most tangible concrete items in the universe (like this book or the chair you are sitting in) are nothing more than energy atoms vibrating at various frequencies. In physics, energy never dies... it just changes forms. It doesn't take too much of a leap of faith to believe that if science can transmit radio and TV waves through the air via sound waves, then our incredibly powerful creative minds can also send and receive messages with the proper training. In fact, you don't have to be religious or even call in any faith. Your mind has already been creating and repelling reality based on your thought structure your entire life. It has even been filtering out opportunities and dangers that you were not ready to see or could handle. Since your mind is already a beacon of energy pulsating and sending messages to the universe... why not spend a few minutes a week programming the messages? You may find 10 minutes a day in silence can reap many times more rewards than ten minutes of busy-ness. (Notice busy-ness sounds a lot like doing business.) Meditation can make you money.

There are thousands of theories on how to meditate properly. In my opinion, all systems have value. Deepak Chopra offers the guidance to quiet the mind of all internal thoughts. He suggests finding the space between the thoughts. The point of mental silence between the thoughts is where you begin to communicate with your higher self. I do know this about Deepak. He is an incredibly wealthy and happy man that has found a way to be "of service" to humanity and walk firmly inside his divine spirit while contributing the betterment of society and his own family. In my mid 20's I volunteered to work on his staff during one of his seminars where he taught many meditation and healing techniques. The staff and I were having lunch in a tiny room in the hotel. My back was to the door and I was visiting with a friend. I felt a powerful and kind energy shift flow over me. In an instant something had changed. I knew someone had entered the room. I turned around to see Deepak had quietly and humbly entered the staff room to grab a piece of fruit. The young lady I was talking to also noticed the profound "wave" of positive energy that went through us. Hmmm? Is it possible that some people that are truly in touch with their "inner God" vibrate at a higher frequency than others? Is energy vibrations like the stations on a radio dials, a personal power we can learn to do control through meditation? Many people believe we can. I have met some amazingly kind, wealthy, happy, and powerful people that I can only describe through a feeling I get... not by what they do, say, or look like. I think meditation is one vehicle to open that energetic channel for you to attract and vibe at that higher level. People sense it.

THREE TECHNIQUES TO TAP INTO
YOUR HIGHER SELF

I will offer just three meditative techniques in this book. !
encourage you to study from other teachers on this topic. In most
meditation techniques you will want to physically become still,
comfortable, and attempt to quiet the mind from external distractions, your to-do list, worries, and turn off all the internal pictures
for a few moments as you take yourself from the waking Beta brain
wave pattern, into a more relaxing meditative Alpha brain wave pattern. Some people count backwards twenty down to one. Others
suggest you focus every aspect of your breathing. Say to yourself,
"I'm breathing in. I'm breathing out."

For many busy minded people, just sitting alone is difficult and
very good for you. I have found that the electronically induced
meditations using "light & sound" machines take me into deep
states of trance even more quickly that simply closing my eyes.
These small glasses with blinking lights actually "pace" my brain
into the altered states of consciousness using scientific research.
Besides being really relaxing, it's actually tons of fun because your
optical nerves are treated to a light show! You can find more about
recommended light & sound machines at:
www.bartbaggett.com/meditation

Whether you are focusing on your breathing, listening to music,
or using a light & sound machine, you will want to quiet your mind.
Once you have reached that quiet place, you will want to begin a
specific technique.

THE NOTHINGNESS TECHNIQUE

If you have no particular outcome in mind for the meditation,
then just let your unconscious mind guide you and focus your attention on the moment between the thoughts. This is harder than you

might think. Thinking about nothing is tricky. But with practice, you can learn to let go of your thoughts. Then, let your mind wander free. I often visualize myself floating through the stars in outer space. I imagine fewer and fewer stars as I travel into total peaceful blackness. Naturally, there is no noise in space except the sound of my own breathing. Eventually, I stop thinking and my unconscious mind takes over. After you come back and open your eyes... you might attempt to analyze the metaphors, stories, or mental imagery for clues to how they might relate to today's issues. Many people keep a notebook or diary of their meditative experiences.

THE EDISON TECHNIQUE

Another powerful creative problem solving technique was first reportedly used by Thomas Edison, the great inventor. Mr. Edison was known for solving his creative roadblocks using short cat naps. If he found himself at an analytical stuck point, he would simply boil down the problem into one simple question. Once he had the right question, he would excuse himself for a nap. In the late 1800's, it wasn't very acceptable in America to fire up some incense and meditate in the lotus position at the factory. His nap was really just a quiet meditative time in which he simply repeated his one question over and over and over in his head until he drifted off into a light sleep. When he woke up, he usually had an answer. In my case, 1 often get the answer hours, days or weeks later. But the answer always comes and it feels like a higher being just hands me the envelope with the correct answer inside. It seems effortless if you let your higher self assist you solve to your problems. Get quiet, ask a question, stop thinking, and let go.

The other technique I am going to share with you is much more pragmatic and self-directed. For those of you who are "take charge" type people, the following time-line visualization technique will appeal to you more than the "let the universe take over" type of meditation I just described. I use both depending on the outcome I desire.

TIME-LINE TECHNIQUE

In a recent chapter you discovered the future value of each hour of your time. I asked you to actually quantify each hour of your day in an effort to make more profitable decisions about where to spend your time. This technique isn't about where you spend your time. This is going to be a lesson on where you store your time in your mind. If this sounds confusing, hang on. I'm about to introduce to you a mental process that can double or triple the speed of the manifestation process of your goals. In fact, discovering how you store "time" can have profound effects on your future goals, your current pleasure in life, and even in dealing with things in your past. I encourage you to utilize this technique in your weekly closed eye meditation sessions. (By the way, this is much more than just another meditative technique. This is also a therapeutic technique used successfully by NLP practitioners, hypnotherapists, and psychologists worldwide to heal past issues and program bright and wonderful future events. I actually have carried a line of cassette tapes that use this technique for the past ten years.)

The animal kingdom doesn't have an exact understanding of time. The clock and the concept of time is a human concept. For animals, now is all there is. It is either time to fly south... or it isn't time to fly south. Birds don't sit around and discuss what mother bird did last week and their plans for next year's summer vacation. You dog doesn't know he has been locked in the house for 12 hours. Your dog only knows that "now" would be good time for you to come home and let him go pee! The present moment is all there is. I mind simply has "storage" of past and possible future moments. Do you agree?

The reason it is important to discover the exact process of how you store time is once you know your own internal map of the past and future - you can chart an exact route to your desired destination. You can be more exact in "installing goals" into your memory banks of your unconscious mind.

Furthermore, if you have memories in your past that are still bothering you (childhood traumas, loss, pain, etc) you have a more direct route to go back and adjust the memory to be less influential over your current state of mind. In reality, your past isn't the problem. The past is over. The problem is your "memory" of the event is stored in a way that drives and directs your current emotions. That is all I am going to say about your past memories. The application of Time-Line is the most effective therapeutic tool I've ever witnessed for overcoming past emotional events. If you are struggling with an event in your past - learn more about the concept or hire a qualified Time-Line Practitioner.

www.bartbaggett.com/timeline

WHY IS HOW YOU STORE TIME SO IMPORTANT?

I have noticed that some people are always on time while others are always late. I noticed in various cultures meetings start at the exact agreed upon time. While in some countries, a meeting could be two days late and nobody seems to care? I have also noticed that some people get totally absorbed in what they are doing and completely forget about obligations. It is as if the current event totally blinded them from seeing that time was moving on. Other people have an internal clock that can wake them up each morning without an alarm no matter how late they stayed up. Some people have a totally organized time schedule while others do not. Some people set goals and achieve them by the exact date. Others set goals and never achieve them. How you store time affects how effectively you live your life and how effectively your future is created.

What I learned is that people do have, inside them, a specific way of coding the past, present and future so they know which is the past, which is the present, and which is the future. Don't you? Tell me, did you pay your rent already? Did you eat today? Have you paid your taxes for last year? Your mind has a way of taking one event and encoding it as part of your past, present, or future. That encoding process can be described in part by your internal time-line.

Most people who have never studied NLP or Time-Line have never thought about the inside of their minds as huge 3-D holographic studios. Instead of just running movies in your mind, you actually have an entire theatre with sound, voices, distance, volume, and the ability to turn your head 360 degrees and view your memories and life from different angles. In an instant, instead of just being inside a theatre, you can be 100 feet above the theatre looking down at the parking lot and the houses around the theatre. Your mind is an amazingly flexible tool. You already have a preferred arrangement of how you store time. You have already given people clues by the language you choose and even the hand motions you display. You may have noticed as people talk, they give you a description of what they are doing inside their mind. Have you ever said, "You are going to look back on this and laugh?"

Have you heard, "Let's put this behind us as soon as possible." What about, "Time is creeping on me." I have also seen people point to places inside the house to describe events that have nothing to do with the house. My friend Chris always points to his right when he describes what he is doing next week. (Is next week in the kitchen?) Likewise, he uses his hand and points to his left when he talks about things that have already happened. I bet he doesn't even notice it, but I do. The use of temporal language and physical gestures are just clues to how people are structuring their own internal time machine.

Universal Truth #24

We never stop dreaming.
Some people just stop believing their
dreams can become reality.
Dream and Believe.

Imagine taking a mental journey out into the future and discovering what's out there. You see, your unconscious mind does have a concept of what it expects to occur in your future. Of course, whatever is out there on your future time line, you can change anytime, as many times as you want. Don't you wonder what your own unconscious has in store for you in your future? Imagine being able to program your future into the future memory banks of your unconscious mind, much like you would transfer a file into the hard disk of your personal computer. What if you could create a mental image of the accomplishment of this goal? And then, in your mind, take that event and mentally place it in your future time line, in the future memory banks of your own conscious mind? And then your unconscious mind would see to it that you do the things you need to do to lead up to the accomplishment of the goal. This is, in a nutshell, how Time-Line works for creating your desired future.

The result is what some researchers call "sustained unconscious motivation". That is, you feel motivated without having to try to do it consciously, because your unconscious mind is working on the goal 24 hours a day and believes that you will achieve your desired future. The mental technique can instantly change how you feel about the goal you've put on your internal time line. Your unconscious believes that the achievement of the goal is real, so you feel confident and certain that you'll succeed. Imagine how that affects your day-to day-performance in any area of your life.

By the way, there is no right or wrong way to store time internally. There are simply effective and non-effective models depending on your desired outcome. Before we analyze this more deeply, take a moment, close your eyes, and find your own internal timeline. Just answer the following questions as completely as you can. If you get to a question where an answer doesn't come to you, go to the next question. One of these following questions will assist you in eliciting your current version of time storage. Most people will have just one time line, some of you might have more than one.

Pick the most comfortable one for the closed eye meditative exercise later in the chapter.

1. Where is the past and where is the future for you? If you could just point to the past and point to the future with your index finger, which way would you point? Which way would be the future? The past?

(Roughly half the people reading this book can get some intuitive answer from this question. If you are not sure yet, go on to the next question. Some people will point their finger out in front of them and say, "There. My future is in front of me." Others will turn their head to the left and say, "Back there, my past is behind me. Isn't everyone's?" No, there are various models for storing time.)

2. "I'd like you to stop and recall a memory from when you were age 16. Now, which direction did that memory come from?" You can choose any age depending on your age. My preferred ages to choose when eliciting a time-line are age 5 to 7, 10 to 13, and 16 to 18, and last week. These ages usually create a clear image or feeling of the direction of the past.

If this worked for you, you are now ready to find out where you store your future. "I'd like you to think of something that's going to happen in the future, say six months from now. Now, what direction did that memory come to you?" The answer you get here will indicate which direction your future is kept.

3. If you still aren't sure about which direction you store time, you might be less visual that the rest of the world. In that case, this question will assist you in discovering the map of your internal 3D world.

"Imagine you are the pilot of a single seat spacecraft that can move effortlessly in any direction (up, down, forewards, backwards, diagonal, fast, slow, etc.) You are docked inside your mind and begin to thrust upwards twenty feet above your own body. You now feel the spaceship moving in the direction of your past... which way is it moving? Do you feel the ship going up, down, backwards, forwards, left, right, etc? Trust your feelings. Allow the ship to take you all the way back to the day of your birth. Then, allow it to take you ten years into the future. The flight path of your spaceship is your time-line.

Is it a straight line from the future to now? Is it a curvy path? Allow yourself to go with your gut instinct. There is no right and wrong answers. Some people have a straight path from back to front. Other people have a straight line from left to right. Some people actually have a spiral time line where the past and future are totally intertwined. (Yes, a bit confusing.) Other people find they have a "V" shaped time-line. Take a moment and use the diagram below to draw a representation of how you see or feel your internal time-line.

Viewpoint when floating above your body looking down at the top of your head.

Notice that you have the option of drawing the line through your own head or drawing the line in front of you own head. That is up to you. Do you feel "inside the time line" or do you feel "you are watching time pass you by?" These are differences you might want to investigate in further study about Time-Line. For now, what is important is that you decide on a time-line model that you can use in order to effectively place future events into your future.

Putting events into your future using your own current time-line will be the most effective accelerated achievement technique you will ever learn. It works because you are installing it within the current operating structure of your own mind. Instead of just placing the "document" on top of the filing cabinet... you are going into the files of your unconscious mind and placing it at the exact time and place you desire. You are leaving nothing to chance.

The next diagram shows an example of how I see my time-line. Don't model me. Use your own time-line unless you feel your time line is a disservice to you. For example, if your past is in front of you and your future is behind you...you obviously have a tendency to focus on the past and find it hard to see the future. In that case, practice switching the time line for experimental purposes. For most people, use your current structure for the following time-line exercise.

I store time with the past behind me to the left and the future in front of me to the right. Because today and tomorrow are "right in front of me" I often let today's activities usurp tomorrow's obligations. I get caught up in today and forget about tomorrow. So, I get lost "in time." Because the future is slightly off to the right, I can see long term goals unconsciously. I don't want to change this because being able to be so "present in time" also makes me very happy in the moment and do well performing "in the moment activities" like speaking and writing.) I prefer to have an accountant and manager who sees time from left to right. Hopefully, they can keep to a tight schedule and help me not miss appointments. These are

This is how some people store time. They have a linear line front to back. Many have curved lines. Some even expand. What does yours look like from above?

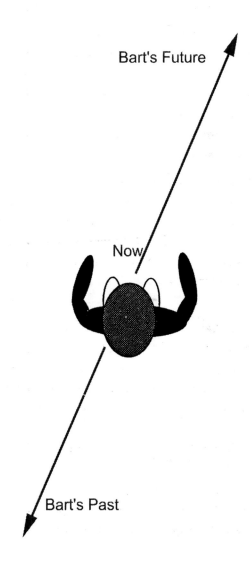

Bart's Future

Now

Bart's Past

just generalizations of certain time lines. Your results might vary.

The reason I have spent this much time asking you about your time is to assist you having a good time creating your future. You will want to use this model of your time-line when you do goal setting exercises and meditation.

During the closed eye meditation, you will be asked to float above your time line and move into the future or past. This is most effective if you can actually see or feel yourself moving up and down the time-line of your life. The image of the actual time-line varies. I have used a golden glowing neon type line as my time line. I have also used purple paint and white light to represent the line. The farther Up, Up, and Up you go above your body, the tinier the time line will become. If you imagine yourself floating far enough above your head, the entire time line of your life will seem less than one inch long. This is a great place to go to get perspective on your life. (I find when I mentally float high enough into space and view the entire planet from outerspace, I feel the one-ness of the planet and my problems seem very insignificant in contrast to the vast universe.) I will ask you to float a few feet above and even inside your time-line during the closed eye mediation.

The following chapter can be used as a template of how you guide yourself through the process of using your own time-line to accelerate achieving your outcomes. I mastered the technique using actual live seminars and guided visual imagery via CD's and audio tapes.

You might want to review chapter 2 and discover if there is anything more you want to program into your future. During the process, it is essential you fully associate with the goals or outcome. You will want to know the texture, feelings, images, sounds, and even the people around you when you accomplish your outcome! Review the art of submodalities from the earlier chapter. When you program your outcomes in the most motivating submodalities, your brain is compelled to make them a reality. (Submodalites are explained in more detail by Richard Bandler in his book *Using Your Brain for a Change*.) Submodalites are the various elements that shape an internal image, thought, or feeling. You could imagine yourself winning a gold medal using a bright image, a dark image, a large image, a small image, a loud crowd, no sound, in full color, in black-n-white, grainy film, clear film, warm feelings, hot sensations, etc. Submodalities assist you in fully associating into any memory or future outcome. The more clarity you have on the submodalities of your outcome... the easier it will be for your unconscious mind to manifest it.)

Other Resources

After you have mastered this technique, I encourage you to use it over and over again in all of your mental processing of future and past events. You can learn more about time-line and even experiment with different closed eye processes at this website:

www.bartbaggett.com/timeline

www.bartbaggett.com/meditation

Universal Truth #24

The future is exactly as bright
as you decide to make it.

CHAPTER 20

INSTALLING YOUR FUTURE WEALTH AND HAPPINESS

Before I walk you through the mental process of installing your goals into your future, I'd like you to answer a hypothetical question. Just for fun, imagine scientists discovered another earth that has been traveling in outer space all these years. The planet is identical in every way. Some people would call this a parallel universe. Regardless of the titles, you have the unique opportunity to enter this exact replica of earth in any role you want. The only requirements are you can't pick a person that already exists and you have to be the same age, and have the approximate same body type (color, height, gender, etc.) as you are today. So, if you could magically appear on earth with none of your own personal history ... who would you choose to be from this point forward?

Would you be a movie star? A teacher? A mom with five kids? The president of your country? Fit and healthy? A billionaire? Would you be an inventor or a musician?

I'm curious, if you have no past and no obligations... what would you create of your life from this point forward? When we play this "what if" game in live seminars, many people re-discover lost dreams and unrealized visions. They had long ago given up on some of their inner most fantasies. What would you do if you knew you couldn't fail? What would you do if you had a sense of absolute certainty you will achieve your outcome?

After you have spent a few minutes visiting this hypothetical future, find a comfortable position and allow me to guide you through a mental journey into your future.

A time-line session will install some of your goals and outcomes directly into the memory banks of your unconscious mind. Because the most effective way to use this visualization process is by closing your eyes, you have three options.

1. Read through the following outline of the time-line process memorizing the key elements. Then do it by yourself in a closed eye meditative trance.

2. Log onto the special webpage and listen to me read the script to you using the power of the Internet and audio files. Just follow the directions on the internet webpage and listen to it via your computer speakers. This audio clip is available at no additional charge. Just log onto www.bartbaggett.com/timeline/chapter20

3. Log onto the special webpage and read the transcript of the time-line script. Then, you can read it into a tape recorder using your own voice and replay it to yourself next time you meditate.

Before you are ready to follow along in this meditative thought process, please gather up notes on the following areas of your life.

1. Your **top three goals or outcomes** for the next **month, year, three years** and **five years**.

2. **How will you know you have achieved these goals**? Have an image prepared in your mind.

3. Know your **#1, #2** and **#3 life** or **career values**.

4. Have a list of **five new beliefs** you want to install.

5. **Visualize any handwriting changes** you have decided to make.

6. **List two key empowering questions** that you would like

answered during the next few months or years.

When you have those items prepared, read the entire script aloud mentally filling in the blanks with the items from your list. Because each person reading this book will have different goals and values, this script will be "general" in nature. You will be asked to use your own images, sounds, and feelings during the process. If my voice were guiding you, I would just be a guide. Even if you listen to my voice on the Internet, there will be places of silence as you fill in the blanks with your own pieces of vital information.

In fact, you don't need my guidance. Once you master the process, you can close your eyes and float out into your future at anytime and energize your future! You can do it in as little as 60 seconds once you master the process!

HERE IS THE PROCESS FOR INSTALLING EVENTS INTO YOUR FUTURE TIME-LINE.

Sit quietly until you have quieted your mind of all outside distractions. Take a few deep breaths.

Think about your internal timeline.

Allow your creative part to imagine a lighter spiritual part of you begin to float out through the top of your head and look down on your peaceful body below.

Feel this spiritual "mind" part of you move toward the future traveling above your own timeline which can be seen below.

You will want to stop at important events along the future time line. I would suggest you stop at one month, one year, three years and five years in the future. Naturally, if there is a specific event you want to program (like New Year's Eve) you would stop above that point in time.

During each stop, you will "lower yourself" into the timeline and have that spiritual mind part of you enter into the physical body of the future you that is already waiting inside the future event.

You must fully associate yourself into that future event. See, hear, and feel the event through the body of your future self. When you are there, you can make changes to make sure the event is exactly like you want it. You can make the picture brighter, add characters, remove characters, increase the volume, win the trophy, cash the big check, or be with your true love. It is your future event — make it compelling. The more emotion you can feel during these visits... the more "automatic sustained motivation" your brain will have to make it become a reality.

Do this at each stop along your future timeline.

During the process, consider incorporating the items and concepts you have listed as part of your notes for meditation. (A few pages ago, I asked that you prepare items relating to six bullet points.)

Make sure that you have the experience of achieving all your outcomes and experiencing the celebration of each achievement.

Also, make sure you feel yourself living all three highest values with emotional intensity.

See yourself saying the new beliefs to yourself in your future times.

See yourself writing with the successful handwriting strokes you want to incorporate into your handwriting.

Hear yourself asking your empowering questions while you are floating above your timeline. Listen and look for what answers appear to you.

Return to your body in the here and now. Smile.

The entire script that you can read to yourself, memorize, follow-along, or just listen to from your own computer is on the internet right now waiting for you.

Hop on the Internet and listen to me walk you through the timeline process. It's a bonus for reading this book.

The audio file is a free to listen to at:

www.bartbaggett.com/timeline/chapter20

Other resources:

www.bartbaggett.com/timeline

Universal Truth #25

Habits are the best of friends
or the worst of enemies.

CHAPTER 21

TURNING WEALTH & HAPPINESS INTO HABITS

I grew up hearing many great one-liners from my father. One phrase that sums up the lives of happy and rich people still holds true today as it did when I was four years old. My dad, Curtis used to say, "Habits can be the best of friends or the worst of enemies." The concept of building habits toward success was illustrated beautifully in Stephen Covey's best selling book *The 7 Habits of Highly Effective People.*

In my life, the healthy habits that I adopted young were the key reasons I achieved such a high level of success at an early age. Even such character traits as honesty, diplomacy, and generosity take conditioning to become habits. Behavioral habits such as turning off the lights when you leave the room, drinking 8 glasses of water per day, or paying your bills before the due date also require a period of conditioning.

If you think back to the chapter relating to handwriting analysis and grapho-therapy, I discussed neuro-logically how habits are formed in the brain. The habit of tying your shoes laces is created the same way the habit of crossing your t-bar at the top of the stem. Practice, practice, practice.

In order to really master the concepts in this book, you have to practice. The art of making a decision to live in a "drama-free" zone takes practice. If you currently live from one crisis to the next, you will have plenty of opportunities to practice starting now.

429

If you are already living a very peaceful life, you will have to look for and even schedule learning opportunities to flex that new mental muscle. One of the reasons people from all over the world have seen dramatic results with the handwriting changes is that they have a daily opportunity to practice. Many people use pen and paper daily, so they have a vehicle for practice. If you never write, you have to schedule the practice. If you are not in the habit of eating vegetables or exercising, you must schedule them until they become habits. If you aren't saving 10% of your income, you start today and do it until it becomes habitual.

Once you create habits out of doing the things necessary to live in the flow of money, good health, and happiness - it seems natural and effortless.

I'll share with you a funny true story that reveals the embarrassing fact that I too still have a lot to learn about life. When I was about 25 years old, I was living in Dallas with a roommate and close friend named Rand Stagen. Because both Rand and I were entrepreneurs, we created our own schedule. Neither one of us had ever developed the habits of getting up early or getting out bed on the first alarm.

I've been reading books and attending self-improvement seminars since I was fourteen. I didn't need any more knowledge. What I needed was better habits.

For Rand, his major problem was he had a lifelong habit of watching television to wind down at the end of the day. He actually had tremendous difficulty falling asleep if he didn't have the TV on! He knew that staying up until 2 am watching reruns of bad sitcoms was not the shortcut to the cover of *Fortune Magazine*!

For me, I preferred to stay up late and didn't seem to wake up in the mornings unless I had an appointment. If I didn't have an appointment, my body would beg me to sleep until 10, 11, even noon sometimes. Naturally, when I finally "got up and moving" I felt like I had lost half the day.

So, as we discussed some mechanisms to "motivate" ourselves to get out of bed at a reasonable time, we concocted a plan. We gave each other permission to dump ice water on the other's head if he didn't get up on the first alarm. Ouch. That's motivation by pain! I remember days hitting the snooze alarm just watching the door of my room, worrying Rand was going to fly in with a bucket of ice water. It worked, the pain of the threat of ice water motivated both of us to create new habits and only two times did our pillows get soaked with water!

If you are thinking that game sounds sophomoric and silly, wait...it gets better. Because of our mutual agreement that not being able to control something as simple as when we get out of bed was childish and embarrassing, we agreed to treat each other like children.

How are kids motivated? Pain vs. pleasure. So, we created a system where we rewarded ourselves like we were in grade school again.

I remember getting gold stars for every book I read in elementary school. That was the ticket. Gold stars for habits we did. No gold star for not doing the habit. So, we bought poster board and created a 3 foot by 2 foot chart with a list of all our habits that we could get gold stars for doing.

We listed all the habits we wanted to do on a daily basis and gave ourselves gold stars at the end of each day. It became a open-to-the-public checklist of our success habits. Rand's list had items such as 50 push ups, daily teeth flossing, no TV, making his bed, and of course, getting up at the first alarm. My list had such items as daily carrot juice, daily teeth flossing, the ancient Tibeten exercises, journal writing, and of course getting up at the first alarm.

To motivate ourselves even more, we posted our charts on the

Healthy Habits Success Checklist

Week of January 14-January 28

Habit	M	T	W	T	F	S	S	Total	Grade
				Day of Week					
Wake	7	8	7:15	8	7	10	9	n/a	B
Total Sleep (hours)	8	9	7	8	8	9	9	58 / 8.28	B
Make bed (7x)	√	√	√	√	√	√	√	7	A
Floss Teeth(2x)	√		√					2	A
Meditate /Time Line Visualization (2x)			√			√		2	A
Tibetan Rites (2x)		√						1	B
No Coffee (4x)								0	F
6 Glasses Of Water (7x)	√		√	√		√	√	5	B
Yoga / Aerobic (2x)				√			√	2	A
No Drama Zone (7x)	√	√	√		√	√		5	B
Talk to parents by phone (1x)							√	1	A
Contribute to Charity (1x)							√	1	A
Read 20 minutes per day (7x)	√	√	√	√	√	√	√	7	A
Review Real Estate in classifieds (1x)							√	1	A
Date with Spouse (1x)				√				1	A
One page of handwriting changes (7x)	√	√	√	√	√	√	√	7	A
Clean Car (1x)								0	F
Don't use the word "try"	√	√			√	√		5	C
Take Vitamins (7x)	√	√	√	√	√	√	√	7	A
No Television (3x)	√		√			√	√	3	A
Put 10% of income into investments.	√							1	A
Clean Desk – End Of Day (5x)	√	√	√		√			4	B
30 Minutes Weekly planning (Sun)							√	1	A
Retire / Bedtime	11	12:15	12	11	1	12	11	n/a	n/a

_____   _____

My Signature   Today's Date

Comments: _____

_____

_____

_____

Special thanks to Rand Stagen at www.stagen.com for sharing the
Success Habits Checklist with us for use in this book.

kitchen wall so all our friends could see what dorks we were. I imagine we had a monthly prize for the guy with the most gold stars. The habit of keeping track of our habits was rewarding enough.

Now, many years later, both Rand and I are professional speakers who teach people how to live more prosperous fulfilling lives. (www.stagen.com) Both of us still use a more advanced form of that silly daily habit success checklist. We don't use gold stars, we use check marks. We don't post the list on poster board, we write inside our daily organizer/ time planner. The principle is the same. Until it becomes a habit, it stays on our healthy habits success checklist.

Sometimes, we have to recycle habits that we forget to keep. I recently saw Rand's Success Checklist and he had written the habit of attending Kung Fu training twice a week. He gets the reward of getting that checkmark twice a week if he keeps that commitment. I had to again add into my success checklist lifting weights three times per week. During the time I wrote the majority of this book, I stopped lifting weights or exercising as often as I would normally do. So, back into the "success checklist" that habit goes. I already turn off the lights when I leave the room, so I don't include that habit on my list.

From a personal growth standpoint, I have committed to meditate at least twice a week. Some weeks I get three checks, some weeks I only get one. In any case, this weekly session of planning and the daily confirmation of keeping track of my healthy habits gives me great perspective on how balanced I am keeping my life. If you found yourself really out of balance using the "life boarding" disk program in chapter 8, you will want to schedule making deposits into the areas of your life you need improvement. If your relationship is suffering, you might schedule "Sincere compliment to my spouse daily." Or, you might schedule one evening per week as a "romantic time with my spouse."

I recently added "No work after 7pm (3x)" I added this because I found myself spending too much time on my "career" quadrant after 7pm. I was becoming a work-o-holic. To change the habit, I now discipline myself to take at least three evenings per week off and play. I use the notation of 3 x to represent three times during the week.

Below is a sample of a healthy habits checklist. I simply use an Excel Spreadsheet to update and make changes each week on my computer. I then print it out at about 60% real size so it fits in my daily organizer. The below checklist is simply a sample of what your's might look like incorporating some of the concepts in this book.

I hope you find the healthy habits checklist one more useful and powerful tool toward more wealth and happiness. In this book, I had shared with you many of the success tools that have helped me live a higher level of wealth and happiness. In fact, all of these tools have been used by other people to various levels of success. You sure don't have to use all of them to live a life of financial and emotional abundance. I would encourage you to share these techniques and tools with your family and friends. When they see the changes in you, they will ask how you did it. You just tell them it is a big secret your friend Bart Baggett told you.

I sincerely appreciate you investing your time and money into this book. I have chosen a path as teacher for the joy and benefits that comes with making a difference in others lives. If you feel the information inside this book has touched you or someone you love in a special way, please share the story with me. It gives me tremendous joy to read mail, e-mail, and especially handwritten letters of people who have been positively affected by my work. My wish for you is a life of emotional and financial abundance!

You can get a weekly dose of Bart Baggett via the Internet by subscribing to Bart Baggett's Weekly Newsletter. Just visit www.bartbaggett.com and enter your e-mail address!

Best of all... it's free!

CHAPTER 22

CONCLUSION

Once again, imagine you are walking along a wooded path on a warm sunny day. The trees are lush and green, the sky a rich cobalt blue. Birds are singing overhead, and the scent of fresh pine fills your nose. You hold close to your heart the ancient scroll of wisdom. You stop, turn around and look down the path behind you. You become entranced by how different your past looks now that you've changed. Notice the long journey of self-exploration you have now completed. Congratulations! You are a success. You have absorbed a lot of new information both consciously and unconsciously and learned several new tools to run your life more successfully. You have learned a roadmap of how to design your life the way ... you choose to live it. You have set goals to create new pathways to your highest outcomes. You now have the wisdom to change your limiting beliefs any time and create better values to pull you toward the pleasures of living your dreams. You are more aware of how your handwriting reveals your strengths and your internal roadblocks, and how to change your handwriting to model highly successful people and remove those roadblocks. You may have already removed your roadblocks, or planted the seeds in your unconscious mind to begin removing your roadblocks now. The power for you to change is just pen strokes away.

Happy that your past has changed, you look down at your feet and see you are standing on your very own life-board. It is saucer-shaped, and customized to fit you. You see the areas in your life that you need to focus on, so that you stay in balance all the time, and that all your basic human needs are getting met. You are aware that your internal rules affect the quality of your experiences and ... you may have changed some of your limiting rules so that your life has less drama and more joy. You have discovered that you can gain rapport with anyone just by matching their posture, voice and breathing. This tool, now deeply ingrained into your awareness, empowers you to have deeper, more authentic relationships with the people who come into your life.

You move your attention to your body, the vessel you have chosen to encapsulate yourself as you walk this planet in search of ... you know deep down what you are searching for. Pay close attention to how you take care of your body. You need it to be healthy for your journey. As you eat properly, exercise regularly, and take measures to prevent dis-ease, you will have the abundant energy necessary to live a long happy life.

Now you look straight ahead. The path curves through the woods along your future time-line. You walk forward, quickly, picking up your pace, jogging toward ... running now, sprinting, once again dropping any limiting beliefs that no longer support the new you. You let go of the past, keeping the positive learnings and storing them in that place in your mind where you store such learnings. You race over a new bridge in your life, feeling the unlimited possibilities moving toward you and you moving toward them. On the other side of the bridge you see the wealthy life that is possible for you to create now.

You know which questions to ask, how to structure your money, to pay yourself first, and share your wealth with those in need. You see yourself in the universal flow of money, and everyday your unconscious mind is learning better ways to direct money toward you.

Walking confidently now, you continue along this wooded path until it opens up into a wide clearing. The sun is shining brightly. You can clearly see several new paths have opened up before you. You now have unlimited opportunities. From this point on you can choose any path that draws you toward your happiest outcomes. In fact, as you look around, you will see that the positive outcomes you have now programmed into your mind are beginning to manifest in your world.

You unravel the scroll and see that it is blank except for one question.

Which highest outcome do you want to achieve first?

The choice is yours. All you have to do is make the decision now and ... step forward toward the new path that calls you most, and enjoy the journey.

APPENDIX
OTHER RESOURCES & PRODUCTS

MyHandwriting.com
International Handwriting Analysis Training

Sign up for your free weekly e-mail Newsletter written by Bart Baggett.
Just visit our website and type in your e-mail. It's free.

myhandwriting.com/newsletters
Also visit:
bartbaggett.com/catalog
botmarketing.com
(Internet Marketing)

sexsecretsrevealed.com
HandwritingUniversity.com
e-onlinepublishing.com
(put the dash after the e -)

mentalfitnessproducts.com (Affiliate program for resellers)

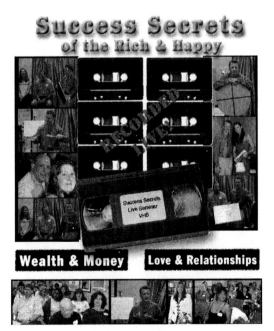

www.e-onlinepublishing.com

www.BartBaggett.com

Success Secrets
of the Rich & Happy

Wealth & Money   Love & Relationships

Toll Free 1-800-398-2278 or 01-214-651-8880

mail@myhandwriting.com

Direct all mail to:
Bart Baggett
c/o Empresse Publishing
PO Box 720355
Dallas, TX 75372 USA

The Handwriting Analysis Certification Home Study Course

THIS COURSE CAN BE YOUR GOLDEN KEY TO UNLOCKING YOUR HIDDEN POTENTIAL!

You can now enroll in our comprehensive home study course and graduate a Certified Handwriting Expert in a few fun filled short months!

That's right! You can take your enthusiasm about understanding human behavior to a whole new level by becoming a Certified Handwriting Expert. You can now get all the education you need, without ever attending a live class or traveling hundreds of miles for a boring intensive, expensive, instructional session at some highbrow university.

Bart Baggett has captured the highlights of live classes on over 16 audio cassettes and packaged them with easy to follow, fascinating lesson handouts. You can get a comprehensive education on handwriting analysis without ever leaving the comfort of your home or car.

This program has that personal touch at just a fraction of what it would cost to attend such a program live. If you are busy and you value your time and money, this is the best program available to advance your knowledge and move to the next level: a Certified Handwriting Expert.

Think About How Learning More Can Benefit Your Life:

- Increase your confidence and self-esteem.
- Set and achieve higher goals without a fear of failure.
- Make a difference in everyone you meet.
- Understand all the handwriting strokes beyond the basic books and cards and even learn how to evaluate and stack traits!

Bart Baggett - Your Virtual Instructor

- Master the science of Grapho-Therapy!
- Earn recognition and respect by becoming a Certified Expert.
- Be invited to be a guest speaker all around town.
- Earn extra income... Upwards of $100 an hour if you enroll into the Deluxe course!

It will teach you how to explain hundreds of traits in such a way that you can inspire others to live their dreams, rather than be discouraged by their differences, limitations, and possible shortcomings. It really is a remarkable sight to see a person's attitude transform like an awakening butterfly. Just think, you can be the catalyst to such optimism, hope, and transformation in others' lives. This course really takes you beyond where any single book can take you.

Some of the most rewarding events in our lives come when we can sincerely make a difference in other people's lives. After you learn to be a Certified Handwriting Expert, that satisfaction tends to be a common experience.

This course is led by expert instructors who explain all the many variables and exceptions of handwriting analysis. You will have a clear picture for understanding people by their handwriting.

1-800-398-2278

The <u>Deluxe</u> Handwriting Analysis Home Study Course: Includes over 16 Hours of Audio lectures, Handout Supplement, Textbook, Video, Kid's and Adult's Workbook, Emotional Gauge,Certificate, and Marketing System and much more!

6 Good Reasons For You To Enroll Today:

1. Learn at your own pace, using audio cassettes and the home study materials. Remember, there is no time limit on the completion of your training.
2. Extra Income: Earn $50-$125 per hour analyzing handwriting in your spare time.
3. Expanded insight and advanced knowledge - Hundreds of insights not included in the Basic Course.
4. Rare Handwriting Samples: Dozens of celebrities, millionaires, psychopaths, politicians and criminals!
5. Master the Science of Grapho-Therapy.
6. Graduation Diploma. Upon your successful completion of your exams and passing an oral test, a frameable blue and gold diploma will be awarded to you. Issued by the Grapho-Analytics Institute of Handwriting Analysis and authorized by the signatures of the Directors.

Just imagine... You, the expert, having fun and getting paid for talking to people, just by looking at others' handwriting. If you really want to go for it, consider the option of investing in the Standard or Deluxe Handwriting Home Study Course.

The Standard Handwriting Analysis Certification Course Includes:

- 14 hours of classroom instruction on audio tape
- Special 70 page Handouts Supplement of Unusual Samples
- Dr. Ray Walker's Textbook
- Emotional gauge
- 21 Tests for Certification
- Complete Trait Dictionary and Review Sections
- Two Bonus Tapes: Grapho-Therapy and Common Questions
- Plus: The How Anyone Can Analyze Handwriting In Ten Minutes or Less Basic Home Study Program. (see page 289)
- And Change Your Life in 30 Days Adults & Kids Workbooks and Tapes
- Plus the bonus... One Hour of Live Consultation/ Testing Coupon $100 value
- Much, much, more...

Standard Certification Home Study Course

ITEM# Hacert-Stnd	**$649.00**
Deluxe Course	**$1397.00**

Visit the website now to enrol, request more detailed course descriptions, and see what current discount coupons or special offers are available on-line!

www.myhandwriting.com/learn

Double Your Income

Time Line / NLP / Hypnosis Audio Course by Bart Baggett

"Bart, *I have only completed the first track so far. However, let me say this section alone is worth it's weight in Gold. Why? Just using two powerful concepts I learned was enough to increase my income. Using these concepts I booked a Stage Hypnosis Show that I performed last weekend in Minneapolis, MN and was paid the highest fee I've ever earned for such an engagement. I can't wait to see what happens when I complete the rest of these powerhouse audios.* "

—*Jona McKee, Washington DC.*

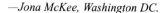

The 2 CD Double Your Income Set is pictured above with two of Bart's New VHS videos - sold separately. You can buy the entire "Abundance Course Live Seminar" that includes all this and six live cassette tapes. Visit the the catalog page at www.bartbaggett.com

This is one of the most amazing courses I have ever published or been a part of. Literally within hours or days of using this program, people get immediate results measureable in cold hard cash. Even I "magically" create more money after I listen to this program using the closed eye process that you are led through on this on this audio soundtrack.

This breakthrough mental programming audio product will open your mind to new ways of thinking about money while attracting wealth and abundance in every area of your life. It doesn't matter what career or job you have now or how much (or how little) money you are making currently. Your mind has the power to open new doors and find ways to create wealth. This mental imagery programming tape unlocks those doors and breaks down limiting beliefs using the power of NLP, Hypnosis, and Time Line Guided Mental Imagery.

The Double Your Income is a two-part program. The first part is a discussion/ lecture about wealth and the belief systems that surround money and abundance. You will learn how you can overcome a lifetime of limiting programming using just your own mind. Part two of the Double Your Income Program is a closed eye process where you use your own internal "Time Line" to install new events and future earnings into your own unconscious mind.

The mental imagery technique called TIME LINE is an advanced technique that is very powerful and effective if performed properly. To insure you follow along properly in your mind's eye... please listen the to the two introductory soundtracks that completely explain and assist you in eliciting your own internal time line. After you have listened to both of these soundtracks, then you can listen to the guided mental imagery section of the Double Your Income Course.

As a bonus, you can listen to the audio "Discovering Your Internal Time Machine - Session" anytime in the future to install ANY goal or desire into your unconscious mind. And, you don't have to wait for shipping. This entire course is now available via Real Audio from the comfort of your own computer just seconds after you place your on-line order.

e-onlinepublishing.com
mentalfitnessproducts.com/products/tltapes/

$67

BART BAGGETT

To inquire about attending a live seminar, receive Bart's free e-mail newsletter or having Bart speak at your next event, please visit his website or contact his corporate office.

You can access his biography, testimonials, media credentials, and view at his on-line speakers kit here:

www.bartbaggett.com/

1-800-398-2278

GRAPHO-DECK FLASH CARDS

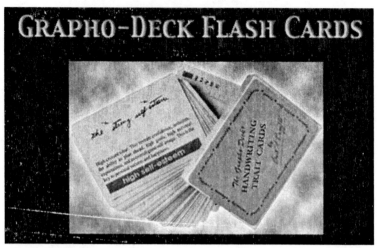

52 Flash Cards for Instant, Fun, Portable Handwriting Analysis!
All Time Best Seller! Just $15.95 at MyHandwriting.com

Handwriting Analysis Basic Home Study Course. (code: hand5)
Includes Bart's first book "The Secrets to Making Love Happen, 4 audio
tapes, VHS video!   Just $99.95 at MyHandwriting.com

MyHandwriting.com
International Handwriting Analysis Training

Subscribe Now to Bart Baggett's Weekly Strokes Newsletter. Get weekly success tips, fresh ideas, current stories, new concepts, get the inside scoop on "in the News Personality Handwriting Samples", and even have Bart personally answer your questions in the "From the Mailbag" section.

This is a short 2 page weekly e-mail newsletter that is always jammed packed with helpful tips and live changing concepts that you can apply immediately to your life. What's more... its FREE! Sign up now and share it with your friends.

Go to this Internet page to subscribe for free and get your first issue right now:

http://www.myhandwriting.com/newsletters/subscribe.html

Read Past Issues
http://myhandwriting.com/newsletters/

Your Name:	
Your e-mail:	

For more information about Bart Baggett's books, tapes, programs, or speaking engagements call his office at 1-800-398-2278, email: mail@myhandwriting.com, or visit www.BartBaggett.com